## Are We Getting Smarter?

The "Flynn effect" is a surprising finding, identified by James R. Flynn, that IQ test scores have significantly increased from one generation to the next over the past century. Flynn now brings us an exciting new book which aims to make sense of this rise in IQ scores and considers what this tells us about our intelligence, our minds, and society. *Are We Getting Smarter?* features fascinating new material on a variety of topics including the effects of intelligence in the developing world; the impact of rising IQ scores on the death penalty, cognitive ability in old age, and the language abilities of youth culture; as well as controversial topics of race and gender. He ends with the message that assessing IQ goes astray if society is ignored. As IQ scores continue to rise into the twenty-first century, particularly in the developing world, the "Flynn effect" marches on!

JAMES R. FLYNN is Professor Emeritus at the University of Otago, New Zealand, and a recipient of the University's Gold Medal for Distinguished Career Research. He is renowned for the "Flynn effect," the documentation of massive IQ gains from one generation to another. Professor Flynn is the author of 12 books including *Where Have All the Liberals Gone?* (Cambridge, 2008) and *What Is Intelligence?* (Cambridge, 2007), which caused many to rethink the prevailing theory of intelligence.

# Are We Getting Smarter?

## *Rising IQ in the Twenty-First Century*

JAMES R. FLYNN

CAMBRIDGE UNIVERSITY PRESS
Cambridge, New York, Melbourne, Madrid, Cape Town,
Singapore, São Paulo, Delhi, Mexico City

Cambridge University Press
The Edinburgh Building, Cambridge CB2 8RU, UK

Published in the United States of America by Cambridge University Press, New York

www.cambridge.org
Information on this title: www.cambridge.org/9781107609174



First published 2012

Printed and Bound in the United Kingdom by the MPG Books Group

*A catalogue record for this publication is available from the British Library*

*Library of Congress Cataloguing in Publication data*
Flynn, James Robert, 1934–
Are we getting smarter? : rising iq in the twenty-first century / James R. Flynn.
p. cm.
Includes bibliographical references and index.
ISBN 978-1-107-02809-8 – ISBN 978-1-107-60917-4 (pbk.)
1. Intelligence tests – History. 2. Intelligence levels – History. I. Title.
BF431.F565 2012
153.9′309–dc23 2012015437

ISBN 978-1-107-02809-8 Hardback
ISBN 978-1-107-60917-4 Paperback

To Arthur Jensen
Whose integrity never failed

# Contents

# Figures

# Tables

# Boxes

# Acknowledgments

As stated in the text, Chapter 2 is a summary of my book, *What Is Intelligence? Beyond the Flynn Effect* (expanded paperback edition), Cambridge University Press (2009). An earlier version appeared in R. J. Sternberg and S. B. Kaufman (eds.), *The Cambridge Handbook of Intelligence* (2011).

The section on British Raven's gains in Chapter 3 is based on "Requiem for nutrition as the cause of IQ gains: Raven's gains in Britain 1938 to 2008," *Economics and Human Biology* 7, 18–27 (2009). The section on *Daubert* motions in Chapter 4 is based on "The WAIS-III and WAIS-IV: Daubert motions favor the certainly false over the approximately true," *Applied Neuropsychology* 16, 1–7 (2009). Chapter 6 draws heavily on two articles: "The spectacles through which I see the race and IQ debate," *Intelligence* 38, 363–366 (2010); and "Modern women match men on Raven's Progressive Matrices" (with L. Rossi-Casé), *Personality and Individual Differences* 50, 799–803 (2011).

# Acknowledgements

# 1 Opening windows

Are we getting smarter? If you mean "Do our brains have more potential at conception than those of our ancestors?" then we are not. If you mean "Are we developing mental abilities that allow us to better deal with the complexity of the modern world, including problems of economic development?" then we are. For most people, the latter is what counts, so I will let the affirmative answer stand. But scholars prefer to ask a different question, to which they attach a special meaning, namely "Are we getting more intelligent?" I will answer that question at the end of Chapter 2.

Whatever we are doing, we are making massive IQ gains from one generation to another. That in itself is of great significance. IQ trends over time open windows on the human condition that make us conscious of things of which we were only half aware. This book attempts to make sense of what time and place are doing to our minds. It has new things to say about cognitive trends in both the developed and the developing world and where they may go over the rest of this century. It falsifies a major hypothesis that suggests that IQ differences between the two worlds are set in the stone of genetic differences. It addresses the most recent debate about the death penalty, particularly attempts to obscure the relevance of IQ gains to who lives or dies. It shows that cognitive trends have rendered inaccurate the diagnosis of memory loss. Perhaps most disturbing, it adds a new dimension to the tendency of western adults and teenagers to grow apart since 1950.

However, all the topics covered do not fit neatly into the box of IQ trends over time. I have included new thinking and data on subjects of general interest: whether race and gender IQ differences are genetic or environmental in origin; how modernity (or lack of it) affects the cognitive abilities of women; whether old age has a darker side hitherto unperceived. And finally, I offer a diagnosis suggested by some 30 years in the field: that psychology has somehow drifted away from sociology and suffered thereby.

Five years ago I published *What Is Intelligence? Beyond the Flynn Effect* (2007) and updated it two years later in the expanded paperback edition (2009). I thought of updating it again. However, as indicated, my new thinking and discoveries did not advance the theory of intelligence so much as a whole range of issues concerning economic growth, the death penalty, aging, and group differences.

Nonetheless what was said in the previous book colors my approach and therefore, the next chapter summarizes its contents. I do not flatter myself that everyone who reads this will have read (or will want to read) my previous work. Still, even those who have read *What Is Intelligence?* may find the next chapter interesting. It gives, for the first time, a full account of adult gains on the WAIS (Wechsler Adult Intelligence Scale), and compares them to child gains on the WISC (Wechsler Intelligence Scale for Children). Moreover, when a book is condensed, connections emerge that were not so clear in the lengthy original.

As for the remainder of this book, Chapter 3 speculates about the distant past and cognitive trends over the rest of this century. It also traces trends on Raven's Progressive Matrices in the UK over the last 65 years, and gives a final verdict on the role of nutrition. Chapter 4 criticizes those who make *Daubert* motions, so they can go on using uncorrected IQ scores to multiply death sentences. It also presents evidence that instruments in current use misdiagnose memory loss in both Britain and Sweden.

Chapter 5 looks at American vocabulary trends over the last half-century. It assesses whether adult gains are the result of the spread of tertiary education or the expansion of cognitively demanding work, and notes a worrying trend for the language used by parents and the language used by their children to diverge. It also analyzes whether high-IQ or low-IQ people are more at risk of a radical loss of cognitive ability in old age. The evidence suggests that while there is a bonus for being bright in retaining vocabulary, there is a levy on being bright in retaining analytic skills.

Chapter 6 argues that the differential performance of black and white Americans on Wechsler subtests does not indicate whether the black/white IQ gap is genetic or environmental in origin. It also shows that modern women match men on Raven's Progressive Matrices, despite the fact that university women have a slightly lower IQ than university men.

Chapter 7 argues that something peculiar happens to the study of intelligence when it becomes sociologically blind. Chapter 8, the last chapter, offers a brief summary and ends with a tribute to *g* and Arthur Jensen.

# 2 IQ and intelligence

Whether the twentieth century has seen intelligence gains is controversial. Whether there have been massive IQ gains over time is not. I will: (1) describe the range and pattern of IQ gains; (2) discuss their historical and social significance; (3) argue that they suggest a new theory of intelligence; and (4) urge that understanding them is more important than classifying them (as either intelligence or non-intelligence gains).

## The evidence and its peculiarities

Reed Tuddenham (1948) was the first to present convincing evidence of massive gains on mental tests using a nationwide sample. He showed that US soldiers had made about a 14-point gain on Armed Forces tests between World War I and World War II or almost a full standard deviation (SD = 15 throughout). The tests in question had a high loading on the kind of material taught in the classroom, and he thought the gains were primarily a measure of improved schooling. Therefore, they seemed to have no theoretical implications, and because the tests were not among those most often used by clinical psychologists the practical implications were ignored.

When Flynn (1984, 1987) showed that massive gains had occurred in America on Wechsler and Stanford–Binet IQ tests, and that they had occurred throughout the industrialized world even on tests thought to be the purest measures of intelligence, IQ gains took center stage. Within a decade, Herrnstein and

Murray (1994), the authors of *The Bell Curve*, called the phenomenon the "Flynn effect."

Nations with data about IQ trends stand at 31. Scandinavian nations had robust gains but these peaked about 1990 and since then, may have gone into mild decline. Several other nations show persistent gains. Americans are still gaining at their historic rate of 0.30 points per year (WAIS 1995–2006; WISC 1989–2002). British children were a bit below that on Raven's from 1980 to 2008, but their current rate of gain is higher than in the earlier period from 1943 to 1980. German adults were still making vocabulary gains in 2007 at a slightly higher rate than US adults. South Korean children gained at double the US rate between 1989 and 2002 (Emanuelsson, Reuterberg, & Svensson, 1993; Flynn, 2009a, 2009b; Pietschnig, Voracek, & Formann, 2010; Schneider, 2006; Sundet, Barlaug, & Torjussen, 2004; Teasdale & Owen, 1989, 2000; te Nijenhuis, 2011; te Nijenhuis *et al.*, 2008).

Other recent gains cover long periods, so whether the rate varied approaching the present is unknown. Urban Argentines (ages 13 to 24) made a 22-point gain on Raven's between 1964 and 1998. Children in urban Brazil (1930–2002), Estonia (1935–1998), and Spain (1970–1999) made gains akin to the US rate. All in all, gains from the developed world cover the United States; 15 European nations or peoples; four Asian nations (urban China, India, Japan, and South Korea); three Commonwealth nations (Australia, Canada, and New Zealand); urban Brazil and urban Argentina; Israel; and white South Africa (Colom, Flores-Mendoza, & Abad, 2007; Colom, Lluis Font, & Andres-Pueyo, 2005; Flynn, 1987, 1998b, 2009c; Flynn & Rossi-Casé, 2011 ; Murphy, te Nijenhuis, & van Eeden, 2008; Must, Must, & Raudik, 2003; te Nijenhuis, 2011).

The developing world has begun to show explosive gains in rural Kenya, Dominica, Turkey, and Saudi Arabia. In Sudan, large gains on the WAIS Performance Scale were accompanied by a small loss for tests closer to school learning (Batterjee *et al.*, in press; Daley *et al.*, 2003; Kagitcibasi, & Biricik, 2011; Khaleefa, Afra Sulman, & Lynn, 2009; Meisenberg *et al.*, 2005).

The Dutch data made the greatest impact. Between 1952 and 1982, young Dutch males gained 20 IQ points on a test of 40 items selected from Raven's Progressive Matrices (Flynn, 1987). The sample was exhaustive. Raven's was supposed to be the exemplar of a culturally reduced test, one that should have shown no gains over time as culture evolved. These 18-year-olds had reached the age at which performance on Raven's peaks. Therefore, their gains could not be dismissed as early maturation, that is, it was not just a matter that children today matured a few years earlier than the children of yesterday. Current people would have a much higher IQ than the last generation even after both had reached maturity.

The Dutch gains created a crisis of confidence. How could such huge gains be intelligence gains? The gains amounted to 1.33 SDs. This would put the average Dutch person of 1982 at the 90th percentile of Dutch in 1952. Psychologists faced a paradox: either the people of today were far brighter than their parents or, at least in some circumstances, IQ tests were not good measures of intelligence.

Box 1 shows how large American gains have been on the most frequently used tests, namely, the WISC (Wechsler Intelligence Scale for Children) and the WAIS (Wechsler Adult Intelligence Scale). These show Full Scale IQ gains proceeding at 0.30 points per year over the last half of the twentieth century, a rate often found in other nations, for a total gain of over 15 points. If we link these to earlier data, such as that of Tuddenham, the gain over the last century has been at least 30 points.

The Dutch gains on Raven's run at over 0.60 points per year, double the rate for Wechsler tests. This is the case for most nations, at least at the time of their peak gains, and focuses us on how IQ tests differ. Raven's measures what is

**Box 1**

The magnitude of US gains on Wechsler tests for both children (WISC) and adults (WAIS) have been comparable, at least for Full Scale IQ. Setting IQs at 100 at the beginning of the period the data cover:

| | | | | |
|---|---|---|---|---|
| WISC: | 100.00 (1947–48) | 107.63 (1972) | 113.00 (1989) | 117.63 (2002) |
| WAIS: | 100.00 (1953–54) | 107.50 (1978) | 111.70 (1995) | 115.07 (2006) |

*Sources:* Flynn, 2009b, 2009c, 2010.

called *fluid intelligence,* solving problems on the spot. You have to identify the missing piece of a design based on its logic, rather like (although often more demanding than) identifying the missing number in a series, say 2-4-8-10 (6 is missing). The Wechsler tests measure *crystallized intelligence,* which is knowledge of a sort you could not acquire unless you were capable of absorbing certain concepts; for example, you could not attain a large vocabulary unless you were good at grasping the concepts behind words. International Raven's data suggest that people have gained 50 points over the twentieth century. It has one rival. The Wechsler test battery consists of 10 subtests, ranging from vocabulary to three-dimensional jigsaw puzzles. One subtest shows gains near the magnitude of Raven's gains. It is the similarities subtest, which tests your ability to classify things that have something in common (e.g. dogs and rabbits are both mammals).

The pattern of IQ gains over time has a final peculiarity, namely, it is not factor-invariant (Wicherts *et al.*, 2004). Factor analysis is a technique that measures the extent to which those who excel on some IQ subtests also excel on others. The tendency toward general excellence is not peculiar to cognition. Just as those with larger vocabularies also tend to be better at arithmetical reasoning and solving matrices problems, so people who are good at one musical instrument are often good at another, and people good at one sport are often good at almost all sports. When a variety of cognitive skills tend to intercorrelate, the measure of the tendency is called *g* (the general intelligence factor).

If the rank order of people on all subtests of the WISC were identical (one person topped them all, another person was second on them all, etc.), *g* would "explain" most of the pattern of test performance and have a high value, perhaps 0.80. If a person's score on each subtest were no more of an indication of their performance on any other subtest than a score chosen at random, *g* would be low or perhaps nil.

One subtest may have a higher "*g*-loading" than another. This means that it is a better guide as to who will do well on the other subtests. For example, if you added an eleventh WISC subtest on shoe tying, it would have a *g*-loading of close to zero: how fast you tie your shoes would have little relation to the size of your vocabulary. On the other hand, your score on the vocabulary subtest might be a pretty good predictor of your scores on the other subtests (except shoe tying) and get a *g*-loading of 0.75. You can rank the subtests into a hierarchy according to the size of their *g*-loadings.

## A pause to make a point

When tests or subtests are ranked according to their *g*-loadings, the skills with the greatest cognitive complexity tend to top the hierarchy, which is to say that the more complex the task, the more high-IQ people open up a gap on the average person. This is an intuitive judgment in that we have only our sense of what is complex to rely upon. But there are enough clear cases to establish the connection.

Imagine I was trying to convince someone that the intensity of heat was correlated with thermometer readings (and lacked a sophisticated knowledge of the science, which I do). I would first choose clear cases; for example I would choose pairs of days during which the temperature had obviously risen and say, "You see that the thermometer shows that it is 10 degrees (Fahrenheit) hotter than it was yesterday." After several such demonstrations, I would urge him to trust the thermometer on days that were close calls, days on which we disagreed about whether or not it was a bit hotter than it was yesterday. Sometimes he would be right, of course, which would fortify his confidence.

There are many clear cases in which differences of cognitive complexity are caught by differences in *g*-loadings. Making a soufflé is more *g*-loaded than scrambling eggs. Digit span backward (repeating numbers in the reverse order you heard them) is more *g*-loaded than digit span forward (repeating numbers in the same order you heard them). Coding (simply pairing symbols and numbers) has by far the lowest *g*-loading of all the Wechsler subtests. Mental arithmetic is far more *g*-loaded than when you are allowed to do the mathematics with a calculator. When we coach people to take IQ tests, we reduce problems that make them think on their feet to problems they can solve merely by applying a method they have been taught; and the *g*-loading falls dramatically.

Its correlation with cognitive complexity gives *g* a good case to be identified with intelligence. If you are still unconvinced, imagine that there were lower *g*-loadings for making soufflés and digit span backward and so forth. Surely this would falsify the claim of *g* to represent intelligence (or at least a certain kind of intelligence). Jensen goes on to suggest that there might exist a latent trait, general intelligence; and that to the extent to which a person possesses that trait the better he or she will do on a whole range of cognitive tasks.

We can now understand why it is thought significant that IQ gains are not consistently factor invariant. As far as *g* is concerned, this means that when we rank subtests by their *g*-loadings, we find that the magnitude of IQ gains on the various subtests do not tally. The largest IQ gain over time may be on a subtest with an average *g*-loading, with a smaller gain on the subtest with the highest *g*-loading. This convinced Jensen (1998) that the bulk of IQ gains were not *g* gains and therefore, were not intelligence gains. He suggests that IQ gains may be largely "hollow"; that is, they are a bundle of subtest-specific skills that have little real-world significance.

## Two kinds of significance

Before we accept the interpretation of IQ gains as hollow, it is useful to supplement factor analysis with functional analysis. Factor analysis may disclose latent traits but no one can do latent traits. What we do in the real world is perform, better or worse, functional activities, such as speaking, solving arithmetic problems, and reasoning about scientific and moral questions. To contrast the two, I will use a sports analogy.

If we factor analyze performances on the 10 events of the decathlon, a general factor or *g* would emerge and very likely subordinate factors representing speed (the sprints), spring (jumping events), and strength (throwing events). We would get a *g* because at a given time and place, performance on the 10 events would be intercorrelated; that is, someone who tended to be superior on any one would tend to be above average on all. We would also get various *g*-loadings for the 10 events, that is, superior performers would tend to rise further above average on some of them than on the others. The 100 meters would have a much higher *g*-loading than the 1,500 meters, which involves an endurance factor not very necessary in the other events.

Decathlon *g* might well have much utility in predicting performance differences between athletes of the same age cohort. However, if we used it to predict progress over time and forecast that trends on the 10 events would move in tandem with their *g*-loadings, we would go astray. That is because decathlon *g* cannot discriminate between pairs of events in terms of the extent to which they are functionally related.

Let us assume that the 100 meters, the hurdles, and the high jump all had large and similar *g*-loadings as they almost certainly would. A sprinter needs upper body strength as well as speed, a hurdler needs speed and spring, a high jumper needs spring and timing. I have no doubt that a good athlete would beat the average athlete handily on all three at a given place and time. However, over time, social priorities change. People become obsessed with the 100 meters as the most spectacular spectator event (the world's fastest human). Young people find success in this event a secondary sex characteristic of great allure. Over 30 years, performance escalates by a full SD in the 100 meters, by half a standard deviation in the hurdles, and not at all in the high jump.

In sum, the trends do not mimic the relative *g*-loadings of the "subtests." One pair of events highly correlated (sprint and hurdles) shows a modest trend for both to move in the same direction and another pair equally highly correlated (sprint and high jump) shows trends greatly at variance. Factor loadings have proved deceptive about whether various athletic skills are functionally independent. We can react to this in two ways: either confront the surprising autonomy of various skills and seek a solution by deep analysis of how they function in the real world; or deny that anything real has happened and classify the trends over time as artifacts. The second option is sterile. It is equivalent to saying that if trends are not factor invariant, they are artifacts by definition.

It is better to talk to some athletics coaches. They tell us that over the years, everyone has become focused on the 100 meters and it is hard to get people to take other events as seriously as in the past. They point out that sprint speed may be highly correlated with high jump performance but past a certain point, it is actually counterproductive. If you hurl yourself at the bar at maximum speed, your forward momentum cannot be converted into upward lift and you are likely to time your jump badly. They are not surprised that increased sprint speed has made some contribution to the hurdles because speed between the hurdles is important. But it is only half the story: you have to control your speed so that you take the same number of steps between hurdles and always jump off the same foot. If you told coaches you found it surprising that real-world shifts in priorities, and the real-world functional relationships between events, ignored the factor loadings of the events, they would find your mind-set surprising.

Factor analysis does not capture the dynamic scenario of social priorities altering over time. Thus, *g*-loadings turn out to be bad guides as to which real-world cognitive skills are merely correlated and which are functionally related. To anticipate, a social change over time such as people putting on scientific spectacles might greatly enhance the ability to classify (similarities) without much affecting everyday vocabulary or fund of general information. Nonetheless all these trends would be of great significance, and to dismiss them as "hollow" would be a barrier to understanding the cognitive history of our time.

## Similarities and Raven's

Five years ago, I tried to simplify the task of explaining massive IQ gains over time by focusing on the tests that showed the largest gains, that is, Raven's Progressive Matrices and the similarities subtest of the Wechsler battery. I tried to identify the "habits of mind" people needed to get the right answers.

When similarities asks "What do dogs and rabbits have in common?" the correct answer is that they are both mammals, rather than that we use dogs to hunt rabbits. The right answer assumes that you are conditioned to look at the world in a certain way: through scientific spectacles – as something to be understood by classification; and not through utilitarian spectacles – as something to be manipulated to advantage. Raven's is all about using logic to deal with sequences of abstract shapes that have no counterpart in concrete reality. If a mind is habituated to taking hypothetical problems seriously, and using logic to deal with the hypothetical, this seems perfectly natural. If you are unaccustomed to using logic for anything but to deal with the concrete world, and indeed distrust reasoning that is not grounded in the concrete, you are not amenable to the change of gears that Raven's requires. Like classification, the reasoning rewarded is of the sort that science, which is all about taking explanatory hypotheses seriously, entails.

The next step toward understanding is rather like an archaeological excavation. Dig into the past hoping to find evidence that appears relevant and assemble it bit by bit. Fortunately, Luria recorded interviews with isolated rural people (Russians in the 1920s) who still lived in pre-scientific cognitive environments.

Here is an interview about classification: fish and crows (Luria, 1976, p. 82).

Q: What do a fish and a crow have in common?

A: A fish – it lives in water. A crow flies. If the fish just lies on top of the water, the crow could peck at it. A crow can eat a fish but a fish can't eat a crow.

Q: Could you use one word for them both?

A: If you call them "animals," that wouldn't be right. A fish isn't an animal and a crow isn't either. A crow can eat a fish but a fish can't eat a bird. A person can eat a fish but not a crow.

Note that even after an abstract term is suggested the "correct" answer is still alien. Today we are so familiar with the categories of science that it seems obvious that the most important attribute that things have in common is that they are both animate, or mammals, or chemical compounds. However, people attached to the concrete will not find those categories natural at all. First, they will be far more reluctant to classify. Second, when they do classify, they will have a strong preference for concrete similarities (two things look alike, two animals are functionally related; e.g. one eats the other) over a similarity in terms of abstract categories. The similarities subtest assumes exactly the opposite; that is, it damns the concrete in favor of the abstract.

Here is an interview about using logic to analyze the hypothetical: camels and Germany (Luria, 1976, p. 112):

Q: There are no camels in Germany; the city of B is in Germany; are there camels there or not?

A: I don't know, I have never seen German villages. If B is a large city, there should be camels there.

Q: But what if there aren't any in all of Germany?

A: If B is a village, there is probably no room for camels.

Today, we are accustomed to detaching logic from the concrete, and say, "of course there would be no camels in this hypothetical German city." The person whose life is grounded in concrete reality rather than in a world of symbols is baffled. Who has ever seen a city of any size without camels? The inhibition is not primarily a result of limited experience but rather of a refusal to treat the problem as anything other than concrete. Imagine that the syllogism said there were no dogs in a large German city. The concrete response is that there must be dogs in German cities – who would want or be able to exterminate them all? And if one is not practiced in dealing with using logic on hypothetical problems that at least use concrete imagery, what of the hypothetical problems of Raven's that are stated in terms of abstractions with no concrete referent?

Today, we are bombarded with symbols. The only artificial images the Americans of 1900 had were representational drawings or photographs, basic arithmetic, musical notation (for an elite), and playing cards (except for the religious). They saw the world through utilitarian spectacles. Their minds were focused on ownership, the useful, the beneficial, and the harmful; and not on the hypothetical and abstract classification.

Genovese (2002) has done his own dig into America's past. He compared the exams the state of Ohio gave to 14-year-old schoolchildren between 1902 and 1913 with those they gave between 1997 and 1999. The former tested for in-depth knowledge of culturally valued information; the latter expected only superficial knowledge of such information and tested for understanding complex relationships between concepts. The former were likely to ask you to name the capitals of the (then) 45 states. The latter tended to ask you why the largest city of a state was rarely the state capital (rural members dominated state legislatures, hated the big city, and bestowed the capital on a rural town). Genovese (2002, p. 101) concludes: "These findings suggest that there have been substantial changes in the cognitive skills valued by Ohio educators over the course of the 20th century." We now have a clue as to why children have made virtually no score gains on the WISC general information subtest.

Thus far, the proffered causes of the huge gains on similarities and Raven's have to do with the minds that took the tests. A full analysis would be multilayered. The ultimate cause of IQ gains is the Industrial Revolution. The intermediate causes are probably its social consequences, such as more formal schooling, more cognitively demanding jobs, cognitively challenging leisure, a better ratio of adults to children, richer interaction between parent and child (Neisser, 1998). Donning scientific spectacles with the attendant emphasis on classification and logical analysis is only the proximate cause. (See Appendix V for a wonderful new paper about Raven's gains.)

## IQ trends and the real world

If IQ trends are mere artifacts they should not predict or explain anything about the real world outside the test room. If it be legislated that they are artifacts unless *g* (or some important cognitive skill akin to *g*) lurks behind them, the debate is over before it begins. We must open our minds to the possibility that, despite the fact that they are not factor invariant, IQ trends have something to do with whether society's cognitive capital is waxing or waning. The significance of cognitive trends is too rich and diverse to be captured by any one construct.

Here are some predictions about the real world that are based on American and world IQ trends: (1) tutoring children on Raven's should do little to improve their mathematical problem-solving skills; (2) enhanced performance on school reading and English courses should decline after the age of 14; (3) enhanced performance in school mathematics should show the same pattern; (4) TV shows should have become more cognitively complex and less "literal" in their plot lines; (5) cognitively demanding games such as chess should show large performance gains over time; (6) the quality of moral debate should have risen over time; (7) American parents and their children are becoming more culturally segregated; and (8) modernity promotes gender parity for on-the-spot problem solving. The last two of these are sufficiently novel or controversial to get lengthy treatment in later chapters. I will discuss the others one by one.

It is tempting to identify mathematical thinking with Raven's. Raven's demands solving nonverbal problems on the spot without a previously learned method for doing so. Mathematics requires mastering new proofs dealing with nonverbal material. Raven's and mathematics tests are highly correlated, which seems to signal that they require similar cognitive skills. Therefore, it appears sensible to teach young children Raven's-type problems in the hope that they will become better mathematics problem solvers. US schools have been doing that since 1991 (Blair *et al.*, 2005, pp. 100–101).

Here IQ gains validate their credentials as diagnosticians of functional relationships between cognitive skills. The large gains on Raven's since 1950 and the virtually nil gains on the Wechsler arithmetic subtest show that the relationship between the two is not functional. It is rather like the relationship between sprinting and the high jump. And sadly, our understanding of the functional processes for learning arithmetic is far behind our understanding of the high jump. Some speculation: except for mathematicians who link the formulas with proofs, mathematics is not a purely logical enterprise. It is more like exploring a separate reality with its own laws, laws that are at variance with those of the natural world. Therefore, just as infants explore the natural world, children must explore the world of mathematics themselves and become familiar with its "objects" by self-discovery.

Subtests that show minimal gains have as much explanatory potential as those that show huge gains. Since 1950, children have made very minimal gains not only on the subtest that measures whether children feel comfortable with the world of mathematics, but also on WISC subtests that measure whether children have an adequate fund of general information and a decent vocabulary. These are very close to school-taught skills. Let us see what they tell us about US trends on the National Association of Educational Progress (NAEP) tests, often called the Nation's Report Card. These tests are administered to large representative samples of 4th, 8th, and 12th graders.

From 1971 to 2002, 4th and 8th graders (average age 11 years old) made a reading gain equivalent to almost four IQ points. However, by the 12th grade, the reading gain dropped off

**Box 2**

I often read my students a stanza from Browning's wonderful poem:

Over the Kremlin's pavement bright
With serpentine and syenite,
Steps, with other five generals
That simultaneously take snuff,
For each to have pretext enough
And kerchiefwise unfold his sash
Which, softness self, is yet the stuff
To hold fast where a steel chain snaps,
And leave the grand white neck no gash.

If you do not know what the Kremlin is, or what "serpentine" means, or that taking snuff involves using a snuff rag, you will hardly realize that these generals caught the Czar unaware and strangled him.

to almost nothing (US Department of Education, 2000, pp. 104, 110; USDE, 2003, p. 21). The IQ data suggest an interesting possibility. For the sake of comparability, we will focus on WISC trends from 1972 to 2002. Between 1972 and 2002, US schoolchildren made no gain in their store of general information and only minimal vocabulary gains (Flynn, 2009c). Today's children may learn to master basic reading skills at a younger age, but are no better prepared for reading more demanding adult literature. You cannot enjoy *War and Peace* if you have to run to the dictionary or encyclopedia every other paragraph (see Box 2).

From 1973 to 2000, the Nation's Report Card shows 4th and 8th graders making mathematics gains equivalent to almost seven IQ points. These put the young children of 2000 at the 68th percentile of their parents' generation. But once again, the gain falls off at the 12th grade, this time to literally nothing (US Department of Education, 2000, pp. 54 & 60–61; 2001, p. 24). And once again, the relevant WISC subtest suggests why.

The arithmetic subtest and the NAEP mathematics tests present a composite picture. An increasing percentage of young children have been mastering the computational skills the Nation's Report Card emphasizes at those ages. However, WISC arithmetic measures both computational skills and something extra. The questions are put verbally and often in a context that requires more than a times-table-type answer. For example, take an item like: "If 4 toys cost 6 dollars, how much do 7 cost?" Many subjects who can do straight paper calculations cannot diagnose the two operations required: that you must first divide and then multiply. Others cannot do mental arithmetic involving fractions.

In other words, WISC arithmetic tests for the kind of mind that is comfortable with mathematics and therefore, likely to find advanced mathematics congenial. No progress on this subtest signals why by the 12th grade, American schoolchildren cannot do algebra and geometry any better than the previous generation.

We turn to the worlds of leisure and popular entertainment. Greenfield (1998) argues that video games, popular electronic games, and computer applications require enhanced problem solving in visual and symbolic contexts. If that is so, that kind of enhanced problem solving is necessary if we are fully to enjoy our leisure. Johnson (2005) points to the cognitive demands of video games, for example, the spatial geometry of *Tetris*, the engineering riddles of *Myst*, and the mapping of *Grand Theft Auto*.

Johnson analyzes television. It is aimed at a mass audience and its level of complexity is based on an estimate of what the average person can assimilate. Johnson shows convincingly that today's popular TV programs make unprecedented cognitive demands. The popular shows of a generation ago, such as *I Love Lucy* and *Dragnet*, and *Starsky and Hutch*, were simplistic, requiring virtually no concentration to follow. Beginning in 1981 with *Hill Street Blues*, single-episode drama began to be replaced with dramas that wove together as many as ten threads into the plotline. An episode of the hit drama *24* connected the lives of 21 characters, each with a distinct story.

Howard (1999) uses traditional games as an informal measure of cognitive gains. He speaks of "cascading feed-back loops." More people want to play chess, the average skill rises, chess clubs form, coaching and chess books improve with rising demand, so you have even better average performance, and so on. He evidences the trend toward enhanced skills by documenting the decline in the age of chess grandmasters. There is no doubt that the standard of play in chess tournaments has risen (Nunn, 1999). Howard makes the same case, although the evidence is less compelling, for other leisure activities that are cognitively demanding such as bridge and go.

I know of no study that measures whether the quality of moral debate has risen over the twentieth century. However, I will show why it should have. The key is that more people take the hypothetical seriously, and taking the hypothetical seriously is a prerequisite to getting serious moral debate off the ground. My brother and I would argue with our father about race, and when he endorsed discrimination, we would say, "But what if your skin turned black?" As a man born in 1885, and firmly grounded in the concrete, he would reply, "That is the dumbest thing you have ever said – whom do you know whose skin has ever turned black?" I never encounter contemporary racists who respond in that way. They feel that they must take the hypothetical seriously, and see they are being challenged to use reason detached from the concrete to show that their racial judgments are logically consistent.

**Box 3 (see Table AIII2 in Appendix III for more detail)**

The WISC and WAIS have shared eight subtests over a roughly common period of 54 years (1950 to 2004). I will rank them from the subtest on which adult gains have most exceeded child gains to the subtest on which children have been most impressive. A difference proceeded by a plus favors adults and a minus favors children. All values are in an IQ metric (SD = 15).

| | | | |
|---|---|---|---|
| Vocabulary | 17.80 (WAIS) | 4.40 (WISC) | +13.40 (difference) |
| Information | 8.40 (WAIS) | 2.15 (WISC) | +6.25 (difference) |
| Comprehension | 13.80 (WAIS) | 11.00 (WISC) | +2.80 (difference) |
| Arithmetic | 3.50 (WAIS) | 2.30 (WISC) | +1.20 (difference) |
| Picture Completion | 11.20 (WAIS) | 11.70 (WISC) | −0.50 (difference) |
| Coding | 16.15 (WAIS) | 18.00 (WISC) | −1.85 (difference) |
| Similarities | 19.55 (WAIS) | 23.85 (WISC) | −4.30 (difference) |
| Block Design | 10.25 (WAIS) | 15.90 (WISC) | −5.65 (difference) |

*Sources:* Flynn, 2009b, 2009c, 2010.

## Trends test by test

It is instructive to examine score trends on Raven's and the various Wechsler subtests one by one. Where relevant, I will remark on different trends for adults (WAIS) and children (WISC). Box 3 provides the necessary comparisons.

• **Vocabulary:** A huge gulf has opened up between parent and child. As foreshadowed, this will dominate a later chapter, but it must say something about the cultural segregation of adults and children. The adult gains imply that serious writers today have a larger target audience capable of reading their works, although the visual culture of our time may limit the number of those willing to do so.

- **Information:** The fact that adults have gained eight points and children only two points probably reflects the impact on adults of the expansion of tertiary education.
- **Comprehension:** Large gains by both adults (almost 14 points) and children (11 points). This subtest measures the ability to comprehend how the concrete world is organized (why streets are numbered in sequence). The greater complexity of life today poses a challenge that people have met successfully throughout their life spans.
- **Arithmetic:** The small gains reveal the failure of education on any level, from primary to tertiary, to habituate people to the world of numbers. The tertiary failure was unexpected and shocking.
- **Picture Completion:** It is easy to say that large gains at all ages reflect a more visual culture. But this is unsatisfactory until we can be more precise about proximate causes; that is, just what cognitive shift allows us to better perceive what is missing in a picture (better mapping skills?).
- **Coding:** Very large gains (16 to 18 points) at all ages. This is an information-processing test that utilizes working memory. The modern world has demanded (and gotten) people who can assimilate information at a faster and faster rate.
- **Block Design:** Like Raven's, this subtest signals enhanced ability to solve problems on the spot that require more than the mere application of learned rules. The schoolchild gains (almost 16 points) are significantly greater than the adult gains (10 points). This makes it tempting to hypothesize that the modern school has increased its demands on analytic ability even more than the modern world of work. However, Raven's data show just the reverse pattern, namely, larger adult gains than child gains (Flynn, 2009a). Clearly the two tests make significantly different demands.

• **Similarities:** The huge gains mark a transition from regarding the world as something to be manipulated for use to classifying it using the vocabulary of science. This habit of mind is a prerequisite for higher education. The fact that the gains are huge throughout life (20 points for adults and 24 for children) shows that this "habit of mind" is not something that a few years of formal schooling inculcates, or a "trick" easily acquired, but a gradual process.

• **Raven's:** Massive gains show that people have freed logic from analyzing concrete situations to deal with problems put abstractly. This too is a prerequisite for the vast expansion of tertiary education and professional jobs requiring university skills and the creative solution of problems on the spot (Schooler, 1998). Taking hypothetical situations seriously may have rendered moral debate more reflective. The full potential of liberated logic has not been realized because universities do not give their graduates the tools they need to analyze the modern world (Flynn, in press).

## Measuring intelligence versus historical narrative

The phenomenon of IQ gains has created unnecessary controversy because of conceptual confusion. Imagine an archaeologist from the distant future who excavates our civilization and finds a record of performances over time on measures of marksmanship. The test is always the same, that is, how many bullets you can put in a target 100 meters away in a minute. Records from 1865 (the US Civil War) show the best score to be five bullets in the target, records from 1898 (Spanish-American War) show ten, and records from 1918 (World War I) show 50.

A group of "marksmanship-metricians" looks at these data. They find it worthless for measuring marksmanship. They make two points. First, they distinguish between the measure and the trait being measured. The mere fact that performance on the test has risen in terms of "items correct" does not mean that marksmanship ability has increased. True, the test is unaltered but all we know is that the test has gotten easier. Many things might account for that. Second, they stress that we have only relative and no absolute scales of measurement. We can rank soldiers against one another at each of the three times. But we have no measure that would bridge the transition from one shooting instrument to another. How could you rank the best shot with a sling against the best shot with a bow and arrow? At this point, the marksmanship-metrician either gives up or looks for something that would allow him to do his job. Perhaps some new data that would afford an absolute measure of marksmanship over time such as eye tests or a measure of steady hands.

However, a group of military historians is also present and it is at this point they get excited. They want to know why the test got easier, irrespective of whether the answer aids or undermines the measurement of marksmanship over time. They ask the archaeologists to look further. Luckily, they discover battlefields specific to each time. The 1865 battlefields disclose the presence of primitive rifles, the 1898 ones repeating rifles, and the 1918 ones machine guns. Now we know why it was easier to get more bullets into the target over time and we can confirm that this was no measure of enhanced marksmanship. But it is of enormous historical and social significance. Battle casualties, the industries needed to arm the troops, and so forth altered dramatically.

Confusion about the two roles has been dispelled. If the battlefields had been the artifacts first discovered, there would have been no confusion because no one uses battlefields as instruments for measuring marksmanship. It was the fact that the first artifacts were also instruments of measurement that put historians and metricians at cross-purposes. Now they see that different concepts dominate their two spheres: social evolution in weaponry – whose significance is that we have become much better at solving the problem of how to kill people quickly; marksmanship – whose significance is which people have the ability to kill more skillfully than other people can.

The historian has done nothing to undermine what the metrician does. At any given time, measuring marksmanship may be the most important thing you can do to predict the life histories of individuals. Imagine a society dominated by dueling. It may be that the lives of those who are poor shots are likely to be too brief to waste time sending them to university, or hiring them, or marrying them. If a particular group or nation lacks the skill, it may be at the mercy of the better skilled. Nonetheless, this is no reason to ignore everything else in writing military history.

Some years ago, acting as an archaeologist, I amassed a large body of data showing that IQ tests had gotten easier. Over the twentieth century, the average person was getting many more items correct on tests such as Raven's and similarities. The response of intelligence- or *g*-metricians was dual. First, they distinguished IQ tests as measuring instruments from the trait being measured, that is, from intelligence (or *g* if you will). Second, they noted that in the absence of an absolute scale of measurement, the mere fact that the tests had gotten easier told us nothing about whether the trait was being enhanced. IQ tests were only relative scales of measurement ranking the members of a group in terms of items they found easy to items they found difficult. A radical shift in the ease/difficulty of items meant all bets were off. At this point, the *g*-metrician decides that he cannot do his job of measurement and begins to look for an absolute measure that would allow him to do so (perhaps reaction times or inspection times).

However, as a cognitive historian, this was where I began to get excited. *Why* had the items gotten so much easier over time? Where was the alteration in our mental weaponry that was analogous to the transition from the rifle to the machine gun? This meant returning to the role of archaeologist and finding battlefields of the mind that distinguished 1900 from the year 2000. I found evidence of a profound shift from an exclusively utilitarian attitude to concrete reality toward a new attitude. Increasingly, people felt it was important to classify concrete reality (in terms the more abstract the better); and to take the hypothetical seriously (which freed logic to deal with not only imagined situations but also symbols that had no concrete referents).

It was the initial artifacts that caused all the trouble. Because they were performances on IQ tests, and IQ tests are instruments of measurement, the roles of the cognitive historian and the *g*-metrician were confused. Finding the causes and developing the implications of a shift in habits of mind over time is simply not equivalent to a task of measurement, even the measurement of intelligence. Now all should see that different concepts dominate two spheres: society's demands – whose evolution from one generation to the next dominates the realm of cognitive history; and *g* – which measures individual differences in cognitive ability. And just as the *g*-metrician should not undervalue the nonmeasurement task of the historian, so the historian does nothing to devalue the measurement of which individuals are most likely to learn fastest and best when compared to one another.

I have used an analogy to break the steel chain of ideas that circumscribed our ability to see the light IQ gains shed on cognitive history. I hope it will convince psychometricians that my interpretation of the significance of IQ gains over time is not adversarial. No one is disputing their right to use whatever constructs are best to do their job: measuring cognitive skill differences between people.

But an analogy that clarifies one thing can introduce a new confusion. The reciprocal causation between developing new weapons and the physique of marksmen is a shadow of the interaction between developing new habits of mind and the brain.

The new weapons were a technological development of something outside our selves that had minimal impact on biology. Perhaps our trigger fingers got slightly different exercise when we fired a machine gun rather than a musket. But the evolution from preoccupation with the concrete and the literal to the abstract and hypothetical was a profound change within our minds that involved new problem-solving activities.

Reciprocal causation between mind and brain entails that our brains may well be different from those of our ancestors. It is a matter of use and structure. If people switch from swimming to weight lifting, the new exercise develops different muscles and the enhanced muscles make them better at the new activity. Everything we know about the brain suggests that it is similar to our muscles. Maguire *et al.* (2000) found that the brains of the best and most experienced London taxi drivers had enlarged hippocampi, which is the brain area used for navigating three-dimensional space. Here we see one area of the brain being developed without comparable development of other areas in response to a specialized cognitive activity. It may well be that when we do "Raven's-type" problems certain centers of our brain are active that used to get little exercise; or it may be that we increase the efficiency of synaptic connections throughout the brain. If we could scan the brains of people in 1900, who can say what differences we would see?

Do huge IQ gains mean we are more intelligent than our ancestors? If the question is "Do we have better brain potential at conception, or were our ancestors too stupid to deal with the concrete world of everyday life?," the answer is no. If the question is "Do we live in a time that poses a wider range of cognitive problems than our ancestors encountered, and have we developed new cognitive skills and the kind of brains that can deal with these problems?," the answer is yes. Once we understand what has happened, we can communicate with one another even if some prefer the label "more intelligent" and others prefer "different." To care passionately about which label we use is to surrender to the tyranny of words. I suspect most readers ask the second question, and if so, they can say we are "smarter" than our ancestors. But it would probably be better to say that we are more modern, which is hardly surprising!

## The theory of intelligence

The thesis about psychometrics and cognitive history, that they actually complement one another, and the remarks made about the brain imply a new approach to the theory of intelligence. I believe we need a BIDS approach: one that treats the brain (B), individual differences (ID), and social trends (S) as three distinct levels, each having equal integrity. The three are interrelated and each has the right to propose hypotheses about what ought to happen on another level. It is our job to investigate them independently and then integrate what they tell us into a coherent whole.

The core of a BIDS approach is that each level has its own organizing concept, and it is a mistake to impose the architectonic concept of one level on another. We have to realize that intelligence can act like a highly correlated set of abilities on one level (individual differences), like a set of functionally independent abilities on another level (cognitive trends over time), and like a mix on a third level (the brain), whose structure and operations underlie what people do on both of the other two levels. Let us look at the levels and their organizing concepts.

- **Individual Differences:** Performance differences between individuals on a wide variety of cognitive tasks are correlated primarily in terms of the cognitive complexity of the task (fluid *g*) – or the posited cognitive complexity of the path toward mastery (crystallized *g*). Information may not seem to differentiate between individuals for intelligence but if two people have the same opportunity, the better mind is likely to accumulate a wider range of information. I will call the appropriate organizing concept "General Intelligence" or *g*, without intending to foreclose improved measures that go beyond the limitations of "academic" intelligence (Heckman & Rubenstein, 2001; Heckman, Stixrud, & Urzua, 2006; Sternberg, 1988, 2006; Sternberg *et al.*, 2000).

- **Society:** Various real-world cognitive skills show different trends over time as a result of shifting social priorities. I will call this concept "Social Adaptation." As I have argued, the major confusion thus far has been as follows: either to insist on using the organizing concept of the individual differences level to assess cognitive evolution, and call IQ gains hollow if they are not *g* gains; or to insist on using the organizing concept of the societal level to discount the measurement of individual differences in intelligence (e.g. to deny that some individuals really do need better minds and brains to deal with the dominant cognitive demands of their time).
- **The Brain:** Localized neural clusters are developed differently as a result of specialized cognitive exercise. There are also important factors that affect all neural clusters such as blood supply, dopamine as a substance that renders neurons receptive to registering experience, and the input of the stress-response system. Let us call its organizing concept "Neural Federalism." The brain is a system in which a certain degree of autonomy is limited by an overall organizational structure.

Researchers on this level should try to explain what occurs on both of the other two levels. The task of the brain physiologist is reductionist. Perfect knowledge of the brain's role would mean the following: given data on how cognition varies from person to person and from time to time, we can map what brain events underlie both social and life histories. To flesh this out, make the simplifying assumption that the mind performs only four operations when cognizing: classification or CL (of the similarities sort); liberated logic or LL (of the Raven's sort); practical intelligence or PI (needed to manipulate the concrete world); and vocabulary and information acquisition or VI. And posit that the brain is neatly divided into four sectors active respectively when the mind performs the four mental operations; that is, it is divided into matching CL, LL, PI, and VI sectors.

Through magnetic resonance imaging scans (MRI) of the brain, we get "pictures" of these sectors. Somehow we have MRIs from 1900 that we can compare to MRIs of 2000. When we measure the neurons within the CL and LL sectors, we find that the later brains have "thickened" neurons. The extra thickness exactly predicts the century's enhanced performance on similarities and Raven's.

As for individual differences, we have pictures of what is going on in the brains of two people in the VI sector as they enjoy the same exposure to new vocabulary. We note that the neurons (and connections between neurons) of one person are better nourished than those of the other because of optimal blood supply (we know just what the optimum is). We note that when the neurons are used to learn new vocabulary, the neurons of one person are sprayed with the optimum amount of dopamine and the neurons of the other are less adequately sprayed. And we can measure the exact amount of extra thickening of grey matter the first person enjoys compared to the second. This allows us to actually predict their different performances on the WISC vocabulary subtest.

Given the above, brain physiology would have performed its reductionist task. Problem-solving differences between individuals and between generations will both have been reduced to brain functions. It will explain both the tendency of various cognitive skills to be correlated on the individual differences level, and their tendency to show functional autonomy on the societal level. That does not, of course, mean that explaining human cognition on the levels of individual differences or social demands have been abolished. Even if physiology can predict every right and wrong answer of people taking IQ tests, no one will understand why these tests exist without knowing that occupation is dependent on mastering certain cognitive skills (social level) and that parents want to know whether their children have those skills (individual differences).

## Closing windows

IQ trends over time turn the pages of a great romance: the cognitive history of the twentieth century. I may have made mistakes in interpreting their significance, but I hope I have convinced you that they are significant. Those who differ about that must, in my opinion, assert one or both of two propositions. That since IQ tests measure *g*, they cannot possibly signal the ebb and flow of anything else. I doubt anyone will defend that proposition. That nothing save *g*, or the special factors that fit under the umbrella of *g*, interests them. I believe that some feel that way, which is sad. They will always view the history of cognition through one window.

# 3 Developing nations

Will the developing world attain mean IQs that match those of the developed world in the foreseeable future? There is no doubt that a significant IQ gap between the two exists. Lynn and Vanhanen (2002, 2006) recorded it and suggested that the developing world does not have the intelligence to equal the record of the developed world for economic growth. I suspect it is not that simple. In 1917, Americans had a mean IQ of 72 (against today's norms) and a good estimate for 1900 would be 67. Only two developing nations fall significantly below this (Saint Lucia and Equatorial Guinea). The US did not leap from 67 to 100 as a prerequisite for industrial development; rather it was a matter of reciprocal causality. The first step toward modernity raised IQ a bit, which paved the way for the next step, which raised IQ a bit more, and so on. It was like climbing a ladder: start with one foot, next step up with the other foot, until you reach the top.

First, I will argue that the evidence that inferior genes for intelligence handicap the developing world is suspect. Second, I will note something unexpected: the IQ gains of the developed world seem to be persisting into the twenty-first century. If this continues, it will be more difficult for the developing world to catch up. Third, I will show that even so, the developing world has the potential to gain at a faster rate. Malnutrition, inbreeding, and ill health are present there and, if overcome, promise dividends. By contrast, these factors have had little effect on IQ in the developed world since 1950. Fourth, I will give evidence that IQ gains in the developing world have begun.

## Parasites versus the Ice Ages

Lynn and Vanhanen (2002, 2006) collected data about IQ differences from 113 nations. Later they expanded the list to 192 by adding estimated scores. Eppig, Fincher, and Thornhill (2010) asked what factor most parsimoniously accounted for these differences. When they controlled for temperature, distance from Africa, gross domestic product per capita, and education, multiple regression analysis showed parasitic stress was the most powerful predictor of national IQ by a large margin. The correlations are preceded by a minus because there was a negative correlation between untreated parasitic conditions and mean IQ. The correlation was –0.82 for both the set of 113 nations and the set of 192. They also found correlations of similar size within the world's six major geographic regions with the exception, oddly, of South America.

Eppig *et al.* controlled for temperature and distance from Africa to test an evolutionary scenario called "out of Africa." Lynn (1987) and Rushton (1995) posit that extreme cold creates a more challenging environment, one that maximizes selection for genes for intelligence. During the Ice Ages, the ancestors of East Asians are supposed to have been north of the Himalayas where the cold was most intense, the ancestors of whites north of the Alps where the cold was next worst, and the ancestors of blacks still in Africa where it was relatively warm. Therefore, we have a racial hierarchy of better genes for intelligence running from East Asians to whites to blacks.

The scenario is ad hoc. If subtropical Africans had the highest IQs today, we might say that competition between people was most intense where humanity evolved, and initially lessened as people moved out of that area, or something of that sort. But better an ad hoc evolutionary scenario than the intellectual bankruptcy of none at all.

The map shows the patterns and timing of human migration with particular reference to China. Note that a group

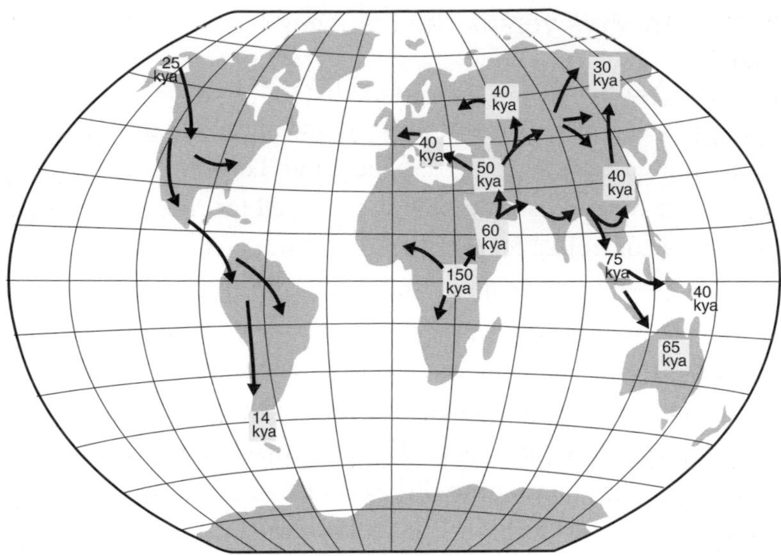


*Figure 1 Human migration with particular reference to China.*

whose history of migration never put it north of the Himalayas settled China about 40,000 years ago. As the map implies some believe there was also a significant migration from Central Asia by a group that had been north of the Himalayas during the Ice Ages.

Thanks to DNA sequencing, virtually all geneticists now believe that there was a large migration from the south into China. The dispute is between those that believe that migration from Central Asia by groups that did suffer from extreme cold was also significant (Zhong *et al.*, 2010); and those who believe it was trivial (Shi & Su, 2009). If the latter prove correct, Lynn and Rushton's scenario is wrong.

Even if the former prove correct, all of the recent data show that there is a genetic divide between north and south (Cavalli-Sforza, 1997, was the pioneer). The incidence of southern or non-Ice-Age genes increases as you go from north China toward the south, with the greatest concentration found in Guandong Province (Chen *et al.*, 2009). Therefore, mean IQ should decline as we go along this vector. We have no IQ data from China itself that allows us to compare the south to the north. But we have a wonderful substitute: the DNA of the Chinese of Singapore shows that they are overwhelmingly from Guandong (the province in which non-Ice-Age genes are most dominant). Those who came to Singapore from Guandong were not a random sample. But if they were elite, they were only mildly so (Ee, 1961).

Therefore, the IQs of Singapore Chinese should be below mainland China. Lynn and Vanhanen (2006) put Singapore at top of the world with a mean IQ of 108. If one isolates the 74 percent of Singapore's people that are Chinese, their mean rises to 114. Mainland China gets only 105. If these values hold, we can forget about the Ice Ages. In passing, all East Asians are supposed to have profited by being north of the Himalayas during the Ice Ages. In fact, no one knows where the ancestors of the Japanese were at that time (Diamond, 1998; Japan Reference, 2011). The Koreans are such a mix of peoples that no clear answer as to their Ice Age whereabouts may be possible. Only a minority came from the Tibetan Plateau (Jung *et al.*, 2010). See Box 4.

History keeps climate scenarios for intelligence differences at bay. Over the past 2,000 years, wonderful cultural achievement moved from the Mediterranean (Greece and Rome), to the crescent from the Middle East through North Africa to Spain (the Arabs), back to Italy again (the Renaissance) and, over the last four hundred years, to northern Europe and the British Isles. The role of IQ is to diagnose potential for cognitively complex cultural achievement. Either other factors can do the job (and modest IQ differences between nations are not that important) or the genes that would later generate IQ advantages were once adequately represented in the south.

**Box 4**

The collapse of the Ice Ages hypothesis does not, of course, settle the debate about whether there are racial differences for genes for intelligence. If universities have their way, the necessary research will never be done. They fund the most mundane research projects, but never seem to have funds to test for genetic differences between races. I tell US academics I can only assume that they believe that racial IQ differences have a genetic component, and fear what they might find. They never admit that the politics of race affects their research priorities. It is always just far more important to establish whether squirrels enjoy *The Magic Flute*.

## The developed world

After 1990, IQ gains in Scandinavia tended to grind to a halt. These nations have a claim to be considered the terminus of many social trends in Europe and North America. In 2000, I speculated that they might foreshadow the end of IQ gains in the developed world. After all, sooner or later formal education gives everyone scientific spectacles, one or two child families put the ratio of adults to children in the home at a maximum, or indeed the ratio worsens with the rise of solo parenthood, richer interaction between parent and child approaches a point beyond which parents will drive children crazy, schooling competes with a teenage subculture that limits commitment to education, economic efficiency forbids featherbedding more and more professional jobs, and too much cognitively challenging leisure becomes like too much hard work.

Over the past decade, I have been shaken by the fact that data, from highly developed nations, signal the persistence of IQ gains even though the first decade of the twenty-first century is over. Box 5 presents gains in four developed nations for recent

**Box 5**

The five most recent estimates of IQ gains from developed nations:

| | | |
|---|---|---|
| South Korea (ages 6–16) | 9.40 points on WISC | 1986–1999 (0.723 pts./year ) |
| United States (ages 5–16) | 4.63 points on WISC | 1989–2002 (0.363 pts./year) |
| United States (ages 16–89) | 3.37 points on WAIS | 1995–2006 (0.306 pts./year) |
| German speakers (median age 42) | 3.50 points on Vocabulary | 1997–2007 (0.350 pts./year) |
| United Kingdom (ages 5–15) | 6.23 points on Raven's | 1980–2008 (0.221 pts./year) |

periods, only one of which begins before 1986 and all of which terminate from 1999 to 2008.

The recent gains of South Korean children on the WISC are based on only 89 subjects but other data sets of reasonable quality confirm at least the Full Scale IQ gain. The WISC rates from 1986 to 1999 are almost exactly double those of US children. The Korean rates were as follows: Full Scale IQ 0.723 points per year; Verbal 0.315 points per year; Performance 1.046 points per year. US children from 1989 to 2002 show the following: Full Scale IQ 0.363; Verbal 0.155; Performance 0.572. Taking the WISC and WAIS together, it is clear that Americans of all ages are still matching their historic rate of 0.300 points per year (Flynn, 2007, 2009a, 2009b; te Nijenhuis *et al.*, 2008).

An analysis of 500 studies with a total of 45,000 subjects, with a median age of 42 years, from German-speaking nations (Germany, Austria, and Switzerland) showed vocabulary gains averaging at 0.350 points per year between 1997 and 2007. The gains were uniform over the whole IQ curve, and were as robust in recent years as in earlier years. They were only slightly lower than the gains that US adults made on the WAIS vocabulary subtest between 1995 and 2006 (rate of 0.455 points per year). The gains of British children on Raven's are lower, but the rate from 1980 to 2008 is actually higher than during the preceding period from 1943 to 1980 (Flynn 2009a, 2009b; Pietschnig, Voracek, & Formann, 2010).

It is always interesting to study trends on Wechsler subtests. I collected a basket of subtests I call "modern-age subtests," because their gains seem to be a response to the increasing complexity and expanding visual culture of the modern world. It is possible that the impact of these facets of the modern world is still escalating. They include comprehension, picture completion, block design, and coding. Then there is similarities, whose gains are a result of more and more people donning scientific spectacles. I suspected that this factor was more fragile in that by now people might have become thoroughly habituated to classifying the world rather than partitioning it. Thus my prediction was that similarities gains would gradually lose ground to the "modern-world" gains, and that a projection into the future would put similarities into the shade.

Box 6 traces the relevant trends over time from the original Wechsler tests to the WISC-IV and WAIS-IV versions; and based on the most recent trends, gives estimates of what the WISC-V and WAIS-V may show in 2012 and 2016 respectively. It is based on Tables AI1 to AI4 in Appendix I. These should interest specialists, in that while a table of gains over time for WISC subtests appeared in *What Is Intelligence?* (2007), the table of WAIS subtest gains has only appeared in journal articles. The values in Box 6 are useless except for the comparisons. The periods between the WISC and WISC-R, and between the WAIS and WAIS-R, were each 24.5 years. After that, the periods were shorter, so I pro-rated the gains over 24.5 years to get comparable values.

The WISC or schoolchild trends in Box 6 seemed to validate my predictions. Circa 1960 (1948–1972), similarities gains

**Box 6 (see Tables AI1 to AI4 in Appendix I)**

This is an attempt to predict whether gains on similarities will be as prominent in the future as they were in the past. "Modern age" refers to the average gain on a group of four subtests causally distinct from similarities. The question is whether similarities gains fall above or below their average. The gains are expressed in an IQ point metric (SD = 15). Their size should not be taken literally; they are devised to facilitate the comparisons. Isolating block design for comparison is less important (see text).

**WISC**
Similarities: **13.85** (1948–72); **9.36** (1972–89); **6.72** (1989–2002); **4.84** (2002–12)

Modern age: **6.78** (1948–72); **5.58** (1972–89); **6.72** (1989–2002); **8.39** (2002–12)

**WAIS**
Similarities: **11.00** (1954–78); **6.48** (1978–95); **7.80** (1995–2006); **9.36** (2006–16)

Modern age: **8.00** (1954–78); **5.04** (1978–95); **5.01** (1995–2006); **5.01** (2006–16)

**WISC**
Block design: 6.40 (1948–72); 6.48 (1972–89); 9.60 (1989–2002); 14.21 (2002–12)

**WAIS**
Block design: 5.00 (1954–78); 5.04 (1978–95); 3.34 (1995–2006); 2.20 (2006–16)

are double the rate of the comparison tests; by circa 1995 they merely match them; and the projection for 2012 shows similarities with a rate only 58 percent of that of the comparison tests.

The scientific spectacles factor seemed to be fading. Then I calculated the WAIS or adult trends, and it was just the reverse. If anything the gains on similarities were drawing away from those of the comparison tests. Since block design is supposed to have some tie to Raven's, and Raven's is the other test affected by scientific spectacles, I charted the course of its gains. This time it is the WAIS that shows a decline, and it is the WISC that shows escalation. Collectively, the American subtest data suggest that all the familiar causes of IQ gains are still potent in the developed world.

## Requiem for nutrition

Hunger is the specter that haunts the developing world. But while large pockets of substandard diet persisted in the developed world into the twentieth century, improved nutrition has not been an important cause of IQ gains there for many years.

At one time, when I saw that massive IQ gains in the Netherlands were accompanied by height gains, I thought there might be a link. During much of the twentieth century East Asia, the Americas, and Europe enjoyed both massive height gains and massive IQ gains. Many have posited enhanced nutrition as a cause of both (Lynn, 1989, 1990, 1993, 1998a, 2009; Storfer, 1990). Later, a wide range of evidence convinced me that the coincidence is deceptive. First, I will survey evidence from general trends here and there. Then I will use the UK to show that the history of IQ gains there cannot be reconciled with any plausible history of how the quality of nutrition has varied over time.

## The Dutch

Recall that comprehensive samples tested in 1952, 1962, 1972, and 1982 show that Dutch males made a 20-point gain on a Raven's-type test (Flynn, 1987, p. 172). The latest period shows a huge gain; that is, the Dutch 18-year-olds tested in 1982 outscored the Dutch 18-year-olds tested in 1972 by fully eight IQ points. Did the quality of the Dutch diet really escalate that much in ten years?

The gains posted by the 1962 males over the 1952 males are interesting. The Dutch 18-year-olds of 1962 had a known nutritional handicap. They were either in the womb or born during the great Dutch famine of 1944 when German troops monopolized food and brought sections of the population to near starvation. Yet, they do not show up even as a blip in the pattern of Dutch IQ gains. It appears as if a brief period of food deprivation has little impact if mother and child are well nourished throughout life.

## Top and bottom of the curve

The major argument for nutrition as a post-1950 factor rests on a hypothesis about the pattern of IQ gains. It assumes that the affluent had an adequate diet in 1950 and dietary deficiencies were mainly in the lower classes. Therefore, improved nutrition would affect primarily the latter. Since the lower classes are more represented in the bottom half of the IQ curve, IQ gains should be larger in the bottom half than the top half.

There are seven nations for which we have the whole IQ distribution: France (1949 to 1974); the Netherlands (1952 to 1982); Denmark (1958 to 1987); the USA (1948 to 1989); Spain (1970 to 1999); Norway (1957 to 2002); and Britain (1938 to 2008). Spain, Denmark, and Norway show gains larger in the bottom half of the curve. But France, the Netherlands, and the USA show uniform gains over the whole curve. Britain is strange, as we shall see (Colom, Lluis Font, & Andres-Pueyo, 2005; Flynn, 1985, p. 240; 1987, Table 3; 1998c; Sundet, Barlaug, & Torjussen, 2004; Teasdale & Owen, 1989, 2000; Vroon, 1984; Wechsler, 1992, Table 6.9).

Where we do not have the full distribution, a sign that gains might be concentrated in the lower half would be that the range or variance (the SD) of IQ scores has lessened over time. If the lower half has gained, and the upper half has not, the bottom scores will come closer to the top scores. The best data show that Belgium, Argentina, Sweden, Canada, New Zealand, and Estonia have no pattern of declining variance. In Israel, males show no SD decline but females do. However, the female data are inferior in quality, and it is hardly plausible that the latter had a worse diet than the former (Bouvier, 1969, pp. 4–5; Clarke, Nyberg, & Worth, 1978, p. 130; Emanuelsson, Reuterberg, & Svensson, 1993; Flynn, 1987, Table 5; 1998b, Table 1a; Flynn & Rossi-Casé, 2011; Must, Must, & Raudik, 2003).

Therefore, as far as we know, nutrition is viable as a causal factor in only three nations post-1950 (Spain, Denmark, and Norway). Even in those nations, it has merely escaped falsification. There are other factors that may have been present among the affluent in 1950 and moved down to benefit the less affluent after that date, such as urbanization, decent education, modern parenting behavior, or fewer children.

## IQ and height

The connection between height gains and IQ gains over time is significant only because it may signal nutrition as a common cause. Coupled with the assumption that nutritional gains have affected the lower classes disproportionately, this brings us back to the IQ curve. Wherever height gains persist, presumably nutritional gains persist, and where nutritional gains persist, IQ gains should show the predicted pattern, that is, gains mainly in the lower half of the curve.

This is not always the case. Martonell (1998) evidences that height gains persisted in the Netherlands until children born about 1965. Yet, cohorts born between 1934 and 1964 show massive Raven's-type gains throughout the whole range of IQs. The French gained in height until at least those born in 1965.

Yet, cohorts born between 1931 and 1956 show massive Raven's gains that were uniform up through the 90th percentile.

In addition, when height gains escalate, presumably significant nutritional gains have occurred, and the rate of IQ gains should increase. Kolmos and Breitfelder (2008) trace US height trends for those born after 1942 and find gains from 1970 to 2002 that dwarf the up and down fluctuations of earlier years. The oldest member of the WISC-III (Wechsler Intelligence Scale for Children – third edition) sample had a birth date of 1973 and the youngest member of the WISC-IV sample, one of 1996. The height pattern predicts that IQ gains in the US should escalate during the period after the WISC-III. They do not. The gains are constant from the original WISC all the way to the WISC-IV.

## Norway and two kinds of nutrition

Norway was cited above as a nation in which the nutrition hypothesis is viable thanks to greater IQ gains in the lower half of the distribution. Actually, it counts against the posited connection between height gains and IQ gains. The upper classes tend to be taller. Yet, height gains have been larger in the upper half of the height distribution than in the lower half (Sundet, Barlaug, & Torjussen, 2004). This combination, greater height gains in the upper half of the distribution, greater IQ gains in the lower, poses a serious problem. Are there two kinds of enhanced nutrition, one confined to the upper classes that raises height more than it does IQ, the other affecting the lower classes that raises IQ more than it does height?

## Raven's data from Britain

British IQ data are so rich as to be worthy of special attention. They come from several versions of Raven's Progressive Matrices. The Coloured Progressive Matrices (CPM) is designed for younger schoolchildren, primarily for those under 11 (Raven, Court, & Raven, 1986, pp. 2–3). Until 2008, the Standard Progressive Matrices (SPM) was used for older schoolchildren. In that year, the SPM PLUS was introduced as a revised version of the SPM. It introduces new items, most of which have been equated to match the old items in difficulty, but some are more difficult than any that appear on the SPM. Tables allow scores on the two versions to be equated.

The CPM was normed three times and all samples were of reasonable quality (Raven, 1986, p. 33; Raven, Court, & Raven, 1986, pp. 19–20; Raven, Rust, & Squire, 2008). The SPM was also normed three times. For details see Flynn (1987) and Raven, Rust, and Squire (2008). All data herein are from the standardizations. All estimates of gains were made in SDUs (Standard Deviation Units) and multiplied by 15 to convert them into IQ equivalents.

## The Coloured Progressive Matrices results

Box 7 gives the CPM results. Between 1947 and 2007, children aged from 5 to 11 gained 15.59 IQ points. The rate was less between 1947 and 1982 (0.170 points per year) than between 1982 and 2007 (0.386 points per year). Gains declined beginning about the age of 9. It was difficult to estimate the gains of older children. By 1982, the CPM had become too easy for bright children aged 11 and by 2007, too easy for children aged 8.

This means you cannot get good estimates of gains over the top half of the curve (see the note in Box 7). Nonetheless, we can say with assurance that the top half outgained the bottom half prior to 1982 for ages 5 to 10 (by the huge ratio of 2.5 to 1); and that the same was true prior to 2007 for ages 5 to 7 (at a ratio of 1.5 to 1). Recall what the nutrition hypothesis asserts: that as time passed, the lower classes made larger nutritional

**Box 7 (see Table AI5 in Appendix I)**

Estimating IQ gains (whole curve) during various periods on the CPM.

| | | |
|---|---|---|
| 1947–1982 (ages 5.5–11): | 5.93 IQ points | 0.170 points/year |
| 1982–2007 (ages 5.5–11.5): | 9.66 IQ points | 0.386 points/year |
| 1947–2007 (ages 5.5–11): | 15.59 IQ points | 0.260 points/year |

Comparing gains over the top and bottom halves of the IQ curve wherever possible.

| | | |
|---|---|---|
| 1947–1982 (ages 5.5–10.5): | 8.63 IQ points (top half) | 3.49 IQ points (bottom half) |
| 1982–2007 (ages 5.5–7.25): | 12.97 IQ points (top half) | 8.92 IQ points (bottom half) |

*Note:* Originally, both the CPM and SPM had levels of item difficulty that were appropriate. But over time, children got better and better at the items, and the tests became too easy for those at and above the 50th percentile. When these children began to get 30 or more items correct (out of 36), the range was too narrow to differentiate them for performance. As Jensen (1980, p. 646) asserts, "Some scores above 30 are underestimates of the child's ability, due to the ceiling effect." A ceiling effect also afflicts scores in the top half on the 1979 SPM distributions. For example, by age 9.5 years, the raw score difference between the 95th and 50th percentiles is about half of that between the 50th and 5th percentiles.

gains than the always reasonably well-fed upper classes; and that therefore, IQ gains should be concentrated in the lower half of the curve.

## The Standard Progressive Matrices results

Box 8 summarizes results for the Standard Progressive Matrices (SPM). These show that between 1938 and 2008, children aged from 7 to 14 gained 13.65 IQ points. Contrary to the CPM, gains

**Box 8 (see Table AI6 in Appendix I)**

Estimating IQ gains (whole curve) during various periods on the SPM.

| | | |
|---|---|---|
| 1938–1979 (ages 8–14): | 9.39 IQ points | 0.229 points/year |
| 1979–2008 (ages 7.5–15.5): | 4.26 IQ points | 0.147 points/year |
| 1938–2008 (ages 7.5–14.5): | 13.65 IQ points | 0.195 points/year |
| 1979–2008 (ages 14.5–15.5) | – 1.88 IQ points | |

Comparing gains over the top and bottom halves of the IQ curve wherever possible.

| | | |
|---|---|---|
| 1938–1979 (age 9.5): | 7.95 IQ points (top half) | 10.71 IQ points (bottom half) |
| 1979–2008 (ages 7.5–15.5): | 2.07 IQ points (top half) | 7.06 IQ points (bottom half) |

on the SPM appear greater in the earlier period than in the later: between 1938 and 1979 the rate is 0.229 points per year; between 1979 and 2008 it is 0.147 points per year. In both periods, gains declined beginning about the age of 12.

At that age and above, ceiling effects are profound and the estimates of gains are based on comparisons at the lower percentiles. But the gains over the bottom half are so small that no plausible gains over the missing part of the distribution would give high overall gains. Therefore, I conclude that the decline in gains beginning at age 12 is real. After 1979, ages 14–15 actually show small losses. This tallies with Piagetian data (Shayer, Coe, & Ginsburg, 2007; Shayer & Ginsburg, 2009). Perhaps the cognitive demands of teenage subculture have been stagnant over the last 30 years.

More to the point, the SPM shows the opposite of the CPM: the gains were larger in the bottom half of the curve. It is true that in the earlier period (1938–1979), only one genuine comparison is possible. But at that one age (9.5 years of age), the

**Box 9 (see Table AI7 in Appendix I)**

The rate of gain from the CPM and the SPM fall into line when compared over the ages they have in common, namely, ages 7 (or 7.5) to 11.

| | | |
|---|---|---|
| CPM 1947–1982 | 6.56 points | 0.187 points/year |
| SPM 1938–1979 | 10.44 points | 0.255 points/year |
| CPM 1982–2007 | 9.58 points | 0.382 points/year |
| SPM 1979–2008 | 9.28 points | 0.320 points/year |

bottom-half gains were clearly larger; and the bottom-half gains are so large at other ages, I suspect that the same was generally true throughout the period. Therefore, the SPM gains seem favorable to the nutrition hypothesis.

In sum, the Coloured Progressive Matrices and the Standard Progressive Matrices told different stories over roughly similar periods. Then I matched the two tests for the ages that they had in common, namely, ages 7 to 11. Box 9 shows that comparing common ages dissolves the conflict over which period showed the larger IQ gains. Both tests now gave a higher rate of gain for circa 1980 and after. The match is as good as can be expected as the periods do not quite correspond. The cause of the apparent "mismatch" was the groups aged older than 11. They show a dramatic drop in gains in the later period. Their exclusion from the CPM data left it unaffected. Their inclusion in the SPM data dragged its overall estimate of gains for the later period well down.

## The merged data

This suggested that the other anomaly, the CPM and SPM giving different estimates as to whether gains were larger in the top or bottom half of the curve, might be a function of age. Therefore,

**Box 10 (see Table AI8 in Appendix I)**

Raven's rates of gain by age when CPM and SPM data are merged. Size of rates over the top of the curve is compared to their size over the bottom half. The rates of gain are expressed in IQ points per year. It also shows how much the gap between the top and bottom halves closed or widened between those born in certain years. A – sign means the gap closed, a + sign means it widened.

| **Rates 1943–1980** | | | | Top/Bot. |
|---|---|---|---|---|
| Ages | | | Born | Gap |
| 5.5–8.25 | 0.255 (top half) | 0.073 (bot. half) | 1936 & 1973 | +6.7 pts. |
| 9.25 | 0.208 (top half) | 0.200 (bot. half) | 1934 & 1971 | +0.3 pts. |
| 10.25 | 0.193 (top half) | 0.227 (bot. half) | 1933 & 1970 | –1.3 pts. |
| 11.21–12.37 | lower (top half) | higher (bot. half) | 1932 & 1969 | (closed) |
| **Rates 1980–2008** | | | | |
| 5.5–6.25 | 0.513 (top half) | 0.352 (bot. half) | 1974 & 2002 | +4.5 pts. |
| 7.37 | 0.430 (top half) | 0.416 (bot. half) | 1973 & 2001 | +0.4 pts. |
| 8.25 | 0.318 (top half) | 0.488 (bot. half) | 1972 & 2000 | –4.8 pts. |
| 9.25–15.5 | –0.035 (top half) | 0.206 (bot. half) | 1968 & 1996 | –6.7 pts. |

I merged the two data sets to see if such a pattern emerged. Fortunately, the Coloured Matrices and the Standard Matrices data share a roughly common time frame. The two earlier periods are 1947 to 1982 and 1938 to 1979 respectively, so I group them as applying to approximately 1943 to 1980. The two later periods are 1982 to 2007 and 1979 to 2008, which become 1980 to

2008. For each age, I average the CPM results, for example, I average the gains for ages 8 and 8.5 to get a value simply for age 8.25. Then I average the SPM results in the same way. Finally, after pro-rating them both, I average the two, which gives an overall value for each age.

Box 10 shows that in the earlier period (1943–1980), gains are larger over the top half of the curve from ages 5 to 9, and gains are larger over the bottom half from ages 10 to 12. In the later period (1980–2008), gains are larger over the top half of the curve from ages 5 to 7, and gains are larger over the bottom half from ages 8 to 15. It can hardly be that over time, the diet of lower-class children deteriorated compared to upper-class children from ages 5 to about 8, and then suddenly improved from ages 9 to about 14.

But this does not do the nutrition hypothesis justice. As Lynn (2009) says: "The nutrition theory posits that the crucial effect of the improvement in nutrition impacts on the fetus and on infants when the brain is growing, and has little subsequent effect." If so, cohorts that differ profoundly in the pattern of their IQ gains (and by inference differ in nutrition) have life spans that differ primarily by birth year. To be plausible, the nutrition hypothesis must single out the year of birth as crucial.

Therefore, Box 10 names the birth years of the cohorts used to measure IQ gains over time. For example, those aged 9 in 1943 were born in 1934, and the comparison cohort aged 9 in 1980 was born in 1971. The box indicates how the upper/lower-half IQ gap fared between those two cohorts: it widened by 0.3 points, which means it was essentially stable. The pattern the nutrition hypothesis predicts, that later cohorts should consistently show the IQ gap narrowing in response to the nutritional gap between the classes narrowing, is not there. Two cohort comparisons show the gap widening, three show essentially no change, and three show the gap narrowing.

But the issue is not to be decided by counting successes and failures. The question is whether we can write a coherent dietary history to cover the results in Box 10. They show that comparing the early Great Depression years (1932–1933) to the period of 1969–1973, the lower classes gained nutritional ground on the upper classes. Then they show that in the later Depression years (1934–1936), the lower classes suddenly began to lose ground dramatically. The data link the early 1970s (1968–1974) to our own day (1996–2002). And they tell us that in the early 1970s (1968–1972) the nutritional gap was huge compared to today, but by the middle of the 1970s (1973–1974) it had become much less than today. This last leaves open two possibilities: either some dramatic improvement in lower-class diet set in about 1973; or some dramatic deterioration set in about 2001. What an up-and-down roller-coaster ride for the diet of the lower classes!

If you pick your years mischievously, you can get fantastic results. Linking the widened gap of 1936 and 1973 (+6.7 points) with the widened gap of 1974 and 2002 (+4.5 points), you get an incredible deterioration of lower-class diet over time: one that separated the top and bottom of the curve by a total of at least 11 points. Linking the narrowed gap of 1932 and 1969 (no exact estimate but probably at least 2 points) with the narrowed gap of 1968 and 1996 (−6.7 points), you get a large improvement of lower class diet over time: one that closed the top and bottom half of the curve by about 9 points. What you cannot do is get a coherent dietary history of Britain. These difficulties pale beside what a detailed cohort chronology implies (see Table AI9 in Appendix I).

I suspect that the British Raven's gains have little to do with cohorts born earlier or later. I suspect that they are, as they seem on their face, age-specific. But I have no easy explanation as to why among young children, the brighter show larger gains, while among older schoolchildren, it is the less bright. If adult data showed the gains sinking even further down the curve, perhaps dropping off it entirely, there would be a coherent pattern: gains occur at a given intellectual level, one that is high on the curve for young children, low on the curve for older children, and off the curve for adults. But we have already seen that Raven's data for the Netherlands, France, and males in Israel show huge adult gains over the full curve.

I do not say that no hypothesis is possible. Perhaps, smaller families and new parenting practices favor the children of the upper classes when they are young, and the advantage fades away as the leveler of school begins to bite. Perhaps beginning at age 9, gaining in momentum at ages 10–11, and dominating all by ages 12–15, a peer group subculture begins to weigh in. This teenage subculture may have become a leveler, so that the cognitive environment of the top half is no better than in the past. Perhaps when teenagers leave their subculture to go to college and eventually work, greater cognitive demands are made over the whole curve. Here is a puzzle for sociologists to solve.

Those who consult Appendix I will find tables by age for both tests comparing all standardizations. There is also a table on the performance of the sample that normed the new SPM PLUS, one that readers will find helpful if they wish to do their own calculations of British Raven's gains (heaven help them). Finally, there are tables that spell out the implications of the pattern of IQ gains for the nutritional history of Britain in greater detail than is provided in the text.

## Summary on nutrition

If diet has been a factor in advanced nations in the modern era, it was weak enough to be swamped by other causes of IQ gains over time. For example, US IQ gains look fairly constant all the way from 1932 to 2006. The Great Depression would have worsened nutrition but the scientific spectacles and modern world factors would have been humming away. During World War II, father absence would have lowered the ratio of adults to children in the home but women expanded their horizons and industrialization proceeded apace. A multiplicity of factors is at work, and moderate fluctuations of one factor do not count for much.

In passing, there is a debate about whether or not twin studies show that the effects of family environment on IQ fade away by adulthood, at least in the developed world (Jensen, 1998). Those who believe that they do will find it hard to defend early childhood nutrition as an important influence on IQ. Differences in nutrition would be primarily between middle-class families and poor families. If the impact of nutrition persists to adulthood, the effects of family environment would have to persist as well.

## Hybrid vigor

Hybrid vigor refers to the fact that too much inbreeding is a negative influence on a whole range of human traits including intelligence, for example, inbreeding between first and second cousins produces IQ deficits. If a nation's population was divided at the beginning of the twentieth century into small and inbred communities and then, over time, became more mobile, it would reap the benefits of outbreeding (hybrid vigor) and the nation's mean IQ would rise.

Evidence from two nations calls enhanced outbreeding into question as an important cause, at least in developed nations in the twentieth century. The US never was a collection of isolated communities that discovered geographical mobility only in the twentieth century. Right from the start, there was a huge influx of migrants who settled in both urban and rural areas. There were major population shifts during settlement of the West, after the Civil War, and during the World Wars. The growth of mobility has been modest: in 1870, 23 percent of Americans were living in a state other than the one of their birth; in 1970, the figure was 32 percent (Mosler & Catley, 1998).

Recent data from Norway compare the scores of males as they reach 18 with the scores of their older siblings who reached 18 a few years earlier. If the younger sibling outscores the older, this signals an IQ gain over time (the reverse would signal a loss over time). The IQ trends yielded by these comparisons exactly match the magnitude of the nation's IQ trends (Sundet *et al.*, 2010). Because siblings have the same parents, they cannot differ in their degree of outbreeding. Therefore, we know that hybrid vigor has not been a factor in modern Scandinavia. If it had, the within-sibling estimate (from which outbreeding is absent) would fall short of the general population trend. Since it does not, we know that outbreeding was equally absent from both. Unless Norway is atypical of the developed world, any dividends from hybrid vigor are over.

I should add that while there is rural isolation in much of the developing world, and areas of between-cousins marriage in places such as the Middle East, I am unsure that increased outbreeding will cause large IQ gains. Data from Hiroshima show that the offspring of first cousins show only a 3-points deficit for IQ and the offspring of second cousins show less than one point (Flynn, 2009c, p. 223).

## Health and class

Have health advances been important causes of IQ gains in the developed world since 1950? How many IQ points would be gained if developed nations improved the health environment that prevails among them at present? Steen (2009) lists America's health ills by cause, all the way from poverty, through low birth weight (LBW), lead poisoning, childhood neglect, and untreated illnesses, to fetal alcohol syndrome. He attaches an IQ cost to each, and estimates that their elimination would raise America's mean IQ by 5 points.

He does not project his calculations into the past. Perhaps the necessary data or literature did not exist in 1950. About the past he makes some mistakes. He cites the Dutch famine of 1944 as evidence of the potency of nutrition when in fact it shows, as we have seen, that temporary food deprivation has a very small impact in an advanced nation. He grants that he cannot retrospectively match health gains to the recent history of IQ gains. I doubt that anyone could. Sometimes advances in prenatal care, methods of delivering infants at birth, and postnatal care (including nurturing premature babies) are cited as an obvious source of IQ gains. That is not the opinion of Sir Michael Rutter (2000, p. 223). He argues that these improvements have had no net positive effect on mean IQ. For every child who has escaped mental impairment, one or more impaired children have been saved who would have died without modern techniques.

What of the future? To get his estimate of a potential gain of 5 points, Steen adds together the benefits of each health improvement he lists. There is no sign that he has used multiple regression equations to allow for confounding. The IQ cost attached to poverty includes much of the costs of LBW, fetal alcohol syndrome, childhood neglect, untreated illnesses, and lead poisoning, so a proper calculation might show no more than two or three points.

Even this seems too high an estimate of the effects of whatever improved healthcare it is realistic to expect. The children of the upper two-thirds of American homes ranked by occupation (children of professional, technical, managerial, and white-collar workers) have had a mean IQ steady at 102.5 from 1932 to the present (Flynn, 2008). Let us say we enhance the health environment of the lower third of children to match that of the upper two-thirds of American homes. We would get an overall gain of 2.5 points (102.5–100). In fact, this estimate entails two false assumptions: that there are no genetic differences for intelligence between the classes; and that we can give the children of the lower classes all of the benefits, not just the health benefits, of better homes.

This is of course a purely static analysis of a dynamic situation. If medical breakthroughs bring dramatic health improvement to all Americans, if brain-altering drugs upgrade intelligence and are confined to the developed world, all bets are off.

I endorse Steen's plea to give America's poor decent healthcare. But alleviating misery and salvaging wasted human potential are reason enough: to predict sizable IQ dividends is problematic. Without doubt, he is correct about the adverse effects of the poverty and ills of the developing world. Eliminating parasitic stress would cause some IQ gains. However, the results will be limited unless the elimination is accompanied by modernity. The developed world did not cure its health problems by benevolent outsiders applying bandages. They cured them by becoming functional modern societies. It is that whole package that caused the massive IQ gains of the twentieth century.

## The developing world

Despite the fact that developed nations are entering the twenty-first century with their traditional rates of IQ gains intact, the developing world may overtake them. We have seen that the developed world long ago largely exhausted sources of IQ deficits still present in the developing world (rural isolation, hunger, inbreeding, ill health). Are there signs that developing nations are beginning to make IQ gains at high rates? Kenya yes, Saudi Arabia yes but doomed, Turkey probably, Dominica probably but grave problems, Sudan no. The name of each nation is followed by Lynn and Vanhanen's estimate of its mean IQ in 2006.

## Kenya (IQ 72)

Daley *et al.* (2003) collected data from two large studies of 7-year-olds in Embu, Kenya, in 1984 and 1998. Gains on the Coloured

Progressive Matrices totaled 13.85 points over the 14 years for a rate of gain of almost 1 point per year.

As Box 11 shows, this huge rate has only two rivals in a literature covering 15 nations or peoples, and these two rates lie well in the past. Children from Leipzig, then in East Germany, reported a rate that was marginally higher back in 1968 to 1978. Youths reporting for military service in France matched it back in 1949 to 1974, but only on paper. The French samples probably exaggerate gains by 5 points, which would reduce the rate to 0.805 points per year, which is in line with near-by Belgium (Flynn, 1987, p. 174). No nation in the developed world shows a Raven's gain beginning as late as 1984, except for adults in Norway where by 1993, gains had virtually ceased.

The authors attribute the Kenyan gain largely to increased parental literacy, family structure, and improved children's nutrition and health. Kenya is the most industrially developed country in East Africa, but manufacturing still accounts for only 14 percent of gross domestic product (GDP). Small-scale manufacturing (household goods, car parts, farm implements) is expanding and its telecommunications sector is highly successful. There is a large pool of English-speaking professional workers, and a high level of computer literacy among the youth.

On the debit side, 10 percent of the people live on the verge of starvation without any state support (they pay to use a latrine). Politics turns around which of the three most powerful tribes (out of 452) will use office to favor their own tribe. GDP growth was low from 2000 to 2005, averaged at over 6 percent from 2006 to 2008, and dipped during 2009 (the financial crisis, drought, and tripled food prices). A recovery began in 2010.

## Saudi Arabia (IQ 84)

Batterjee (2011) report results for children aged 8 to 15 between standardizations of the Standard Progressive Matrices in 1977

**Box 11**

The Kenyan Raven's gains are ranked against all others on record. I calculated the Kenyan gains as follows: 4.49 raw score points; divided by 4.863 (British SD for 7-year-olds in 1982); equals 0.923 SDs; times 15 equals 13.85 IQ points.

| | | |
|---|---|---|
| **Children** | | |
| Leipzig (1968–78, aged 11–16) | 10 plus points | rate 1.000+ per year |
| **Kenya (1984–98, aged 7)** | **13.85 points** | **rate 0.989 per year** |
| La Plata, Argentina (1964–98, aged 13–18) | 21.35 points | rate 0.628 per year |
| Edmonton, Canada (1956–77, aged 9) | 8.44 points | rate 0.402 per year |
| New Zealand (1956–81, aged 15–16) | 9.26 points | rate 0.370 per year |
| Saudi Arabia (1977–2010, aged 8–15) | 11.70 points | rate 0.355 per year |
| Australia (1950–76, aged 10–16) | 8.76 points | rate 0.337 per year |
| Great Britain (1938–2008, aged 7.5–14.5) | 13.65 points | rate 0.195 per year |
| **Adults** | | |
| France (1949–74, aged 18+) | 25.12 points | rate 1.005 per year |
| Belgium – Flemish (1958–67, aged 18+) | 7.82 points | rate 0.869 per year |
| La Plata, Argentina (1964–98, aged 19–24) | 27.66 points | rate 0.814 per year |
| Belgium – Walloon (1958–67, aged 18+) | 6.47 points | rate 0.719 per year |
| Spain (1963–1991, aged 18+) | 19.20 points | rate 0.686 per year |
| The Netherlands (1952–82, aged 18) | 20.10 points | rate 0.667 per year |
| Israel female (1976–84, aged 17.5) | 5.09 points | rate 0.637 per year |
| Norway (1954–68, aged 19–20) | 8.80 points | rate 0.629 per year |
| Israel male (1971–84, aged 17.5) | 7.35 points | rate 0.565 per year |
| Great Britain (1942–92, aged 18–67) | 27.00 points | rate 0.540 per year |
| Dominica (1968–2003, adults) | 18.00 points | rate 0.514 per year |
| Norway (1968–93, aged 19–20) | 7.90 points | rate 0.316 per year |
| Norway (1993–2002, aged 19–20) | 0.33 points | rate 0.033 per year |

*Sources:* Flynn (1987, 1998a, 1998b); Flynn and Rossi-Casé (2011); Box 10 above. See text for an explanation of Dominica's dates as being 1968 to 2003.

and 2010. The gain of 11.70 points over the 33 years gives a rate of 0.355 points a year, impressive but no higher than rates for Australia and New Zealand 20 years earlier (see Box 11). Both samples were from urban centers in Makka Province.

The economy of Saudi Arabia is dependent on oil. The petroleum sector accounts for over half of the gross domestic product and 95 percent of export earnings. Its population is 27 million of whom 70 percent (about 18.7 million) are Saudis and the rest foreign workers (Saudi Press Association, 2011). At present, thanks to oil revenue, the public sector manages to employ its native population in unproductive work (Mahdi, 2010). In 2030, when the oil runs out, its population is projected to be 44 million.

Despite brave talk about alternative sources of energy and tourism, disaster looms. It may achieve IQ parity with the developed world but that will hardly determine its fate.

## Dominica (IQ 82)

Meisenberg *et al.* (2005) used a cross-sectional design to measure Raven's gains in Dominica, an Afro-Caribbean island nation of 76,000 people. They compared two cohorts aged 18–25 and 51–62 respectively, the older born in 1948 and the younger in 1983. Scored against the appropriate British norms, adjusted to allow for British gains, the total gain was 18 IQ points, which over 35 years gives a rate of 0.514 points per year. They concluded that enhanced formal schooling was more important than family structure (Meisenberg *et al.*, 2006). Note that they measure the period of gains by birth date. If they had compared 20-year-olds tested in 2003 with 20-year-olds tested in 1968, the usual research design, the years would be 1968 to 2003. The period is too long to allow us to estimate recent trends. If it is escalating, it now exceeds any rate of gain we have reason to believe exists in the developed world today.

Despite a strong ethos in favor of education and a literacy rate of 87 percent, Dominica has 30 percent of its people below the poverty line. It is not clear that any enhancement of academic skills (or IQ) can deal with its main economic problem: natural disasters. Hurricane David in 1979 had the most catastrophic effects in modern times, but there were also severe storms in 1989, 1995, and 1999. Landslides are common. Benson *et al.* (2001) spells out its vulnerability with a list that sounds as bad as the Biblical plagues of Egypt. Aside from storms, potential hazards include volcanic activity, earthquakes, drought, floods, bush fires, and tsunamis.

## Turkey (IQ 90)

Kagitcibasi, & Biricik (2011) opens a window on Turkey. In 1977, the Draw-a-Person test was administered to 5th graders (N = 218) in five schools located in the city of Bursa and rural villages. In 2010, it was administered to 5th graders (N = 258) in six schools. Thanks to access to the paper in draft, I have more detailed data than appear in the published version (which I will furnish on request).

At both times, one school was a moderate distance from the city and another was in a remote village. I averaged these to get a rural comparison at each time. In 1977 there were three "urban" schools: one from a middle-class urban area, one from a lower-income urban area, and one from a nearby village. In 2010, there were four urban schools: one from a middle-class urban area and three from lower-income urban areas. I assumed that increased sampling of poor schools reflected a change in the balance between the classes in the metropolitan area. Owing to a huge migration into the city, Bursa went from being a small city to a huge metropolis during the 33 years. I calculated a weighted average of the urban school sample for both years to get an urban comparison.

**Box 12**

Calculating Turkey's IQ gains between 1977 and 2010 requires a mean IQ for urban and rural dwellers at both times, plus the percentage of the population that were urban and rural at both times. The method of deriving the means is described in the text. As for the percentages: 1977 – 42.4 % urban, 57.6 % rural; and 2010 (projected) – 75.0% urban, 25% rural.

The calculations using Kagitcibasi, & Biricik (2011), Table 1:

---

1977 rural mean: (63.50 + 74.05)/2 = 68.78

2010 rural mean: (89.22 + 95.67)/2 = 92.45

1977 urban mean: ((85.29 × 14) + (90.11 × 80) + (102.09 × 93))/187 = 95.71

2010 urban mean: ((97.94 × 163) + (103.19 × 52))/215 = 99.21

1977 national mean: ((42.4 × 95.71) + (57.6 × 68.78))/100 = (4058.10 + 3961.73)/100 = **80.20**

2010 national mean: ((75.0 × 99.21) + (25.0 × 92.45))/100 = (7440.75 + 2311.25)/100 = **97.52**

Gain: 97.52 – 80.20 = **17.32 IQ points**/33 years = **rate of 0.525 points per year**

---

Box 12 details the calculations that suggest that Turkey gained more than 17 IQ points over the last 33 years for a rate of gain of 0.525 points per year. This is more of a guess than a solid estimate. The rural samples are very small. No doubt, better census data would alter my urban values. Still, if the rural means are approximately correct, they alone entail a large gain. Assume that the mean in urban centers was no higher in 2010 than in 1977: the rural gains would still boost the nation's overall IQ by 14.70 points for a rate of 0.445 points per year.

Note that the calculations assume that Bursa's IQ trends were typical of urban Turkey after 1977. This cannot have been the case. Between 1970 and 2009, Turkey's population doubled (from 36.1 to 72.6 million) and her urban population increased by almost four times (from 14 to 54 million). Bursa's population increased by 25.5 times: it went from 100,000 to over 2.55 million. Bursa accommodated a hugely disproportionate share of Turkey's urbanization. If this meant an unusual problem in assimilating rural migrants and modernizing them, Bursa's IQ rise may be below gains in Turkish cities in general; and my calculations would give an underestimate of national gains over this period.

The fact that the Draw-a-Person (DAP) test was used can be counted as either a plus or a minus. In 1977, Turkey's rural population was relatively test naive. Therefore, a test that is non-verbal and designed to be independent of academic skills may have given a fairer picture of Turkey's mean IQ at that time than a test such as the WISC. On the other hand, studies of the correlation between the DAP and the Stanford Binet vary from 0.26 to 0.92; and those with the WISC from 0.38 to 0.77 (Kagitcibasi, & Biricik, 2011). A value just below 0.60 is a reasonable estimate.

A low national IQ 33 years ago did not forbid economic progress in Turkey. Over that time, the usual yearly growth rate has been 6 percent, although there were sharp setbacks in 1994, 1999, and 2001. Well before the end of the twenty-first century, Turkey promises to be as highly developed as France; and have the same mean IQ. If only her people had been trapped north of the Alps during the Ice Ages, what wonders might lie ahead? An interesting trend: in 1977, there was no significant difference between the genders; in 2010, the girls in the sample scored almost 6 IQ points higher than the boys.

## Sudan (IQ 71)

Khaleefa, Afra Sulman, and Lynn (2009) report IQs gains on the WAIS-R in Sudan between 1987 and 2007. The samples were selected to be representative of Sudan minus the southern region, which seceded in July 2011. Most of Sudan has Arab and Nubian roots but the southern region is Christian and animist. It should be noted that even today, five-eighths of the people in the areas sampled are illiterate and would find certain subtests of the WAIS (arithmetic, information) difficult. The overall gains are not large: 4.05 points for Full Scale IQ over a 20-year period gives a rate of 0.203 IQ points per year.

However, the pattern of gains is fascinating. Performance IQ shows a gain of 7.2 IQ points. They gained on all the "modern world" subtests. There was a huge gain on object assembly and a large one on digit symbol or coding, subtests responsive to modernity's emphasis on spatial skills and speedy information processing. And there were moderate gains on picture arrangement and picture completion, subtests responsive to modernity's visual culture. As for the "scientific spectacles" subtests, gains are lower on block design; and similarities shows a loss of 3.45 points, the first such loss I have ever seen in the literature. The "school-basics" subtests of information, arithmetic, and vocabulary collectively show a gain of only 1.4 points over the 20 years. This is even worse than America's record for these subtests, except for arithmetic. Given that schooling in Sudan was starting from a much lower level than prevailed in America two generations ago, this is disturbing.

The 2007 sample had a median age of 50. On average, they were born in 1957, at school from say 1963 to 1972, and were adults from 1976 to 2007. The earlier sample was born in 1937, at school from 1943 to 1952, and adult from 1956 to 1987. The data may be comparing schooling in 1948 with 1968, and comparing two adult populations the later of which was selectively exposed to the modern world more and more as they aged.

My diagnosis would be as follows: the Sudanese had a traditional formal schooling and were taught the basics no better in the 1960s than in the 1940s; they still wear utilitarian rather than scientific spectacles; but they are now being exposed informally to the modern world's culture, probably from radio, television, and the Internet, perhaps because of some contact with foreigners. To test this scenario against the facts, I took a brief look at the history of Sudan since 1940.

Sudan has never had stability since independence in 1956. The first civil war from 1955 to 1972 killed 500,000 people. The second from 1983 to 2005 killed 2 million, and 4 million people were displaced, often more than once. Both devastated the economy. About 80 percent are in agriculture (mainly subsistence farming) and the oil boom since 2006 has left them untouched. The Koran dominates the educational system and its dominance was formalized in 1980. The "Muslim curriculum" is based on the permanence of human nature, religious values, and physical nature (which does not necessarily mean modern science). The majority is still illiterate.

Khaleefa, Abdelwahid, Abdulradi, and Lynn (2008) added to the literature on Sudan by comparing standardizations of the Draw-a-Man test (the old name for Draw-a-Person) held in 1964 and 2006. The subjects were schoolchildren aged from 4 to 10, so the early sample was in school about when the recent WAIS sample was in school (the 1960s). The gains scored against the test manual were 12.19 points, which over 42 years gives a rate of gain of 0.290 IQ points per year. Given the histories of the two nations it is not surprising that the Sudanese gains are lower than my estimate of Turkish gains on the same test.

## Brazil (IQ 87)

Colom *et al.* (2007) compared children aged from 7 to 11 who took the Draw-a-Man test in the city of Belo Horizonte, Brazil: 499 were tested in 1930 and 710 in 2002. They showed an IQ gain of 17 IQ points over the 72 years for a rate of 0.236 points a decade. This rate is even lower than the Sudan, but the period begins at a time too distant to compare with our other data or to shed any light on current trends. Whether or not Brazil is closing the IQ gap with North America and Europe, her mean IQ does not seem to be inhibiting her economic growth. She is one of the world's fastest-growing major economies with an average rate of over 5 percent. Her economy is predicted to become one of the five largest in the world by 2050.

## China (IQ 105)

China's mean IQ is already at least the equal of developed western nations and her high rate of growth appears unstoppable. I include her here only because she still has a huge problem of rural poverty. Raven and Court (1989, p. RS4.8) give data for urban adults on Raven's. I did not include them in Box 11 because the estimates are based on birth dates. Those born earlier scored lower than those born later, but they were older at the time of testing, and performance on Raven's declines with age. This would inflate the rate of gain. In any event, between 1936 and 1986, urban adults "gained" 22 points for a rate of 0.440 points per year, rather less than in Europe.

A recent study by Liu *et al.* (2012) shows that children aged 5 to 6 gained 4.53 points on the WPPSI (Wechsler Preschool and Primary Scale of Intelligence) between 1984 and 2006. This gives a rate of 0.206 points per year, again a bit below that of the United States. The pattern of IQ gains is interesting. Verbal and performance gains are virtually the same, and there was actually a loss on subtests such as similarities and block design. This indicates that better schooling, at least of the traditional sort, was responsible rather than the modernization that promotes better classification skills and the use of logic on abstractions. But these children are very young and the picture might alter with age.

## The twenty-first century

The race is on. Will the developing world catch the developed world for a mix of economic development and mean IQ? This probably depends on some solution of impending energy, pollution, water, food, and population problems. In addition, some nations are disadvantaged because of climate, geography, markets, and scarce resources. I do not believe genes limit their potential. Lynn, ever respectful of evidence and impressed by recent trends, has recently granted that the IQ gap between developed and developing nations may close (Khaleefa *et al.*, 2008).

Always keep in mind: few developing nations have a mean IQ, measured against current norms, as low as the mean the US had in 1900.

# 4 Death, memory, and politics

Some of the implications of massive IQ gains are clear. IQ scores are deceptive unless adjusted for when the test was normed. Indeed, if we fail to adjust IQs, we will make the execution of capital offenders a lottery in which life and death are decided by what test they happened to take as schoolchildren. Judges are becoming aware of this. It is also becoming evident that the problem with IQ scores is the tip of an iceberg. Other scores, such as those used to measure memory loss, are suspect. Scholars should accept these findings with alacrity. However, learned journals still publish a surprising number of papers that use IQ scores uncritically. Other implications of IQ gains are not clear. For example, has political debate in America become more rational over time?

## Death a lottery

The Supreme Court has held, in effect, that a capital offender whose IQ on a reliable test places him in the bottom 2.27 percent of the population has a prima facie case of being exempted from the death penalty. That is the criterion for mental retardation. Ideally, the offender was tested at school prior to the age of 18. But particularly when such scores are not available, or when they seem contradictory, he is tested while on death row.

The other consideration is clinical assessment, based on life history and interview by a psychologist, as to whether the offender is indeed mentally retarded. However, in the American adversarial system of justice, almost inevitably, the defense finds someone who assesses the offender as mentally incompetent and the prosecution finds someone who assesses him as clearly responsible. Therefore, the judge is likely to be heavily influenced by IQ scores as the only thing that cannot be fudged. If your IQ is 70 or below, you are in the bottom 2.27 percent of the population and that is that. But unfortunately, IQ scores cannot be taken at face value. This is because Americans have made score gains on Wechsler and Binet tests since the day they were first published.

As everyone knows, a salary that is average for today (about US$50,000) is well above average if we compare it to salaries 20 years ago. It would be strange to pretend that you made more than the average person by using the wages of 20 years ago as your norms, that is, your standard of measurement. You would be simply ignoring the fact that wages had risen. Similarly, it would be strange to pretend that an IQ test performance (say 20 items correct) put you above the bottom 2.27 percent today simply because it puts you above the bottom 2.27 percent of 20 years ago. People did worse on IQ tests then, so today you might have to get 30 items correct. An IQ below 70 on today's norms would suddenly become well above 70 on yesterday's norms. How much sense would it make to rank you against the norms of the Stone Age? They might make you appear to be a genius.

Unless we adjust IQs for obsolete norms, the death penalty becomes a lottery. You take a test with current norms and your IQ is 70. But if you are unlucky enough to take a test with norms 20 years obsolete, the very same performance will get an IQ of 76 and you will be executed. That is because IQs have been rising at about 0.3 points per year and 0.3 times 20 years equals 6 points. These adjustments are not exact. When I appear as an expert witness, I say: "Of course the rate may vary a bit from year to year and it could be a bit higher at low-IQ levels. But one thing I know for certain. If you fail to deduct the 6 points, in most cases you will be doing a monstrous injustice. You will be executing someone simply because he took an IQ test whose norms were 20 years obsolete. He appears to be above the bottom 2.27 percent but he is not."

Courts have to use rules of evidence, and these were not fashioned with situations of this sort in mind. They assume that expert testimony can meet high tests of reliability. The rules were set out in a decision called the *Daubert* case. In recent years, prosecutors have cited them in an effort to ban testimony about adjusting IQ scores. They argue that this advice lacks the rigor expected of expert testimony. What follows is a plea to the courts to reject *Daubert* motions.

## Daubert motions

The court has before it a capital case. Mr. Smith was murdered at his home and the coroner has established the time of death at 10 am. The defendant admits he entered the home but claims that Smith was already dead. There is a damning piece of testimony against him. A newspaper boy saw him entering the home and heard the town clock strike 10. However, the defense presents three witnesses who passed the town clock on the morning in question and noticed that as usual, the town clerk was some days late in resetting it to mark the start of daylight saving. They were all amused as they checked their watches. One put the actual time at 10.55, another at 11.00, and the third at 11.05. But in any event, the actual time supported the defendant's testimony.

The prosecution argues that only witnesses expert at timekeeping should be allowed to challenge town clocks; and that the three defense witnesses do not qualify as such. It cites the criteria set by the *Daubert* case:

(1) The witnesses' technique was to check the clock against a wristwatch. The scientific community in general has

not yet accepted this method of adjusting time as measured by town clocks.

(2) The theory that lies behind the technique is that reset watches are more likely to capture the actual time (under daylight saving) than nonreset town clocks. The prosecution is unaware of anyone who has rigorously tested that theory.

(3) Articles defending the theory have appeared in peer-reviewed administrative journals (that assess the consequences of lazy town clerks). But not in peer-reviewed chronological journals devoted to the science of measuring time.

(4) The method of correcting the town clock has a margin of error, which is not precisely measurable. Here the prosecution is absolutely correct. The three defense witnesses all offer different corrections ranging from the town clock is slow by 55 to 65 minutes, and for all we know, a fourth would put the correction at 50 to 65 minutes.

(5) Following on from (4), there are no established standards for applying the technique. Adding an hour on to the time of a town clock not reset for daylight saving ignores all sorts of complications. A drunken town clerk might set the clock back an hour, experts note that the task of coordinating any mechanical clock or watch with Greenwich time is complex, and so forth.

The prosecution also makes a point of law. At the time the Supreme Court accepted town clocks as the measure of time, they were all set "in conformity with professional practice" and vouched for by experts as the most accurate measure possible. This was intended to avoid experts wrangling about the "real time," and ever since, courts have been reluctant to question their reliability and invite a new battle of experts.

I take it that anyone would regard all of this as bizarre. It misses the point: failing to question the town clock means putting the time at something that is certain to be misleading. And while taking the average of the three more reliable times leaves us uncertain as to the exact time, it must be done to avoid grievous error.

An additional absurdity: taking town clocks at their face value makes a lottery out of who lives or dies. Surprisingly, there was an identical case in the next town, where the clerk was assiduous and kept the town clock up to date. So whether you live or die depends on whether your town has a lazy or conscientious town clerk.

## The distinction between tests and their norms

There was nothing defective about the town clock. But clocks are not like a ruler that allows me, if it is not defective, to measure height whenever I wish. They require maintenance from time to time and after each intervention they must be accurately reset. The fact that we cannot take IQ scores at face value has nothing to do with the quality of IQ tests. No IQ test has ever classified anyone as gifted, or normal, or suffering from mental retardation. We use the test norms to do that and today, test publishers accept that we must reset the test norms periodically to keep test scores from being deceptive.

You must understand that the test score sends a message that has nothing to do with the test in isolation. Unless you have administered it to a standardization sample, that is, a representative sample of Americans of all ages, or at least all ages in the age range the test covers, the test is useless. A score of 70 is awarded by definition to the exact level of performance that cuts off the bottom 2.27 percent of the population (in statistical terms it is two standard deviations below the mean). If the score of 70 does not do that, no one would trust it. This is because the psychological community believes that the bottom 2.27 percent captures, roughly, the group that suffers from mental retardation.

For particular individuals, they must be compared to their peers. That means to people that are of the same age. They must be of the same age because no 6-year-old can be expected to match the performance of a 12-year-old, and no 70-year-old can be expected to match the performance of a 35-year-old (unless they are superior for their age). They must be of the same age *at the same time*. As we have seen, even people who suffer from mental retardation can rise on the percentile scale if you compare them with people of the past. The average American has gained 30 IQ points over the last century and this appears to be true at all levels of the IQ scale.

Psychologists debate whether twentieth-century IQ gains signal competence gains among the bottom 2.27 percent. If this were so, only those with very low IQs (40 or below) on current norms should strike clinical psychologists as mentally retarded. This is far from the case. My view is that while the bottom 2.27 percent of the population has gained in some ways (a bit more vocabulary and some rudimentary classification skills), they have not enhanced what Stenberg calls practical intelligence: their ability to live autonomous lives. They still need help from others and are subject to manipulation by others. The Vincland Adaptive Behavior Scale measures whether people can cope with everyday life. During a period (from 1989 to 2002) in which American schoolchildren gained over 4 points on the WISC (Wechsler Intelligence Scale for Children), they made (at best) no gains on the Vineland (Flynn, 2009c, pp. 126–127; Vineland, 2006).

But even if we decide one day that the number of mentally retarded is dwindling, we would still have to adjust IQ scores so that individuals were being compared to their own age group at the same time. Let us imagine that we want to isolate only the bottom 1 percent as mentally retarded and made the cutting line an IQ of 65.

Identical twins are both convicted of a capital offense. In 1975, at age 11, one takes the WISC-R. The standardization sample was tested in 1972, so there is only a 3-year lag between himself at age 11 and the 11-year-olds who normed the test. He gets an IQ of 65 and lives. In 1975, his twin attends a different school. There he takes the old WISC whose norms have not been updated since 1947–48 (when its sample was tested). Now there is a 27.5-year lag between himself at age 11 and the 11-year-olds who normed the test. As a result of being compared to 11-year-olds from the distant past, when average performance on the test was worse, he gets an IQ of 72.35 and dies. In other words no matter where we set the cutting line, at 65 or 70, such cases will arise. And the extra points that get one twin killed will be entirely the work of the obsolete norms!

No one felt they could make life and death a lottery in terms of whether a town clerk remembered to reset a clock. Do we want to make life and death the same kind of lottery? To make death depend on whether a school psychologist bought the latest version of the WISC, or whether, perhaps because of a limited budget, decided to use up copies of an older version is unacceptable. No prosecutor or prosecution expert has had the courage to address that question. In sum, whatever we eventually decide about our criterion for mental retardation, we cannot in the meantime "tolerate the infliction of a sentence of death under legal systems that permit this unique penalty to be so wantonly and so freakishly imposed" (Justice Stuart in *Furman* v. *Georgia*, 1972).

## Adjusting obsolete IQ scores

The town clock example was an answer to a prosecution motion to exclude adjusting IQ scores in a recent capital case. The case is

Leon Anthony Winston (Petitioner) v. Loretta K. Kelly (Warden) in the US District Court for the Western District of Virginia. The warden moved that a stay of execution be vacated and supports this motion with a memorandum. The memo urges that the report of a psychologist who wants to adjust the petitioner's IQ scores in the light of the "Flynn effect" (IQ gains over time) should be precluded. It describes itself as a "*Daubert* motion" and argues that IQ adjustments do not qualify as reliable evidence (*Winston* v. *Kelly*, 2008).

I will not repeat my rebuttal of the main drift of this *Daubert* motion. Its core is that no court would argue that a piece of evidence *known* to be radically deceptive be left to stand, simply because evidence to the contrary is not as precise as we would like. *Daubert* motions favor the certainly false over the approximately true. However, there is some detail in this motion worth picking out for comment.

I advocate adjusting WISC (Wechsler Intelligence Scale for Children) and WAIS (Wechsler Adult Intelligence Scale) scores as follows: for every year between the year when a person took a test and the year when the test was normed, deduct 0.3 IQ points from the IQ score. Recall the example of the identical twins. The one who took the WISC-R when its norms were only three years out of date (1975 as compared to 1972) would have 0.9 points deducted, lowering his score from 65 to 64.1. The other who took the WISC when its norms were 27.5 years out of date (1975 as compared to 1947–48) would have 8.25 points deducted, lowering his score from 72.35 to 64.1 as well. Once we adjust their scores, the identity of their performances is clear and both will live.

The *Daubert* memo emphasizes that the formula for adjusting IQ scores assumes a precision that the evidence for the rate of IQ gains over time lacks. It cites a table reproduced in Flynn (2009c) that uses comparisons from Wechsler and Stanford–Binet tests to estimate the rate of recent IQ gains. Table AII1 in Appendix II updates this table.

**Box 13 (see Table AII1 in Appendix II)**

Estimates of IQ gains (points per year) since 1972

| | |
|---|---|
| (1) From 1995 to 2001 | +0.917 |
| (2) From 1978 to 1985 | +0.489 |
| (3) From 1995 to 2001.75 | +0.459 |
| (4) From 1989 to 2001 | +0.417 |
| (5) From 1989 to 2001.75 | **+0.332** |
| (6) From 1972 to 1989 | **+0.312** |
| (7) From 1995 to 2006 | **+0.306** |
| (8) From 2001.75 to 2006 | +0.282 |
| (9) From 1978 to 1995 | **+0.247** |
| (10) From 1972 to 1985 | +0.227 |
| (11) From 1985 to 2001 | +0.173 |
| (12) From 1972 to 1985 | +0.166 |
| (13) From 1972 to 1978 | +0.150 |
| (14) From 1989 to 1995 | −0.117 |
| Average of all 14 comparisons | +0.311 |
| Average of 4 comparisons in bold | **+0.299** |

Box 13 shows that the memo's point is literally correct. The 14 comparisons give an average estimate of 0.311 points per year. But the range is from a huge estimate of 0.917 points per year to one maverick negative estimate. In each case, the same group of subjects took both an older and a newer test. If they did 3.00 points better on the older test (due to its obsolete norms), and the tests were normed 10 years apart, the estimated rate of gain would be 0.300 points per year (3.00 divided by 10 = 0.300).

However, a close inspection of the data reveals two things. The extreme values from (1), (2), (13), and (14) all come from comparing tests normed only 6 or 7 years apart. The reason for this is that any comparison may be a point or two off; and a two-point variation over six years influences the rate by twice as much as a comparison over 12 years. Most impressive are the values in bold. It is well known that the rate of gain can differ from one kind of test to another. Comparisons (5), (6), (7), and (9) compare like with like: either an older with a newer version of the WISC, or an older with a newer version of the WAIS. The values range only from 0.247 to 0.332 points per year and average at 0.299. The evidence suggests that the estimates are converging on 0.300 points per year, and that the deviations from this are measurement error.

The *Daubert* memo quotes me as saying that we will be sure that the WAIS-III (normed in 1995) has been become obsolete at 0.300 points per year only when the WAIS-IV results are published. The WAIS-IV was renormed in 2006 and is included in Box 13 as number (7). It shows a gain over the 11 years at 0.306 points per year. Now it is 2012 and no doubt, the demand will be for results that go beyond 2006.

This demand is not relevant to any test normed before 2006. We now have the data needed to adjust their scores. As for the WAIS-IV itself, we cannot be sure. But every one of us, lacking time machines to go into the future, uses the recent past to make rough predictions, unless there is some clear sign of a change that would undermine continuity. If someone has a case that IQ gains in America should cease, let them bring it forward. Their data should be about America and not about Scandinavia (where gains have stopped) or nations where they are persisting (some at a rate greater than 0.300). We do not predict temperatures in America on the basis of data from the North Pole.

## Analysis of gains from the WAIS to the WAIS-IV

Most cases turn on adjustment of an obsolete IQ score from some version of the WISC taken at school, or some version of the WAIS taken on death row. Since the WAIS-IV data recently came to hand, I will detail WAIS gains over the last half century.

We begin with a group the Wechsler organization gave both the older WAIS (1953–54) and the newer WAIS-R (1978). The group was aged from 35 to 44 and numbered 80 (Wechsler, 1981, p. 47). Some of the eleven subtests used to compute Full Scale IQ had been revised but no subtest was dropped or added. Therefore, the comparison is straightforward: they got a mean IQ of 111.3 on the earlier test and got 103.8 on the later, giving an IQ gain over 24.5 years of 7.5 points.

The group that took both the (by now) older WAIS-R (1978) and the newer WAIS-III (1995) ranged from ages 16 to 74 and numbered 192 (Wechsler, 1997b, pp. 78–79). The list of which 11 subtests were used to compute Full Scale IQ had altered, but they gave the comparison group all 11 of the old WAIS-R subtests. That was fortunate: it meant that the true obsolescence of the WAIS-R could be measured. Flynn and Weiss (2007), the latter being Director of Research and Development at the Psychological Corporation, stress that comparing one set of subtests to a different set distorts results.

Therefore, I calculated the standard score total the group got on the same 11 WAIS-R and WAIS-III subtests. Using these totals and the WAIS-R conversion tables (Wechsler, 1981, pp. 93–109), I calculated Full Scale IQs for the two tests over all the ages covered. Since these gave a 4.2-point difference on average (with little variation), I subtracted that from their WAIS-R mean to get a WAIS-III mean. A Full Scale IQ of 105.8 on the earlier test and 101.6 on the later gave a gain over 17 years of 4.2 points.

The group that took both the WAIS-III (1995) and the newer WAIS-IV (2006) ranged from ages 16 to 88 and numbered 240 (Wechsler, 2008b, p. 75). The list of subtests used to compute Full Scale IQ had both altered and dropped to 10. But, once again, they gave the comparison group all 11 of the old WAIS-III subtests. Therefore, I calculated the standard score total the group got on the same 11 WAIS-III and WAIS-IV subtests. Using these

> **Box 14**
>
> The proper method of comparing the WAIS-III and WAIS-IV is described at the bottom of Table AII2 in Appendix II. The problem was to estimate the mean IQ of the members of a group from one total standard score. When you do this, you must simulate the range of scores of its members. The best way to do that is to use a spread of the standard scores that surround the total standard score. In this case, a simplistic conversion would have inflated the estimate of IQ gains.

totals and the WAIS-III conversion table, I calculated Full Scale IQs for the two tests. Since these gave a 3.37-point difference, I subtracted that from their WAIS-III mean to get a WAIS-IV mean. A Full Scale IQ of 102.90 on the earlier test and 99.53 on the later gave a gain over 11 years of 3.37 points. See Box 14.

For a table that gives trends on all subtests, see Table AII2 in Appendix II. It is also a summary table that traces adult gains all the way from the original WAIS (1953–54) through the WAIS-IV (2006). In Flynn (2007, pp. 180–181), there is a similar summary table that traces child gains all the way from the original WISC (1947–48) through the WISC-IV (2001.75). For convenience, it is reproduced in Appendix II as Table AII3.

Box 15 summarizes these two tables. It shows that the gains of American adults and children are strikingly similar for Full Scale IQ. The subtest gains show equally striking differences, as we shall see in Chapter 5.

## The rate of 0.300 points per year revisited

In Box 15, using the higher rate for the last WISC period, the median of the six period estimates of the rate of IQ gains is 0.308 points per year (the lower value gives 0.306). The variation around the median is plus or minus 0.060 points. The reader can now

**Box 15 (See Tables AII2 and AII3 in Appendix II)**

Full Scale IQ gains on the WISC and the WAIS

| | |
|---|---|
| From WAIS (1953.5) to WAIS-R (1978) | WISC (1947.5) to WISC-R (1972) |
| 111.3 – 103.8 = 7.5 pts. over 24.5 years | 107.63 – 100 = 7.63 pts. over 24.5 years |
| Rate: **0.306 points per year** | Rate: **0.311 points per year** |
| From WAIS-R (1978) to WAIS-III (1995) | WISC-R (1972) to WISC-III (1989) |
| 105.8 – 101.6 = 4.2 pts. over 17 years | 113 – 107.63 = 5.47 pts. over 17 years |
| Rate: **0.247 points per year** | Rate: **0.322 points per year** |
| From WAIS-III (1995) to WAIS-IV (2006) | WISC-III (1989) to WISC-IV (2001.75) |
| 102.90 – 99.53 = 3.37 pts. over 11 years | 116.83 – 113 = 3.83 pts. over 12.75 years |
| Rate: **0.306 points per year** | OR 117.63 – 113 = 4.63 pts.<br>Rate: **0.300 or 0.363 points per year** |
| Average rate from 1953–54 to 2006 | Average rate from 1947–48 to 2001.75 |
| 15.07 points over 52.5 years | 16.93 or 17.73 points over 54.25 years |
| Rate: **0.287 points per year** | Rate: **0.312 or 0.325 points per year** |

appreciate why 0.300 points per year is a good estimate of the rate of obsolescence of the norms of Wechsler tests in America. But there is some unfinished business.

First, are IQ gains the same at the crucial level of mental retardation, that is, for scores from about 55 to 80? Flynn (2009c, pp. 134–137) shows that this is certainly true for all versions of the WISC. The pattern on the older versions of the WAIS was confused by changes over time concerning the bottom threshold of scores (Flynn, 2006b). Fortunately, this has been put right. The rate of gain from the WAIS-III to WAIS-IV is the same at all IQ levels (Wechsler, 2008b, p. 77).

Second, does the WAIS-III inflate IQ scores, over and beyond obsolescence, because they happened to get a substandard standardization sample? In 2007, I hypothesized that they did and suggested that WAIS-III scores be adjusted as follows. (1) Deduct 0.3 points per year for obsolescence. If the test were administered today this would amount to 17 years (1995 to 2012) and equal 5.1 IQ points. (2) Deduct another 2.34 points because its substandard norms inflated IQs by that amount even at the time it was standardized.

Number (2) must be revisited. When calculating WAIS-R to WAIS-III gains some 10 years ago, I took my estimate from a table that gave Full Scale IQs for both tests (Flynn, 1998c). However, the subtests the two tests used to calculate Full Scale IQs differed. It was only after 2007 that I realized that you should keep the basket of subtests unaltered. This correction raised the rate of gain (from the WAIS-R to WAIS-III) to a more respectable level (from 2.9 to 4.2 points). In addition, I lacked two recent data sets: these expand the number of comparisons we can use to test the WAIS-III for eccentricity from 12 to 14.

Thanks to the new data and a revised value for the WAIS-R to WAIS-III comparison, my analysis (at the bottom of Table AII1 in Appendix II) now puts the atypical inflation of WAIS-III IQ scores at 1.65 points. Moreover, when compared to the WAIS-R and WAIS-IV, the WAIS-III is only 0.49 points out of line. Another point: the Wechsler organization was at pains to ensure that the WAIS-III sample included a sufficient number of subjects at low IQ levels, and this could make a difference of as much as 0.554 points (Flynn, 1998c, pp. 1234–1235). In passing, I have not added those points on to my WAIS-R to WAIS-III estimate because one cannot be certain that this is appropriate.

It is difficult enough to convince nonspecialists of the basics of allowing for obsolete norms without making choices that might appear to inflate estimates of IQ gains.

## The WAIS and other tests

Just as I was about to exonerate the WAIS-III from the charge that its standardization sample was substandard, and inflated IQs, I received a copy of Floyd, Clark, and Shadish (2008). A group of 148 college undergraduates scored 8.64 points higher (adjusted for dates of standardization) on the WAIS-III than on the Woodcock–Johnson III; and a group of 99 subjects scored 6.77 points higher (adjusted) than on the Kaufman Adolescent and Adult Intelligence Scale.

These comparisons did not focus on low-IQ subjects. But I then received Silverman *et al.* (2010), which reports results for 76 low-IQ adults that had scores on both the WAIS and the Stanford–Binet. Their WAIS IQs ranged from 39 to 88, and their SB IQs ranged from 23 to 67. On average, the WAIS IQs were 16.7 points higher. If we allow for the fact that the SB tests were normed a few years earlier than the WAIS, this reduces to 15.6 points. The 14 cases whose WAIS IQs were 64 or above, and thus fell into the danger zone of qualifying for the death penalty, scored on average 13.7 points higher than they did on the SB. This reduces to 12.6 points when scores are adjusted. To add detail, not one of the seven people the WAIS put above 70 was also above 70 on the SB; and four of them were below 60.

It is unpardonable that this discrepancy goes unresolved year after year. Surely, in the interim, capital offenders should be given the benefit of the doubt. I strongly recommend setting WAIS-III scores aside. In every such case, the subject should be tested anew on both the WAIS-IV and the Stanford–Binet 5. Even if given today (2012), the results of both will have to be adjusted for obsolescence: WAIS-IV scores lowered by 1.8 points to cover six years; SB-5 scores lowered by 3.3 points to cover 11 years.

## Something new about the very bottom of the curve

There are difficulties with using any standard IQ test, whether Wechsler or Stanford–Binet, to measure IQs at very low levels. The tests are designed to cover the whole population. This means that there are only a handful of mentally retarded subjects (as few as four) at each age in the standardization sample. Therefore, you are unsure that they are really representative of the bottom 2.27 percent of the population, and unsure whether the norms they set for IQs below 70 are very reliable.

What if we had a test that had been normed on a large and truly representative sample of the mentally retarded at two times, all of whose items discriminated in the mentally retarded range? In the Netherlands, Nijman *et al.* (2010) simulated such a situation by using an intelligence test designed for children aged from 3 to 6 years (the Snijders–Oomen Nonverbal Intelligence Test or SON). If adults have a mental age of 3 to 6 years, they are assigned IQs ranging from 35 to 55. In sum, by measuring IQ gains on the SON, we may get a real measure of gains by adults whose mental age matches that of early childhood.

The SON was normed in 1975 and the SON-R in 1996. A group of 39 children aged 3 to 6 of normal intelligence took both versions in counterbalanced order and registered an IQ gain of 5.9 points over the 21 years for a rate of 0.281 points per year, close to the 0.300 that prevails in America. They then followed the same procedure with 69 adults whose mental age was 3 to 6 years, and they showed a raw score gain twice that of the normal children. This does not entail that the mentally retarded made IQ gains twice those of normal children. But it does mean that the mentally retarded were located at some point on the curve where normal children were gaining at twice their overall rate. This is not unprecedented. Recall that between 1943 and 1980, young British children in the top half of the curve made a gain three or four times that of children in the bottom half. Thus, there is at least a suggestion that the mentally retarded in the Netherlands have a rate of gain well above 0.281 points per year.

Dutch data are not American data. But this interesting research design is well worth replicating in the United States.

## Individuals and groups

The *Daubert* memo echoes a point made by virtually every prosecution brief. It notes that while scholars use the formula of 0.3 points per year to adjust Wechsler IQs in America, they are studying groups and not individuals. Well, studying groups is what scholars do: if you want to make generalizations, a sample size of one is too small to be reliable. As for clinical psychologists, they deal with individuals but rely primarily on their clinical judgment and are not swayed much by whether an IQ test gives 67 or 73.

The argument that adjusting an individual's IQ is some sort of leap into the unknown is based on a total lack of understanding of what an IQ is. No individual ever got an IQ score except by comparison with the performance of a group, namely, a standardization sample. If he performs at the cutting line for the bottom 2.27 percent of that group, he gets an IQ of 70. If the sample is not representative, it is biased and gives bad IQs. It gives bad IQs to everyone, individuals, herds, groups, flocks, and the local barbershop quartet.

It makes no difference whether the sample underperformed (and inflated IQs) because it had no college graduates or whether it underperformed because it was peopled by the lower-performing Americans of the past. In either event, if you want to salvage an individual's IQ score, you must allow for the inflation occasioned by the substandard sample. In the first case, you should compare the scores with those based on standardization samples that included all educational levels. In the second case, you should compare the scores with those based on a representative sample of Americans today. Which is to say you should adjust them for obsolescence. It is just that simple.

A final point that should be underlined a hundred times. Adjusting the IQ of an individual is no less or more accurate than adjusting the mean IQ of a group. How could it be? You use the same rate of obsolescence for both: you deduct 0.3 points for every year between the time of norming and the time of testing. If the rate is accurate, both adjustments are accurate. The original IQ of an individual may be less reliable. The day before the test, a woman may find that her husband has run off with the babysitter. Within a large group, few will have suffered that fate. But what caused the original IQ to be unreliable has nothing to do with the effects of adjustment.

## Playing the game

"Professor Flynn, I am phoning you because we do not want anything in an email until we have acquainted you with the case." You bet they don't. Before they use me, they want to find out whether I will interpret the IQ record so as to support a reprieve from execution. Often I disappoint them and am not retained. The prosecution does the same. They phone people to find out what they think about adjusting IQ scores.

Judges know how this game is played. They can put a stop to it. All they need do is comprehend something very simple. An IQ score is not a number but a message. It tells you whether someone's mental competence is in the lower 2.27 percent. Judges can read these messages without the help of lawyers: just use the formula that adjusts for obsolescence. It would be tragic if *Daubert* motions confuse the issue. A mechanical application of the usual rules of evidence about expert testimony would not promote equity. It would perpetuate the monstrous injustice of making the death penalty a lottery. Justice Stewart (*Furman* v. *Georgia*, 1972) deserves the last word: "These death sentences are cruel and unusual in the same way that being struck by lightning is cruel and unusual." Someone who dies because of an inflated IQ score is struck by electricity or injection or the noose, and this happens far more frequently than death by lightning.

## The present state of play

Whatever the merits of adjusting IQ scores for obsolescence, it is important to stay in touch with what is actually being done. Therefore, I offer an overview of what the courts were saying as of April 2011. The US Navy–Marine Corps Court of Appeals flatly states that the Flynn effect is to be considered when evaluating a defendant's IQ (*United States* v. *Parker*, 2007, p. 629). However, since it is a military court, its decisions are not binding on federal district courts or on the states.

There are 13 "civilian" Federal Courts of Appeals but thus far, only three have made a substantive ruling. Their jurisdictions include most of the states that have actually executed anyone during 2009, 2010, and early 2011 (Ohio and Oklahoma are the big exceptions). To be specific, the states they include are collectively responsible for 78 percent of the 110 executions in that period. The Federal Court of Appeals for the 4th Circuit covers Maryland, Virginia, West Virginia, North Carolina, and South Carolina; the 5th Circuit covers Texas, Louisiana, and Mississippi; and the 11th Circuit covers Alabama, Florida, and Georgia. All three appellate courts have taken a neutral stand, namely, that while altering IQ scores in the light of the Flynn effect is not mandatory, it is also not unreasonable.

There are differences of nuance. Criticizing a prosecution case that the defendant was not mentally retarded, the 11th Circuit said: "Moreover, all of the scores were on WAIS tests, which may have reflected elevated scores because of the Flynn effect" (*Holladay* v. *Allen*, 2009, p. 1358; also see *Thomas* v. *Allen*, 2010). The 4th Circuit has held that lower courts must at least discuss whether the Flynn effect is relevant to the evaluation of the persuasiveness of expert testimony (*Walker* v. *True*, 2005, pp. 322–323; *Walton* v. *Johnson*, 2005, pp. 296–297; *Winston* v. *Kelly*, 2008; *Winston* v. *Kelly*, 2010; *Walker* v. *Kelly*, 2010). The 5th Circuit says that it is unproven "whether it is appropriate to adjust an individual's score based on this theory" (*In re Salazar*, 2006). But it has also said that a series of IQ scores, including one adjusted to account for the Flynn effect, provided a valid basis for lower court's finding of sub-average intelligence (*Moore* v. *Quarterman*, June 29, 2006). On another occasion, it chose to set the issue aside by relying "primarily on one IQ score upon which the defendant has no Flynn claim" (*In re Mathis*, April 2, 2007).

The federal appellate courts bind all those courts in their jurisdiction whether federal district courts or state courts. But given the uniformity of their opinions, the ground rules they have set probably apply universally: all trial courts must discuss the relevance of the Flynn effect to the case in hand; having done so they are free to apply or ignore it without much fear of being overruled; unless they do something odd such as applying it eccentrically. Federal district courts have made full use of their freedom and thus, the 11 that have weighed in thus far vary widely in terms of positive or negative attitudes toward the Flynn effect.

Five are favorable. The Eastern District of Maryland "will, as it should, consider the Flynn-adjusted scores in its evaluation of the defendant's intellectual functioning" (*United States* v. *Davis*, 2009, p. 488). The Eastern District of Louisiana found that "the Flynn effect is well established scientifically ... Hence the court will correct for the Flynn effect ... applying Dr. Flynn's formula" (*United States* v. *Paul Hardy*, 2010, p. 33). The Eastern District of Virginia accepted that "that the Flynn effect causes an increase in IQ scores of approximately 0.3 points per year" *(Green* v. *Johnson*, 2006, pp. 45–47; 2007). The Northern District of Alabama said that: "a court should not look at a raw IQ score as a precise measurement of intellectual functioning. A court must also consider the Flynn effect ... in determining whether a petitioner's IQ score falls within a range containing scores that are less than 70" (*Thomas* v. *Allen*, 2009, p. 1281). The Southern District of Texas was also positive (*Rivera* v. *Dretke*, 2006).

Three federal district courts have been more guarded. The Southern District of Alabama held that the Flynn effect could potentially render IQ scores unreliable (*Williams* v. *Campbell*, 2007, p. 47). The Northern District of Mississippi said that failure to apply the Flynn effect was not in itself unreasonable. But that since, in the case at hand, the expert witnesses were unanimous on the existence of and necessity of applying it, the Court would take it into account (*Wiley* v. *Epps*, 2009, pp. 894–895). The Southern District of Texas found that since the trial court had relied on a low estimate of the Flynn effect that could not be supported, the decision could be appealed (*Butler* v. *Quarterman*, 2008, pp. 815–817).

Three federal district courts have been negative, two about the Flynn effect and one about Flynn. The Northern District of Mississippi is a stern advocate of credentialing: "Affidavit on the Flynn effect from Dr. Flynn himself is inadmissible because the standard of *Chase* v. *State*, 873 So.2d 1013 (Miss. 2004), requires that expert testimony on M.R. come from a licensed psychologist or psychiatrist, and Flynn is a political scientist" (*Berry* v. *Epps*, 2006, p. 35). The Northern District of Georgia was "not impressed by the evidence concerning the Flynn effect" (*Ledford* v. *Head*, 2008, pp. 8–9). The Northern District of Texas was also negative (*Hall* v. *Quarterman*, 2009).

As for state courts, California is favorable. Both an appellate court and the Supreme Court upheld a trial court's acceptance of the Flynn effect (*People* v. *Superior Court of Tulare County*, 2004, 2007). Ohio is guarded: the state Court of Appeals for the 10th District held that trial courts must consider Flynn effect evidence but that such evidence is not binding (*State* v. *Burke*, 2005, p. 13). Kentucky is negative. The Supreme Court said that the state legislature knew about and could have chosen to include Flynn in the statute, but did not (*Bowling* v. *Commonwealth of Kentucky*, 2005, p. 375).

The Tennessee Supreme Court has just switched from negative to permissive. In 2004, it said: "[T]he statute should not be interpreted to make allowance for any standard error of measurement or other circumstances whereby a person with an I.Q. above seventy could be considered mentally retarded" (*Howell* v. *State*, 2004, p. 14). In April 2011, it held that state law did "not require that raw scores on IQ tests be accepted at face value," and that a trial court may consider expert testimony by someone who takes the Flynn effect into account (*Coleman* v. *State*, 2011, p. 242, note 55). This is important because the Supreme Court's decisions bind all lower state courts. For example, in 2010, the Tennessee Appellate Court was favorably disposed to the Flynn effect but felt bound to ignore it thanks to its state Supreme Court (*Coleman* v. *State*, 2010, pp. 17–18).

In Texas, the state Appellate Court held that the Flynn effect "does not provide a reliable basis for concluding that an appellant has significant sub-average general intellectual functioning" (*Neal* v. *State*, 2008, p. 275). However, it cites its own earlier decision, which is a bit softer: "This Court has never specifically addressed the scientific validity of the Flynn effect. Nor will we attempt to do so now. Rather than try to extrapolate an accurate IQ by applying an unexamined scientific concept to an incomplete test score, we will simply regard the record as it comes to us as devoid of any reliable IQ score" (*Ex Parte Blue*,

2007, p. 166). It seems to be saying that lower courts cannot use the Flynn effect to adjust IQ scores, but that they could use it to ignore scores unless they were so high as to be clearly damning.

In sum, the "Flynn effect" has had a significant impact on judicial decisions in capital cases. The best hope for the future is that more lower courts, whether federal or state, will use their freedom wisely and opt in its favor. Scholars who write in this area are beginning to urge them to do so (Gresham & Reschly, 2011; Young, 2012).

## Something new about the top of the curve

We leave the bottom of the IQ curve behind to go to the top. There has always been some evidence that the rate of IQ gains that prevails at the mean in America does not fall significantly as you approach high IQs (Flynn, 1985, 1998c; Wechsler, 2003, 2008b). But only recently has anyone isolated large samples of high IQ children for analysis.

Wai and Putallaz (2011) studied schoolchildren who qualified as in the top 5 percent on a variety of standardized academic achievement tests highly correlated with IQ. The EXPLORE project used its own tests to select 89,000 4th and 5th graders aged 10 to 11. The SAT (Scholastic Aptitude Test) was used to select 1,170,000 7th graders aged 13; and the ACT (American College Testing) was used to select 440,000, also 7th graders aged 13. The content of the tests was similar for EXPLORE and the ACT, namely, students got a composite score that combined mathematics, science, English, and reading. The SAT composite score included both the SAT-Mathematics and the SAT-Verbal.

The EXPLORE scores covered the period from 1995 to 2010 and gave a rate of gain of 0.230 points per year for the 10–11-year-olds. The SAT covered 1981 to 2010 and gave 0.060 for the 13-year-olds. The ACT covered 1990 to 2010 and gave 0.100 for that age. Thus the younger children enjoyed a larger rate of gain: perhaps this is explained by the Nation's Report Card data (see Chapter 2), which shows robust mathematics and reading gains among young schoolchildren reducing as they approach the age of 17.

As for the older children, the SAT and ACT match three WISC subtests for test content, namely, arithmetic, information, and vocabulary. Averaging these three subtests, American children gained at 0.080 points per year between 1989 (WISC-III) and 2002 (WISC-IV) – see Table AI1 in Appendix I. That is exactly the average rate yielded by the SAT (0.060) and the ACT (0.100). It remains to be shown whether the top 5 percent match the general population for rate of gain on the other seven WISC subtests. I doubt that the relevant data exist. Still, it is good to know that over the last 30 years, the very bright have made the same gains on the "basics" as schoolchildren in general. It is a pity that these gains have been so modest.

## Other times, other places

Cross-national data now available dramatize the folly of assuming that even kindred nations have identical IQ trends. Roivainen (2009) compared European and US standardization samples on the WAIS-III. These samples were selected to be representative of their nation at the time of testing. She used their raw scores (the number of items got correct) to score five European nations against the US norms.

Look at Box 16. The foreign samples were tested anywhere from two to nine years after the US sample. Therefore, I calculated how many points the US would have gained over the years in question in order to get fair comparisons. This required the rate of US IQ gains since 1997, and Table AII2 in Appendix II provides estimates (the WAIS-III to WAIS-IV period began in 1995). The values used were: 0.30 points per year for Full Scale IQ; and about 0.34 points per year for Performance IQ (the Table shows

**Box 16 (see Table AII4 in Appendix II for the raw data and adjustments)**

WAIS-III scores nation by nation. The IQs reveal how much above or below America each nation would have scored, if the WAIS-III had been normed both there and in America during the same year (America has been set at 100). The years given refer to when the foreign tests were published; these must all be reduced by two to get the years when the samples were actually tested. The Full Scale IQs for France and Germany are based on only 7 of the 10 subtests. The Finnish standardization sample may have been below average at ages 15 to 24. Her scores compare much more favorably at age 45 and over.

| | | |
|---|---|---|
| France (2000) | 104.2 (Full Scale) | 106.2 (Performance) |
| UK (1999) | 103.1 (Full Scale) | 103.6 (Performance) |
| Germany (2006) | 100.2 (Full Scale) | 100.5 (Performance) |
| America | 100.0 (Full Scale) | 100.0 (Performance) |
| Spain (1999) | —(Full Scale) | 97.1 (Performance) |
| Finland (2005) | —(Full Scale) | 93.1 (Performance) |

gains on performance subtests that average higher than those on verbal subtests; digit span is set aside). Look at the values for France and Germany. We do not know where they stood 20 years before the most recent data. If they both had a Full Scale IQ of 102 scored against US norms at that time, France had to gain 2.2 more points to reach its recent mean of 104.2. Germany had to gain 1.8 fewer points to drop to its recent mean of 100.2. Since America gained 6 points over 20 years, France gets a gain of 8.2 points and a rate of 0.41 points per year. Germany gets a gain of 4.2 points and a rate of 0.21.

In capital cases one point often decides between life and death. Foreign data are of great interest to scholars but keep it out of the courts. Despite this admonition, nothing is more certain than that a prosecutor will soon put in evidence a study showing that the rate of IQ gains among vampires in Transylvania is less than 0.30 points per year.

## Tip of the iceberg

Clinical psychologists do other things than diagnose mental retardation among capital offenders. They are beginning to see that obsolete norms on IQ tests are merely the tip of the iceberg. Obsolescence affects a whole range of diagnostic instruments.

Baxendale (2010) compared the performance of standardization samples from 1985 on the AMIPB (Adult Memory and Information Processing Battery) and from 2007 on its successor, called the BMIPB (Brain Injury Rehabilitation Trust Memory and Information Processing Battery). The samples could be compared because tasks on two of the four subtests are identical, and statistical analysis allows scores to be equated on the other two. This battery is the one used most often by clinical neuropsychologists in the UK, for example, to evaluate epilepsy surgery patients for memory loss.

On the test as a whole, the rate of gain for all ages collectively was 0.229 "IQ" points per year over the period of 22 years. But diagnoses are made by age and, as Box 17 shows, some ages gained at higher rates. For both ages 31–45 and 61–75, the rate was close to 0.300. If subjects aged 31–45 took the old AMIPB in 2007, 22 years after it was normed, gains would inflate their overall scores by the equivalent of 6.94 IQ points. What seemed to be an average score would actually mean that they were well below average for their age cohort (at the 32nd percentile). If a psychologist selected out either the visual learning or visual recall subtest, the scores of every age group would be inflated by somewhere between 5 and 10 points.

These findings mean that the reliability of every test of neurological functions, in America as well as Britain, is suspect.

**Box 17**

Over the 22 years between 1985 and 2007, gains inflated scores on the leading British memory test. For each age group, I estimate the inflation both in terms of points (and rate). All values are expressed in an IQ metric (SD = 15).

| | | | |
|---|---|---|---|
| **Ages 18–30** | | | |
| List learning: | 0.90 pts. (.041/yr.) | List recall: | 2.55 pts. (.166/yr.) |
| Visual learning: | 6.15 pts. (.280/yr.) | Visual recall: | 4.65 pts. (.211/yr.) |
| Ave. four subtests: | 3.56 pts. (.162/yr.) | | |
| **Ages 31–45** | | | |
| List learning: | 6.30 pts. (.286/yr.) | List recall: | 2.40 pts. (.109/yr.) |
| Visual learning: | 10.50 pts. (.477/yr.) | Visual recall: | 8.55 pts. (.389/yr.) |
| Ave. four subtests: | 6.94 pts. (.315/yr.) | | |
| **Ages 46–60** | | | |
| List learning: | 0.30 pts. (.014/yr.) | List recall: | 0.00 (.000/yr.) |
| Visual learning: | 7.20 pts. (.327/yr.) | Visual recall: | 7.20 (.327/yr.) |
| Ave. four subtests: | 3.68 pts. (.167/yr.) | | |
| **Ages 61–75** | | | |
| List learning: | 2.85 pts. (.130/yr.) | List recall: | 5.70 pts. (.259/yr.) |
| Visual learning: | 7.05 pts. (.320/yr.) | Visual recall: | 8.25 pts. (.375/yr.) |
| Ave. four subtests: | 5.96 pts. (.271/yr.) | | |
| **All ages** – average of four subtests: | 5.035 pts. (0.229/yr.) | | |

*Note:* Gains over the 22 years were first calculated in SDs: each BMIPB score (later sample) minus the AMIPB score (earlier sample); and the result was divided by the AMIPB standard deviation for each task. The SD differences were multiplied by 15, and the result divided by 22 to get the rate in points per year.

As Baxendale says (2010, p. 703): "It is unknown whether the Flynn effect is evident amongst patients with discreet pathologies that affect memory function, such as hippocampal sclerosis. For example, are the memory deficits associated with moderate hippocampal volume loss less severe now than those seen 20 years ago?" The hippocampus is the main center of visual memory in the brain, and those who suffer from shrinkage of the area are assessed for its effects. Clearly, if their scores are compared to people 20 years ago, whose memory scores were lower than today's population, memory loss may go undetected. When diagnosing whether atypical patterns of memory loss have occurred, scores must be adjusted. The new BMIPB may have been current as of 2007, but its norms are now becoming obsolete.

In Sweden, Rönnlunda and Nilsson (2009) did time-sequential analyses of four age-matched samples (aged 35–80; N = 2996) that were tested on the same memory battery on any one of four occasions (1989, 1995, 1999, and 2004). Excluded were those diagnosed with dementia or mental retardation, and those with a native tongue other than Swedish. Their diagnostic instrument differed somewhat from the UK tests. The *recall* subtest required recollection of commands, sentences, and nouns; the *recognition* subtest recognition of nouns, faces, and family names; the *knowledge* subtest is a vocabulary test: and the *fluency* subtest requires generating words and professions when presented with letters (given letter P: respond with postman, pilot, etc.). Recall and recognition are episodic memory tasks, while knowledge and fluency are semantic memory tasks.

Gains varied somewhat during the four dates of testing. For example, knowledge (vocabulary) showed the largest gains between 1989 and 1999, but was unique in showing a slight decline between 1999 and 2004. Over the whole period of 15 years, the gains ran: recall 2.10 points (0.140 points per year); recognition 2.205 points (0.147/year); knowledge 2.67 pts. (0.178/year); and fluency 3.66 pts. (0.244/year). Note the tendency toward larger gains on semantic memory than on episodic memory. The average rate of gain for the four subtests is 0.177 points per year. Continental Europe joins the English-speaking world as an area in which the diagnostic instruments of clinical psychology must be critically assessed.

## Scandal in the literature

How quickly will clinical psychologists assimilate the fact that their scores are meaningless unless they specify the test used, when it was normed, when subjects were tested, and the test's rate of obsolescence? The precedent of IQ gains over time is discouraging. The first warning was issued 28 years ago (Flynn, 1984) and elaborated in the appropriate journal shortly thereafter (Flynn, 1985). To assess awareness, Laird and Whitaker (2011) analyzed all articles published during 2008 in the two leading journals on mental retardation: *The Journal of Applied Research in Intellectual Disabilities* (UK) and *The American Journal on Mental Retardation* (USA).

Out of 91 articles, 81 used the concept of intelligence. The sins committed were numerous: (1) of nine articles that utilized different IQ tests, four assumed that the scores were equivalent without discussing either dates of norming or type of test; (2) five offered IQs without even naming the test; and (3) four claimed to have measured very low IQs (below the floor level of 40 on Wechsler tests) with no indication of how this was done. If editors and referees are uninformed after 25 years, it is understandable that judges have taken ten years to assimilate the significance of IQ gains over time. Particularly since eloquent clinicians earn their livings by trying to confuse them.

Scholars measuring group differences sometimes neglect the lessons learned since 1984. In 2007, I saw a conference paper with the message that contrary to the claims of other researchers (Rushton and Jensen), students in a sub-Saharan Black African nation had an IQ on Raven's close to American norms. They did not remark on the extraordinary fact that this result implied that Black Africans were far above US blacks (scored versus whites, US blacks aged from 16 to 17 had an IQ of 88 at that time).

When scored against the US Raven's norms of 1982, the African sample did get an IQ of 99.05. But these were all races norms, so scoring against white Americans reduced the mean to 97. Since they were tested circa 2005, we must allow for 23 years of obsolescence. There is no good estimate for US IQ gains on Raven's over those years, but a ball park value from international data would be 0.5 points per year, which over 23 years would equal 11.5 points. Deducting that from 97 equals 85.5, or a plausible result 2.5 points below black Americans. I urged publication (after revision) in that an IQ of 85 from Black Africa would be well above the values usually reported, but the paper seems to have dropped from sight.

## Political debate

The implications of IQ gains over time for diagnostic instruments are beyond dispute. However, for most of us, the question of whether cognitive capabilities have been enhanced is more interesting.

Chapter 2 gave my own opinion. Adults have expanded their active vocabularies and a larger public can read serious literature if they care to do so. Schoolchildren have no greater fund of culturally valued information but adults do (probably thanks to more tertiary education). Both have responded successfully to the greater complexity of everyday life in the modern world, including its visual culture and its demands for faster information processing. Neither has become significantly more at ease with numbers. Both have put on scientific spectacles. They have evolved from mere utilitarian manipulation of the world to classifying it. And they are now accustomed to use logic not only on the concrete but also on abstractions and to take the hypothetical seriously.

I have also contended (although I cannot prove it) that the level of moral debate has risen (because taking the hypothetical seriously is a prerequisite for serious moral debate). Concerning whether politicians debate issues more intelligently, I have always been more tentative. In 2007, I cited Rosenau and Fagan (1997) who show that gender issues were debated in the Congressional Record with more attention to logic and evidence after World War II than at the time of World War I. However, I expressed skepticism about presidential debate. Its purpose, today as in the past, is to use emotive language to get a visceral response from a mass audience and it must do so within strict time constraints (hence the emergence of "spin doctors").

A quotation from *What Is Intelligence?* (2007, p. 162): "That Congressmen have become less willing to give their colleagues a mindless harangue to read does not necessarily mean that Presidential speeches to a mass audience have improved."

Gorton and Diels (2010) have shown that my caution was justified. In a fascinating article, they analyzed the presidential TV debates from 1960 to 2008 and found no evidence that they had become scientifically richer. To be specific, they found no increase in the use of abstract scientific terms or the quality of causal and logical analysis. Scientific discourse with respect to economics had actually declined. I can attest that there are signs the standard of political debate has declined in New Zealand. A few years ago, a party leader catapulted his party up the polls by using the words "family," "moderate," and "reasonable" more often in five minutes than any sane person would think possible.

My choice of words may have encouraged a false impression. As a shorthand, I talk about the transition from people who had utilitarian spectacles to people who have put on scientific spectacles. Realizing that this could mislead, I tried to warn against reading too much into the term "scientific spectacles." The fact that people have absorbed the habits of mind associated with science does not imply that they have become rational, scientifically informed, or knowledgeable about the specific abstract categories that economists, social scientists, and so forth use. I did speak of adopting scientific language but that was careless: I meant basic concepts such as mammal, not the operational concepts used in the sciences. Recently, I made the point explicit: "The full potential of (scientific spectacles) has not been realized because even the best universities do not give their graduates the tools they need to analyze the modern world except perhaps in their area of specialization" (Flynn, in press).

Gorton and Diels are pioneering a significant literature about political debate. I would like to believe that during the twentieth century, the political thinking of presidential candidates has become less awful even if what they say on the stump has not. When William Jennings Bryan gave his mindless "Cross of Gold" speech in 1896, everything about him suggests that he was not tongue-in-cheek. In the film *The Candidate*, Robert Redford is dismayed when his stump speech is reduced to a few clichés and the slogan: "For a better way: Bill McKay!" There is the wonderful scene when he sits in the back of the campaign car mocking himself: "This country cannot house its houseless, blah, blah, blah." We live in hope.

# 5 Youth and age

We return to our old companions the Wechsler subtests. At this point, puzzles begin to emerge. First, over the last half-century, have adults and their children progressively grown apart, rather like partners in a failed marriage who find it more and more difficult to speak the same language? Second, old age seems to levy a penalty on our analytic abilities that becomes more and more onerous the brighter we are. Do bright brains require a higher level of maintenance, one that old age cannot supply? Or does retirement reduce everyone's mental exercise to the lowest common denominator? These speculations strike me as unwelcome if not bizarre, but I will rehearse the evidence that forced them upon me.

## Vocabulary trends since 1950

Comparing WISC and WAIS trends reveals a growing gap between the active vocabularies of American adults and schoolchildren over the last half-century. In order to compare adults and children over the same periods, I averaged the beginning and ending dates of the WISC and WAIS periods. The only complication was posed by the final period of gains. Here the WISC gains represent 12.75 years and the WAIS gains only 11 years. Therefore, I multiplied WAIS gains by 12.75/11 to get values comparable to the WISC.

The vocabulary subtests consists of words used in everyday life, not specialized vocabulary. Box 18 shows a huge adult vocabulary gain of 17.80 points (which divided by 54.25 years, gives a rate of 0.328 points per year). This in itself is not surprising.

The fact that more and more people go to university and graduate to professional jobs ought to count for something. What was unanticipated is the huge difference between adult gains and child gains: adults have opened up a gap of 13.40 IQ points or 0.893 SDs.

What I had expected was a gradually growing gap between adults and children on the information and arithmetic subtests, but only a mild expansion, if that, of a vocabulary gap. As adult Americans enter tertiary education, they should become better informed, more numerate, and expand their general vocabularies. But they should transfer these benefits to the children they raise more effectively going from information to arithmetic to vocabulary. When parents interact with their children, they are not likely to discuss geography or foreign affairs (talk about Paris or Brazil). They are more likely to help them with arithmetic homework and transfer some of their numeracy. But particularly as they age, children should hear their parents' everyday vocabulary used constantly, both when spoken to and when their parents speak to one another.

Box 18 shows some expectations were met. Since 1950, information has behaved well, with a parent/child gap enhanced by a quite sizable 6.25 points or 0.417 SDs. Presumably, this is made up when our children experience tertiary education and expand their store of general information. Arithmetic has not opened up a similar gap but the reason is obvious. Tertiary education, like all levels of education, has failed to improve the arithmetical reasoning skills of Americans. The adult gain since 1950 is only 3.50 points, marginally more than the child gain of 2.30 points, but still pathetic. So let us focus on the real mystery – vocabulary.

## Vocabulary and tertiary education

I tried to simulate vocabulary gains for parents and their own school-age children by plotting WISC and WAIS gains over the same time frame. The match is good in that WAIS samples were

**Box 18 (see Tables AIII1 and AIII2 in Appendix III)**

I have selected three subtests common to the WISC and WAIS so as to compare child and adult gains in America between 1950–51 and late 2004, a period of 54.25 years. They are subtests on which I thought adult gains would be greater than child gains because more and more adults had at least some tertiary education. The subtest gains are expressed in an IQ-point metric (SD = 15). Table AIII2 gives values for eight subtests.

Vocabulary: 17.80 points (WAIS gain) – 4.40 points (WISC gain) = 13.40 (difference)
Information: 8.40 points (WAIS gain) – 2.15 points (WISC gain) = 6.25 (difference)
Arithmetic: 3.50 points (WAIS gain) – 2.30 points (WISC gain) = 1.20 (difference)

tested only 4 to 6 years after WISC samples. There are some discrepancies. For example, the WISC-R children were aged 6 to 16 in 1972. Their actual parents would have been aged 23 to 71 and therefore, 29 to 77 by 1978. The WAIS comparison sample of 1978 was aged 35 to 44, a somewhat younger age range than the target ages. The later WAIS comparison samples included all adult ages and so, beginning with the WISC-III/WAIS-III combination the matches are excellent.

Figure 2 puts the initial "Vocabulary IQ" of both parents and their children in 1947–48 (the years the WISC was normed) at 100. As the percentage of Americans aged 25 years and over with at least one year of tertiary education rises, from 12.1 percent in 1947 to 52.0 percent in 2002, parents gain at an average rate of 0.328 IQ points per year. Their children lag behind at a rate of 0.081 points per year.

Figure 2 appears to make a strong case that greater exposure to tertiary education has increased the size of adult vocabularies. However, if university is potent, the raw scores on

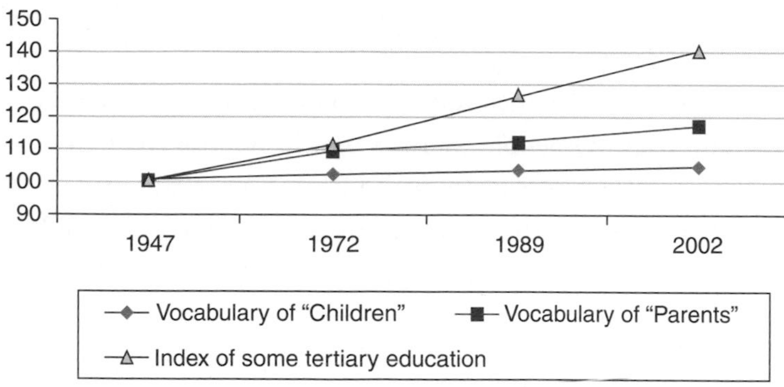


*Figure 2 As the percentage with some tertiary education rises, the gap between "parent" and "child" vocabulary expands. See the comment on this figure in Appendix III (Figure 4).*

vocabulary (number of items correct) should escalate between the age when most people enter university and the age when most people graduate. The WAIS data isolates those years: it tells us how much vocabulary increases between ages 16–17 and ages 20–24. And if greater exposure to tertiary education caused the adult vocabulary gain over time, then age gains between 16–17 and 20–24 should be much smaller in 1947 (when only 12 percent had any tertiary education between those ages) than in 2002 (when 52 percent had at least some tertiary education). Unless, of course, other factors such as going out to work at age 17 (which was far more frequent in 1947 than in 2002) are potent boosters of vocabulary.

To isolate the effects of university from other factors, I divided the population into two groups. The first being those with a mean IQ of 79 (that would be their IQ if they scored one SD below the mean on all 10 WAIS subtests including vocabulary) because the expansion of university education would be unlikely to affect them. Few of them go to university even today. The second being those with a mean IQ from 121 to 146 (that assumes they scored either one or two SDs above the mean on all 10 subtests) on the grounds that greater opportunity to attend university would affect them profoundly. Far more of them attend university today than 50 years ago. The prediction: between ages 16–17 and 20–24, the difference between the vocabulary gains of low- and high-IQ people in 1947 would be less than the difference between the gains of low- and high-IQ people in 2002. The best fit we can get for the years we want is to compare the WAIS sample (1953–54) with the average of the WAIS-III and WAIS-IV samples, which is 2000–1.

Box 19 is based on Table AIII3 in Appendix III. The prediction is vindicated, but the impact of expanded tertiary attendance is disappointingly small at 2.775 IQ points. Our calculation is based on comparing those who were 17 and 22 at the same time (cross-sectional data), rather than following an actual group of students going through university (longitudinal data). But no adjustment for this is in order. Our year 2000 students would have benefited from four years of IQ gains over time as they went through university, but so would our 1953 students. Over 47 years the total adult vocabulary gain was just below 15 points. Expanded university attendance seems to account for only 18.6 percent of that total (2.775 divided by 14.935 = 0.1858).

It appears that the world of work, which follows university, has been the main force behind the adult vocabulary gains of the last half-century. Careful scrutiny of Box 19 reinforces that conclusion. Note that in 1953, low-IQ people enhanced their vocabularies over the ages of 17 to 22 far more than low-IQ people did in 2000. I suggest the hypothesis that they were more likely to be settled in apprenticeships or adult jobs in those days than today. Even the high-IQ people increased their vocabularies more between the ages of 17 to 22 in 1953 than in 2000. Apparently being placed in work was more potent than being in a tertiary institution. On the other hand, tertiary education has played an indirect role by affecting the kind of work we do throughout our adult lives. Its expansion was a prerequisite for filling the

**Box 19 (see Table AIII3 in Appendix III)**

First, I give the 1953–54 values for how much high-IQ subjects enhanced their vocabularies *during the university ages*, then for how much low-IQ subjects did, and finally the difference. Second, I do the same for 2000–1. This tells us whether the differential gains of high IQ versus low IQ *during the university ages* increased between 1953–54 and 2000–1.

All values are expressed in an IQ-point metric (SD = 15).

| | | | |
|---|---|---|---|
| 1953–54: | 9.075 (high IQ) | 8.750 (low IQ) | 0.325 (difference) |
| 2000–01: | 6.500 (high IQ) | 3.400 (low IQ) | 3.100 (difference) |
| How much the difference increased over time: | | | 2.775 IQ points |

new jobs in which far more people played vocabulary-demanding roles as professionals, managers, and technicians.

If you are unconvinced, set all the above aside. Whatever has been responsible for the large vocabulary gains of adults over the last half-century, why have parents been so ineffective in transmitting those gains to their children?

## Active versus passive vocabulary

The General Social Survey administered a vocabulary test to a representative sample of English-speaking adult Americans from 1978 through 2006. It shows that they gained the equivalent of 1.88 IQ points over those years or, if you allow for an item that might have been more difficult by 2006 because less used in ordinary language, the gain was 2.25 points (see Table AIII4 in Appendix III). Even the latter falls far short of the 8 points US adults gained during those years on the WAIS vocabulary subtest. The GSS years were chosen to correspond to the years in which the WAIS-R (1978) and WAIS-IV (2006) standardization samples were tested. Three possible explanations follow.

(1) *Sampling.* This obvious explanation is almost certainly false. What would have to be the case for WAIS samples to uniquely inflate vocabulary gains? They would have to include: people who were average for vocabulary in 1953–54; people who were somewhat above average for vocabulary (but average for everything else) in 1978; more above average for vocabulary (and it alone) is 1995; and still more above average for vocabulary (and it alone) in 2006. No random error would produce such a result. You would have to deliberately oversample the preparers of dictionaries and gradually increase their overrepresentation over time.

(2) *Test content.* The GSS vocabulary test has used the same ten words since its inception in 1972. As indicated above, only one word of the ten looks a bit dated. I cannot name it, but it would be as if today's adults were presented with a word such as "notwithstanding." The 2006 sample outperforms the 1972 sample at all levels below getting a really high score (8 to 10 items correct), as if its best members were finding one item unusually difficult. However, recall that compensating for this item only raises the GSS gain from 1.88 to 2.25 points, still well short of the WAIS gain of 8 points.

(3) *Test format.* The WAIS is a "free recall paradigm" requiring the subject to volunteer the meaning of the words read out. The GSS is a "recognition paradigm." It offers five possible synonyms and the subject must recognize the one that is correct. If we assume that the WAIS and GSS results do not differ because of sampling error, it

must be because the former is testing active vocabulary rather than passive. That is, the WAIS discovers what words people are really likely to use in conversation or composition, while the GSS discovers what words people are likely to understand in context if someone else uses them or if they read them in a book.

It may seem impossible that from 1978 to 2006, American adults would gain 8.00 points for active vocabulary and 2.25 points for passive. The latter is only 28 percent of the former. However, recall and recognition involve different brain structures and processes. It is not uncommon for individuals with traumatic brain injury to be able to recognize a correct answer that they cannot recall. During half a century, the world of work may have altered its verbal demands toward the capacity to actually use more words (more talkers and fewer listeners). If so, the appropriate brain structures would become more developed, just as if we all began to swim a lot our muscles would adapt. No physiological impediment bars a greater increase of active than passive vocabulary over time.

The data suggest this summary for the whole period from 1950 to 2004. Schoolchildren gained 4.4 points for active vocabulary; adults gained 17.8 points for active vocabulary. American adults made a much lower gain for passive vocabulary: assuming it was 28 percent of the active for the whole period, it would have been about 5 points (0.28 × 17.8). We do not know what passive gain children made. Even if they made none, they did not fall far behind adults. We can now restate our central problem: why have parents and the children they raise shown a widening gap in their vocabularies; and why has the active vocabulary gap become wider than the passive gap? The active gap (13.4 points) puts average schoolchildren at the 18th percentile on the adult curve; the posited passive gap (4.98 points) puts them at the 37th percentile.

## Parents talking to teenagers

Circa 1950, when parents addressed their teenage children the latter understood them and answered in kind. Today, their children understand them. But to a significant degree, they cannot answer in kind or use their parents' vocabulary when talking to their peers or anyone from the adult world. The trend is nullified as children become adults. The tertiary years weigh in and then the world of work finishes the job of turning the teenage-speak teenager into an adult-speak adult. So the long-term social consequences are not serious. Even when adults lecture to freshmen at university, students will understand most of their speech even if, at that point in their lives, they cannot imitate it.

Mintz (2004) asserts that teenage subculture did not exist until 1950. Most young people aspired to adulthood as fast as their physical development allowed. In 1950, my friends and I were about 16, and it never occurred to any of us that this was a desirable phase of life to be prolonged into our twenties or even our thirties. Today, the desire of "teenagers" to be treated as both adults (independent decision-makers) and children (cared for financially) for a lengthy period has bemused many parents (see Box 20).

Despite debate about the new teenage subculture, most agree on certain brute facts: it is an increasingly autonomous subculture that has acquired its own dress, hairstyles, music, income for consumption – and dialect. WAIS versus WISC trends since 1950 suggest that teenage subculture has evolved. It always had the power to make its members use an alternative to adult speech. Today it inhibits them from developing the capacity to use adult speech. They have become less bilingual and more monolingual.

Celtic nationalities in the British Isles that resent English as an "alien" language try to revive their traditional languages. Teenagers have not only created an alternative dialect but also

**Box 20**

Some years ago, *The New Yorker* carried a cartoon depicting a scene in a recording studio. The singer was a flamboyantly attired youth weeping as he sang into the microphone: "I feel so sad, sad, sad, when my dad, dad, dad, won't give me the keys to the car." The orchestra was staffed with conventionally dressed middle-aged men. You would have to see their faces to appreciate the look of utter loathing.

withdrawn from their natural speech community. Until recently, US adults did not expect to bear the burdens of parenting beyond the age of 15. Perhaps antagonism between parents and teenagers rises as dependence is prolonged. Perhaps parents have begun to impose goals (get into Harvard) most teenagers cannot attain. Perhaps when teenagers become more alienated from their parents, they reinforce their subculture as a protective barrier. Cognitive trends over time are not events that happen in a test room: they signal the existence of important social trends.

## Trends from youth to old age

More than at any time in the past, those with high analytic ability are advantaged in marketing their skills. Does this asset have a darker side? Perhaps analytic brains that are high performance are also high maintenance in a way old age finds it difficult to satisfy? The four standardizations of the WAIS provide data for levels of ability ranging from those one SD below the median through those 2 SDs above. The trends with age vary from one intelligence level to another in a most surprising way.

I will proceed as follows: organize the WAIS data in terms of four cognitive levels and four kinds of cognition; introduce the concepts of bright taxes and bright bonuses; simulate cohorts; offer explanations of the results ranging from the

**Box 21**

From the WAIS to the WAIS-IV: Indexes and their subtests

| | Verbal Comprehension | Working Memory | Perceptual Reasoning | Processing Speed |
|---|---|---|---|---|
| WAIS-IV | Vocabulary<br>Information<br>Similarities | Arithmetic<br>Digit span | Block design<br>Visual puzzles<br>Matrix reasoning | Coding<br>Symbol search |
| WAIS-III | Vocabulary<br>Information<br>Similarities | Arithmetic<br>Digit span | Block design<br>Matrix reasoning | Coding<br>Symbol search |
| WAIS-R | Vocabulary<br>Information<br>Similarities | Arithmetic<br>Digit span | Block design | Coding |
| WAIS | Vocabulary<br>Information<br>Similarities | Arithmetic<br>Digit span | Block design | Coding |

*Sources:* Wechsler, 1955, p. 4; 1981, p. 10; 1997a, p. 8; 2008a, pp. 2–4.

purely environmental to those that emphasize the role of brain physiology.

## The WAIS and its four indexes

As Box 21 shows, the WAIS divides its subtests into four groups, each of which measures a different cognitive ability. For example, the WAIS-IV uses vocabulary, information, and similarities (classification) to make up an index of *Verbal Comprehension*. It uses arithmetic (mental arithmetic) and digit span (repeating or reordering a series of digits from memory) as an index of *Working Memory*. It uses block design (a sort of three-dimensional jigsaw puzzle), visual puzzles (recognizing what pieces make up a puzzle in obedience to two simple rules), and matrix reasoning (recognizing what image logically completes a series of images) as an index of *Perceptual Reasoning*. It uses coding (how quickly people can pair symbols and numbers) and symbol search (how quickly people can recognize that two groups of symbols have one in common) as an index of *Processing Speed*. "Perceptual Reasoning" is often called fluid intelligence because it challenges the subject to analyze and solve a problem on the spot. I will label it a measure of "Analytic Ability."

The WAIS-III has the same subtests as the WAIS-IV except that it omits visual puzzles. Visual puzzles is one of the three analytic subtests, so I gave block design, another analytic subtest, double weight. In the WAIS-IV data, the two subtests give almost identical estimates for the aging pattern of various levels of performance. The WAIS-R and the old WAIS include all Verbal and Working Memory subtests. However, block design is the only subtest that measures analytic ability. Fortunately, in the WAIS-IV data, it gives nearly the same estimates as the three analytic subtests combined. The early tests use only coding to measure Processing Speed but once again, it gives almost the same results as the combination of coding and symbol search. The four versions of the WAIS are comparable in terms of the four indexes of cognitive abilities.

I analyzed the WAIS data in two ways. Within each cognitive ability, I looked at four levels of intelligence (from 2 SDs above the median to one SD below). Other levels showed "floor" and "ceiling" effects. At 3 SDs above the median, subjects were getting all items correct and one did not know how far above average they really were. At 2 SDs below the median, there was not enough "room" for scores to decline much with age. Between cognitive abilities, I compared to see whether or not trends by age for those more or less intelligent were similar. Box 22 describes the steps (Table AIII5 in Appendix III details the calculations).

**Box 22**

The data analysis involves four steps:

1. **Raw scores**: WAIS tables give raw scores for every subtest at levels from three SDs below the median to three SDs above. The WAIS and WAIS-R do this for groups from ages 16–17 to ages 70–74 (although the WAIS borrowed from an independent study to get some data for older subjects). The WAIS-III and WAIS-IV do the same through ages 85–89 and ages 85–90 respectively. Therefore, all versions can be compared for trends through age 72 and the later versions up through ages 87 or 88 (Wechsler, 1955, pp. 101–110; 1981, pp. 142–150; 1997a, pp. 181–192; 2008a, pp. 206–218).
2. **Scaled scores and IQ scores**: The tables equate raw scores with scaled scores (SD = 3) at various performance levels. These can be equated with IQ scores (SD = 15). If your raw score equates with a scaled score of 10, you were at the median for your age on that subtest. If it equates with a scaled score of 7, you were one SD below the median or minus 15 IQ points. If it equates with 13, you were one SD above or plus 15 IQ points.
3. **Scoring all ages against the norms for 16–17-year-olds**: I equated the raw scores of all age groups with the scaled scores of 16–17-year-olds. An example: if the vocabulary raw score of someone at the median for 67-year-olds put them at a SS of 13 for 17-year-olds, they were one SD above the median for 17-year-olds. This is the equivalent of 15 IQ points, so the average person gained 15 points between the ages of 17 and 67.
4. **Levels of performance scored against the norms for 16–17-year-olds**: Elderly subjects one SD below the median for their age were scored against 17-year-

olds who were one SD below the median for their age. The same kind of comparison was made at the median, one SD above the median, and 2 SDs above the median.

5. **Averaging subtest results to get ability index results:** The Verbal index is the average of vocabulary, information, and similarities subtests. Therefore, if the average person at 67 had gained 15 points for vocabulary (since age 17), 5 points on information, and 10 points on similarities, their gain on the Verbal index was 10 (average of the three).

## Bright bonuses and bright taxes

I was quite unprepared for the results. The trends between youth and age differed by intelligence level, that is, going from the below average to the very bright. And the intelligence differences varied between abilities; for example, verbal showed the intelligent to be privileged and analytic showed them to be disadvantaged.

Box 23 gives results from the WAIS-IV (normed in 2006). Verbal ability shows bright bonuses from an early age. By a *bright bonus* I mean that going from comparisons 1 SD below the median to 2 SDs above, the higher the level the more favorable the comparison between the elderly and their 17-year-old contemporaries. This is apparent at ages 35–44. The least bright (those one SD below the median) are 5.9 points above their juniors, while the brightest (those two SDs above the median) are fully 11.7 points above their juniors. So going from the bottom to the top of the intelligence scale gives a bonus of 5.8 points (11.7 – 5.9 = 5.8). As we go to older age groups, the bright bonus grows to 8.40 points by age 72 and is still the same at age 88. The brightest may be past their peak but their verbal ability at age 88 is still 4.2 IQ points above their 17-year-old contemporaries. The least bright at age 88 have lost 4.2 IQ points on their youthful contemporaries. Therefore, the total bright bonus with age is fully 8.4 IQ points.

However, Analytic Ability shows a huge *bright tax*, that is, the higher the level of intelligence the less favorable the comparison between the elderly and their 17-year-old contemporaries. By age 72, the brightest are 22.50 points below their 17-year-old contemporaries, while the least bright are only 13.35 points below, giving a bright tax of 9.15 points. By age 88, the brightest have a deficit of 35.85 IQ points and the least bright only 21.60 for a tax of 14.25 points.

The IQ of those so penalized is very high indeed. Our brightest subjects are two SDs above the median on every subtest. This might seem to put their Full Scale IQ at age 17 at 130 (15 × 2 SDs). In fact, the WAIS-IV scoring tables show that, to do so well on each and every one of the ten subtests, you need a Full Scale IQ of 143. The tables give the least bright, those who have lost far less ground, an IQ of 79 at age 17.

Box 23 shows that Working Memory is bright neutral. It has no real bright tax or bright bonus at any point in old age. Processing Speed shows a bright tax of 6.20 points at age 72 increasing to 11.25 points at 88. However, this is not so

**Box 23 (see the derivation of the values below described in Appendix III)**

All of the older age groups are being compared to 17-year-olds who were their contemporaries (for example, those 85–90 in 2006 with those 16–17 in 2006).

The WAIS-IV: Trends with age for Wechsler cognitive abilities (SD = 15)

| | 16–17 | 35–44 | 55–64 | 65–69 | 70–74 | Gain or loss | 85–90 | Gain or loss |
|---|---|---|---|---|---|---|---|---|
| **Verbal** | | | | | | | | |
| −1 SD | 85.0 | 90.9 | 90.9 | 89.2 | 88.3 | **+3.3** | 80.8 | **−4.2** |
| Median | 100.0 | 107.5 | 108.7 | 107.0 | 105.4 | +5.4 | 97.3 | −2.7 |
| +1 SD | 115.0 | 127.5 | 128.4 | 125.9 | 124.2 | +9.2 | 118.3 | +3.3 |
| +2 SDs | 130.0 | 141.7 | 143.3 | 143.3 | 141.7 | **+11.7** | 134.2 | **+4.2** |
| | | | | | Bonus | 8.4 | Bonus | 8.4 |
| **Working Memory** | | | | | | | | |
| −1 SD | 85.0 | 86.3 | 85.0 | 82.5 | 81.3 | **−3.7** | 73.8 | **−11.2** |
| Median | 100.0 | 101.8 | 100.8 | 97.8 | 95.3 | −4.7 | 87.6 | −12.4 |
| +1 SD | 115.0 | 113.8 | 116.3 | 111.3 | 110.0 | −5.0 | 98.8 | −16.2 |
| +2 SDs | 130.0 | 135.0 | 131.3 | 130.0 | 127.5 | **−2.5** | 118.8 | **−11.2** |
| | | | | | Bonus | 1.2 | Neutral | – |
| **Analytic** | | | | | | | | |
| −1 SD | 85.0 | 81.7 | 76.7 | 74.2 | 71.7 | **−13.3** | 63.4 | **−21.6** |
| Median | 100.0 | 96.7 | 89.0 | 85.4 | 82.5 | −17.5 | 74.1 | −25.9 |
| +1 SD | 115.0 | 108.3 | 102.5 | 96.7 | 95.0 | −20.0 | 83.4 | −31.6 |
| +2 SDs | 130.0 | 117.6 | 115.9 | 111.7 | 107.5 | **−22.5** | 94.2 | **−35.8** |
| | | | | | Tax | 9.2 | Tax | 14.2 |
| **Processing Speed** | | | | | | | | |
| −1 SD | 85.0 | 82.5 | 75.0 | 72.5 | 70.0 | **−15.0** | 56.2 | **−28.8** |
| Median | 100.0 | 96.8 | 88.5 | 84.3 | 80.5 | −19.5 | 67.8 | −32.2 |
| +1 SD | 115.0 | 111.3 | 103.8 | 96.3 | 95.0 | −20.0 | 80.0 | −35.0 |
| +2 SDs | 130.0 | 125.0 | 115.0 | 111.3 | 108.8 | **−21.2** | 90.0 | **−40.0** |
| | | | | | Tax | 6.2 | Tax | 11.2 |

depressing. If one's analytic abilities are intact, taking longer to process the information to be analyzed is tolerable.

The phenomenon in question is a real-world one that has nothing to do with the statistical artifact of regression to the median or mean. If you select out an elite group from a population, say those who score 2 SDs above the mean, and retest them later, they will regress toward the mean (perhaps be only 1.75 SDs above). This is because they will on average have had a fortuitous performance on the first testing and cannot carry good fortune over to the second. I am comparing two distinct groups tested at the same time: one that is 2 SDs above the median for 17-year-olds with another that is 2 SDs above the median for 88-year-olds. Both are fixed at 2 SDs above the median for their respective populations, it is just that a performance good enough to put you at that level for the aged is not good enough to put you at that level for the youth. There is no retesting or regression present.

To get the point across intuitively, how could regression to the mean dictate a bright bonus for one cognitive ability and a bright tax for another? In the first case the performance loss with age has "regressed" so as to diminish the farther above the median you go, in the second case it has "regressed" or diminished the farther down toward the median you go. And why do those at the median "regress" away from those below the median when a bright bonus is at work?

## Cross-sectional and longitudinal data

Readers may be shocked by the magnitude of losses with age for Analytic Ability and Processing Speed. But note that this is cross-sectional rather than longitudinal data. The elderly are being compared to contemporary 17-year-olds, not what they were like at 17. Those who were 85–90 in 2006 were 16–17 about 1935. During those 71 years, 17-year-old Americans made

Full Scale IQ gains of over 21 points. Those who were 70–74 in 2006 were 16–17 about 1951. During those 55 years, 17-year-olds made Full Scale IQ gains of about 17 points. These estimates come from WISC data covering the 54 years from 1948 to 2002. Fortunately, we have data by subtest and can use them to calculate gains for the four Wechsler cognitive abilities. We also know that Full Scale IQ gains were relatively uniform from high IQs to low IQs (from Chapter 4). We do not know whether high and low IQs made the same gains over time on the four cognitive abilities, but to get some kind of estimate, I assumed that they did.

Box 24 takes IQ gains over time into account. The gains and losses with age of 70–74-year-olds are adjusted by crediting them with the points they "lost" by being compared with current 17-year-olds rather than themselves at 17. The same is done for 85–90-year-olds. The adjustment by definition leaves bright bonuses and bright taxes unaffected. But at least the trends with age are less alarming. All elderly people are better off for Verbal ability than they were at 17 (if we isolated vocabulary the adjustment would be small). For Analytic Ability, the trends are still grim. At circa 72, those average or below average are about where they were at 17, but the brightest are 6.6 points worse off. At circa 87–88, only those who are below average are near where they were at 17. The average have lost 5 points, the superior 11 points, and the brightest 15 points.

Do we have a right to feel somewhat reassured by the adjustments? It may be that between 17 and their present age, the elderly of today enjoyed an enhancement of cognitive environment that merely disguises the "real" losses with age. If the effects of aging are largely physiological, the unadjusted trends with age may give an accurate picture of "brain decline." What if IQ gains stop over the next 50 years? Then it would not matter whether we are comparing the aged with contemporary 17-year-olds or themselves at 17.

**Box 24**

Comparing those aged 70–74 and 85–90 in 2006 with themselves at the age of 16–17.

The WAIS-IV: Trends adjusted for IQ gains over time.

| | 70–74 Gain/Loss | Adjusted | 85–90 Gain/Loss | Adjusted |
|---|---|---|---|---|
| **Verbal** | | (+10.2) | | (+13.2) |
| –1 SD | +3.3 | +13.5 | –4.2 | +9.0 |
| Median | +5.4 | +15.6 | –2.7 | +10.5 |
| +1 SD | +9.2 | +19.4 | +3.3 | +16.5 |
| +2 SDs | +11.7 | +21.9 | +4.2 | +17.4 |
| | Bonus | 8.4 | Bonus | 8.4 |
| **Working Memory** | | (+2.3) | | (+3.0) |
| –1 SD | –3.7 | –1.4 | –11.2 | –8.2 |
| Median | –4.7 | –2.4 | –12.4 | –9.4 |
| +1 SD | –5.0 | –2.7 | –16.2 | –13.2 |
| +2 SDs | –2.5 | –0.2 | –11.2 | –8.2 |
| | Bonus | 1.2 | Neutral | – |
| **Analytic** | | (+15.9) | | (+20.7) |
| –1 SD | –13.3 | +2.6 | –21.6 | –0.9 |
| Median | –17.5 | –1.6 | –25.9 | –5.2 |
| +1 SD | –20.0 | –4.1 | –31.6 | –10.9 |
| +2 SDs | –22.5 | –6.6 | –35.8 | –15.1 |
| | Tax | 9.2 | Tax | 14.2 |
| **Processing Speed** | | (+18.0) | | (+23.4) |
| –1 SD | –15.0 | +3.0 | –28.8 | –5.4 |
| Median | –19.5 | –1.5 | –32.2 | –8.8 |
| +1 SD | –20.0 | –2.0 | –35.0 | –11.6 |
| +2 SDs | –21.2 | –3.2 | –40.0 | –16.6 |
| | Tax | 6.2 | Tax | 11.2 |

## Progressivity of the bright tax

Box 25 averages the results from all versions of the WAIS to compare age 72 with those at corresponding levels of performance at age 17. It averages the WAIS-III and IV to compare age 87/88 with those at corresponding levels of performance at age 17. It confirms what we already suspected. The Analytic bright tax is not like an albatross that hangs around the neck of only the very bright. It is a progressive tax that penalizes being brighter at every rung of the IQ ladder. While the Verbal bright bonus rewards being brighter at every IQ level.

For Analytic Ability, at age 72, the worst escalation of the penalty for being brighter is at the step from those 1 SD below the median to those at the median. At age 88, the worse escalation occurs from the step 1 SD below the median to 1 SD above the median, although the very bright still suffer a substantial extra penalty. In sum, while the escalation of the bright tax is present at every level, the escalation is actually least for the very bright. They still, of course, pay the greatest total tax, almost 16 points. We will soon see that confidence limits mean that our level-by-level analysis should not be taken literally. It is merely offered to demonstrate a negative: there is no reason to believe that going to the highest rung of the IQ ladder is what imposes a bright tax. For Verbal Ability, as usual, the pattern is different. The extra bonuses accrue mainly to those who are at least above average.

## Confidence limits

The nature of the data imposes wide confidence limits. An in-depth statistical analysis would almost undoubtedly give much narrower ones but that requires data on individual scores. Having values only for levels of the total standardization sample, the best we can do is use the fact that we have several independent

**Box 25 (see Table AIII5 in Appendix III)**

Versions of the WAIS averaged: Analytic tax and Verbal bonus compared

| *Analytic Ability* | *Age 72 compared to age 17* |
|---|---|
| At –1 SD: | Worse off by 12.05 IQ points |
| At Median: | Worse off by 17.70 IQ points |
| At +1 SD: | Worse off by 19.58 IQ points |
| At +2 SDs: | Worse off by 21.05 IQ points |

Total tax for being at +2 SDs rather than –1SD: 21.05 – 12.05 = 9.00 IQ points

| *Verbal Ability* | *Age 72 compared to age 17* |
|---|---|
| At –1 SD: | Better off by 1.05 IQ points |
| At Median: | Better off by 1.15 IQ points |
| At +1 SD: | Better off by 3.55 IQ points |
| At +2 SDs: | Better off by 7.13 IQ points |

Total bonus for being at +2 SDs rather than –1 SD: 7.13 – 1.05 = 6.08 IQ points

| *Analytic Ability* | *Age 87–88 compared to age 17* |
|---|---|
| At –1 SD: | Worse off by 17.45 IQ points |
| At Median: | Worse off by 23.75 IQ points |
| At +1 SD: | Worse off by 29.95 IQ points |
| At +2 SDs: | Worse off by 33.35 IQ points |

Total tax for being at +2 SDs rather than –1SD: 33.35 – 17.45 = 15.90 IQ points

| *Verbal Ability* | *Age 87–88 compared to age 17* |
|---|---|
| At –1 SD: | Worse off by 4.20 IQ points |
| At Median: | Worse off by 3.45 IQ points |
| At +1 SD: | Worse off by 0.85 IQ points |
| At +2 SDs: | Better off by 2.10 IQ points |

Total bonus for being at +2 SDs rather than –1 SD: 2.10 + 4.20 = 6.30 IQ points

| | |
|---|---|
| Verbal: | All four data sets suggest that a bonus begins between ages 18 and 24. |
| Analytic: | Data sets vary as to when a tax begins, but suggest between ages 55 and 69 with median at 65. |

data sets. Box 26 shows beyond a doubt that things such as bright bonuses and bright taxes exist.

At age 72, the two that concern us most are the Verbal bright bonus and the Analytic bright tax; and the odds that these arose by chance are only one in 167. The Verbal bonus has confidence limits of plus or minus 2.77 points, so can be put at about 3 to 9 points. The Analytic tax has limits of 4.04 points and can be put at 5 to 13 points. At age 88, thanks to the fact that we have only two data sets, we cannot set confidence limits, but can say that the odds are one in five that the Verbal bonus arose by chance and only one in 15 that the Analytic tax did so. If the WAIS-V (due in about 2018) shows the same results, the situation will be remedied. If not, the whole issue will have to be revisited anyway.

The existence of a Processing Speed bright tax is overwhelmingly probable at both age 72 and age 88, but the range of possible estimates is very large, from about 3 to 21 points. The results for Working Memory are consistent with its having neither a bright bonus nor tax.

## Simulating cohorts

The above attempt to simulate longitudinal trends with age did not test for what we want most: to determine whether longitudinal data would give different estimates of bright taxes or bonuses than those our cross-sectional data engender. Indeed, no attempt to simulate a genuine longitudinal study can be entirely successful. None will give the history of a real cohort that took the WAIS-IV at age 17 and then retook it as they aged. But as a second best, we can trace artificial cohorts that took the WAIS at the various times it was normed. For example, we can compare those aged 60 from the WAIS-R (1978), with those aged 77 from the WAIS-III (1995), with those aged 88 from the WAIS-IV (2006). We can at least determine whether a rough approximation of longitudinal data alters bright bonus/tax trends with age.

**Box 26**

Here are estimates of the size of all bright bonuses/taxes. Also the minimum and maximum values that set probable limits on their sizes; that is, the odds are 19 to 1 that their sizes fall somewhere between those limits. Also the possibility they arose by chance. WM refers to Working Memory and PS to Processing Speed.

| **Age 72** | Estimate | Min. | Max. | Possibility arose by chance |
|---|---|---|---|---|
| Verbal bright bonus | 6.08 | 3.31 | 8.85 | 1/167 |
| Analytic bright tax | 9.00 | 4.96 | 13.04 | 1/167 |
| PS bright tax | 12.45 | 3.38 | 21.52 | 1/45 |
| WM bright bonus | 3.13 | – 2.15 | +8.41 | 1/6 |
| **Age 88** | | | | |
| Verbal bright bonus | 6.30 | – | – | 1/5 |
| Analytic bright tax | 15.95 | – | – | 1/15 |
| PS bright tax | 11.85 | 3.60 | 20.10 | 1/29 |
| WM bright tax | 4.35 | – | – | 1/2 |

I have traced the history of three cohorts. Some pro-rating is necessary to get comparable values for each cohort at the same ages during their lives but it can be done.

(1) The 88-year-old cohort that took the WAIS-IV in 2006. They were 77 in 1995, 60 in 1978 (and with a bit of reverse projecting we can get an age 72 estimate as well), and 35.5 in 1953–54. If we compare these age groups, we are progressively cutting the age gap between the 17-year-olds (with whom they were compared) and themselves at 17 from 71 years to 19 years. (2) The cohort that was 72 in 2006. The same procedure catches them at 61 in 1995 (or 60 in 1994). (3) The cohort that was 60 in 2006.

A point of information: shifting the age that is the base for calculating bonuses/taxes affects even the cross-sectional values a bit. For example, when you calculate the total bright tax of 88-year-olds in 2006 from WAIS-IV data, you are no longer comparing their raw scores to those of 17 years but to those of 35.5-year-olds. Otherwise the cross-sectional data would not be comparable to "longitudinal" data. This increases the bright tax at age 88 by 1.4 points, and shifts values for other ages by small amounts. A word of warning: the standard errors of estimate do not apply to different results between one data set and another, which means that confidence limits for "shifts" over time are unknown. Nonetheless, what I will now say must be qualified by the fact that it would be foolish to take differences of three or four points too seriously.

Box 27 gives the bright bonuses/taxes of our three cohorts at elderly ages. It seems plausible that both bright bonuses and bright taxes would become more pronounced with age, that is, for them to become larger as we go from age 60 to 72 to 88 (certainly that makes sense if there is a physiological component). When we compare "longitudinal" trends with the cross-sectional trends, the results are mixed.

(1) For Verbal Ability, the longitudinal results make more sense than the cross-sectional. Take the cohort born in 1918. The values across (longitudinal) show a slight increase of the bright bonus from 7.90 at age 60 to 9.45 points at age 88. The diagonal values (cross-sectional) show a slight decline from 11.10 to 9.45. However, the cohort born in 1934 seems to confirm that (at best) there is no increase between ages 60 and 72.
(2) For Analytic Ability, longitudinal and cross-sectional results are much the same. Both yield trends that show the bright tax increasing sharply with age from 4 or 5 points to 15.65 points.
(3) For Processing Speed, the longitudinal results make less sense than the cross-sectional. Take the cohort born

in 1918. The longitudinal trend shows the bright tax as essentially stable with age varying around 13 points. The cross-sectional trend shows a sharp increase at age 72.

(4) For Working Memory, both the longitudinal and cross-sectional results are consistent with its being bright neutral. The values bob around a bit but there is no obvious trend toward the bright having either an advantage or a disadvantage as they age.

In sum, simulating longitudinal values offers rough confirmation of the cross-sectional data. Everyone would prefer genuine longitudinal data. But unless those conducting longitudinal studies take the possibility of bright taxes/bonuses seriously, there is no chance that the relevant longitudinal data will be collected. Moreover, even their putative existence suggests interesting lines of research, as will become apparent.

## Causes

Let us address the bright tax on Analytic Abilities in conjunction with the bright bonus for Verbal Abilities. These could be purely environmental phenomena. Following the Dickens–Flynn model of cognitive development, I will focus on interaction between genes and environment. High cognitive ability begins with genetic potential for a better-engineered brain and when that better brain becomes operational, it begins to access environments that give it unusual cognitive exercise. This enhances the cognitive advantage further, which accesses an even better exercise environment, and so forth. In other words, those whose brains are best wired for analytic and verbal skills become professionals and technicians who build up a huge exercise advantage on those in less cognitively demanding jobs and with less articulate friends.

Assume a division of labor. The analytic exercise advantage is connected primarily to work; the verbal advantage

**Box 27**

Comparing three cohorts to determine whether longitudinal patterns differ from cross-sectional patterns. For longitudinal look at the values in bold straight across. For cross-sectional patterns look at the values in bold going diagonally upward.

| | | | |
|---|---|---|---|
| **Verbal** | | | |
| Born 1918 | Age 60 (in 1978) | Age 72 (in 1990) | Age 88 (in 2006) |
| Bright bonus | **7.90** | **7.27** | **9.45** |
| Born 1934 | Age 60 (in 1994) | Age 72 (in 2006) | |
| Bright bonus | 10.50 | **9.85** | |
| Born 1946 | Age 60 (in 2006) | | |
| Bright bonus | **11.10** | | |
| **Analytic** | | | |
| Born 1918 | Age 60 (in 1978) | Age 72 (in 1990) | Age 88 (in 2006) |
| Bright tax | **3.85** | **13.25** | **15.65** |
| Born 1934 | Age 60 (in 1994) | Age 72 (in 2006) | |
| Bright tax | 1.00 | **10.70** | |
| Born 1946 | Age 60 (in 2006) | | |
| Bright tax | **5.62** | | |
| **Processing Speed** | | | |
| Born 1918 | Age 60 (in 1978) | Age 72 (in 1990) | Age 88 (in 2006) |
| Bright tax | **11.70** | **16.71** | **13.00** |
| Born 1934 | Age 60 (in 1994) | Age 72 (in 2006) | |
| Bright tax | 12.45 | **9.00** | |
| Born 1946 | Age 60 (in 2006) | | |
| Bright tax | **8.58** | | |
| **Working Memory** | | | |
| Born 1918 | Age 60 (in 1978) | Age 72 (in 1990) | Age 88 (in 2006) |
| Bonus/tax | **+4.15** (bonus) | **−3.93** (tax) | **−0.75** (tax) |
| Born 1934 | Age 60 (in 1994) | Age 72 (in 2006) | |
| Bonus | 0.00 | **+1.75** (bonus) | |
| Born 1946 | Age 60 (in 2006) | | |
| Bonus/tax | **−2.70** (tax) | | |

primarily to leisure, that is, to the informal interaction with the other professionals who are your friends and companions (often including a professional spouse and budding professional children).

Both of these exercise advantages persist up to the retirement age of 65. But after retirement from the job, you are no longer doing cognitively demanding work, and the average person is no longer doing less demanding work. You are like a runner who stops training. The main advantage you now have is the genetic one and the exercise gap between you and the less able has much diminished. Hence the bright tax on Analytic Abilities. On the other hand, more of your time is devoted to leisure and compared to the average person it is a talkative leisure. No longer dealing with subordinates, you converse more exclusively with family and friends. Your verbal exercise advantage over the average person has actually increased. Hence the bright bonus on Verbal Abilities.

If less analytic exercise after retirement is the cause of the bright tax, and if you resent the relative decay of those abilities (you may just want to relax), the remedy is clear. Keep doing research, keep teaching complex material, play more chess, keep up with developments in mathematics, and so forth. Adam *et al.* (2007) compared performance on a test of episodic memory between two age groups: males aged 50 to 54 and 60 to 64 respectively. Obvious confounds were obviated by ranking 12 nations in terms of persistence of employment into old age. If the percentage of males in work dropped by 90% as men aged (Austria, France), there was a 15% decline in episodic memory. If the percentage in work dropped by 25% (the USA, Sweden), the decline was only 7%. It is a pity that the test did not include a measure of Analytic Abilities, but unless they are atypical, exercise in old age would benefit them as well.

On the other hand, the bright tax on Analytic Abilities could be an effect of the physiology of the aging brain. Imagine a number of cars, some of which are engineered for higher performance than others. While all are maintained properly, the performance advantage of the better cars persists in its entirety. But the high-performance cars are also high-maintenance cars. As the mechanics that service the cars age, they lose the energy to give the best cars what they need for top performance. The less needy cars require less maintenance and therefore, do not show as sharp a downward curve for performance. Logic does not forbid the hypothesis that the analytic portions or circuits of the brain become more high maintenance the better the engineering. Therefore, they may be more subject to decay as the efficiency of whatever services them declines with age.

These causes are not mutually exclusive: a combination of less exercise in old age and more vulnerability to reduced maintenance in old age may be at work. But the exercise component is easy (in theory at least) to evidence: we just need the kind of data Adams *et al.* (2007) had but inclusive of Analytic Abilities. We could then see whether the bright tax is postponed to the retirement years, no matter whether they begin at 60 or 65 or 70. So I will focus on how we might evidence the posited physiological component. The following is an amateur effort to summarize what we know about brains that explains individual differences in cognitive performance.

## What we know about the brain

Deary, Penke, and Johnson (2010) begin by distinguishing grey and white matter. Nerve cells or neurons actually carry on mental functions, such as analysis or information processing, and they are the grey matter of the brain (about 40%). Some nerve cells have fibrous extensions or axons. These are the communications networks from one neuron to another (and between neurons and the other parts of the body), and they constitute the white matter of the brain (60%).

Crude correlations between IQ and greater volume of matter run at about 0.25 for the frontal cortex and the parietal and temporal cortices (all of which have been long thought to be the "seat" of intelligence); and for the hippocampus (spatial mapping). Correlations with the volume of grey and white matter respectively run a bit higher at 0.31 and 0.27 respectively. The correlations with grey matter appear to have more to do with its thickness than sheer volume. Its thickness can be enhanced by mental exercise. Dopamine appears to make neurons more efficient with use. Mental exercise sprays them with dopamine, which thickens them, and makes them operate more efficiently the next time they are used; thus learning. The white matter (axons) is sheathed in myelin, which is rather like wires being insulated. The myelin prevents the communications network between neurons from leaking electrical energy and losing efficiency.

As for the crucial role of the white matter communications network (the axons that connect neurons), there is a growing consensus for the concept of a "small-world network." The optimum seems to be a high level of local clustering and short pathways that link them, that is, the most efficient network is few paths and short paths to link the clusters. The best brains appear to be more efficient in the sense that they use fewer brain resources to do reasoning tasks. The average brain has to be very active to deal with a mental task of moderate difficulty, while a superior brain solves it with less effort. For difficult tasks, the average brain is inactive because it gives up, while the superior brain now mobilizes all of its resources.

Aging has important effects. Neurons lose plasticity, and dopamine has less effect in repairing and improving them. The communications system between neurons becomes less efficient. When the axons of the elderly develop lesions, these show a negative correlation with IQ, at present probably lowered by subjective assessment of the presence of a lesion. Recall that myelin insulates the axons. Myelin breakdown and repair is continually occurring over the brain's entire neural network. But in old age, we begin losing the repair battle. The average performance of the communications network declines with age at an accelerating rate.

## Pointers

What, then, would we look for in order to detect a physiological cause of the bright tax? First, we would have to isolate the brain areas and circuits that are relevant to Analytic Abilities. We would look to see if the rate of decay for the analytically bright was greater than for the analytically average as follows. (1) Is the plasticity of the neurons fading at a faster rate? (2) Is the myelin sheath around the axons thinning at a greater rate and are more lesions apparent? (3) Are the number and length of the pathways at work during analysis increasing at a faster rate? And is all this occurring despite the fact that high-performing elderly people persist in vigorous analytic exercise? If so, it appears that the analytic brains of the high performing, compared to the analytic brains of the average performing, are more high maintenance; and more vulnerable to the decline of maintenance quality that accompanies old age. You will still drive a high-performance car but its condition will deteriorate faster than those less blessed.

Genes may be involved in the bright tax. Erickson *et al.* (2008) found that adults with a certain genotype performed better on a measure of executive function at around 65 years of age, when compared to individuals who carried a mutant. However, when they followed up the participants ten years later at the age of 75, the *unmutated* genotype was the only one to show a significant decline in executive function. Executive function has some relationship to fluid intelligence, but more convincing would be a positive link between the unmutated genotype and analytic skills. There are some hints in the literature. Tsai *et al.* (2004) found that those with the val/val genotype performed better as young adults on the WAIS-R Performance Scale; but sadly their greatest advantage was on object assembly rather than the more directly relevant block design. Harris *et al.* (2006) did not focus on the analytic bright tax or the verbal bright bonus but relevant correlations may be hidden in their huge array of raw data.

Erickson *et al.* (2008) furnishes genuine longitudinal data that suggest a bright tax. But it is possible to give their results an environmental interpretation. Those with the val/val genotype, being on average brighter and thus more frequently in cognitively demanding jobs, may suffer from a greater loss of analytic exercise when they retire (at, say, 65). If they examined their val/val subjects and found that a larger proportion had not retired, or that they had enjoyed no higher occupational status, the possibility that this gene confers a high-maintenance brain physiology would be much enhanced.

## Ignorance and puzzles

Clancy Blair (Nisbett *et al.*, 2012) shows that locating different cognitive functions in different brain areas is possible. He cites the study that found that the hippocampi (seat of navigating through three-dimensional space) of taxi cab drivers enlarged in proportion to their time on the job (Maguire *et al.*, 2000). Three months of playing the visual-spatial game Tetris gave increased cortical thickness in two regions and brought functional changes in other areas. Three months of juggling increased the size of grey matter in the mid-temporal and left-posterior areas. Three months after juggling ceased, some expansion was lost. Figure 3 maps the WAIS cognitive functions on areas of the brain, and offers comments about the effects of aging on those areas.

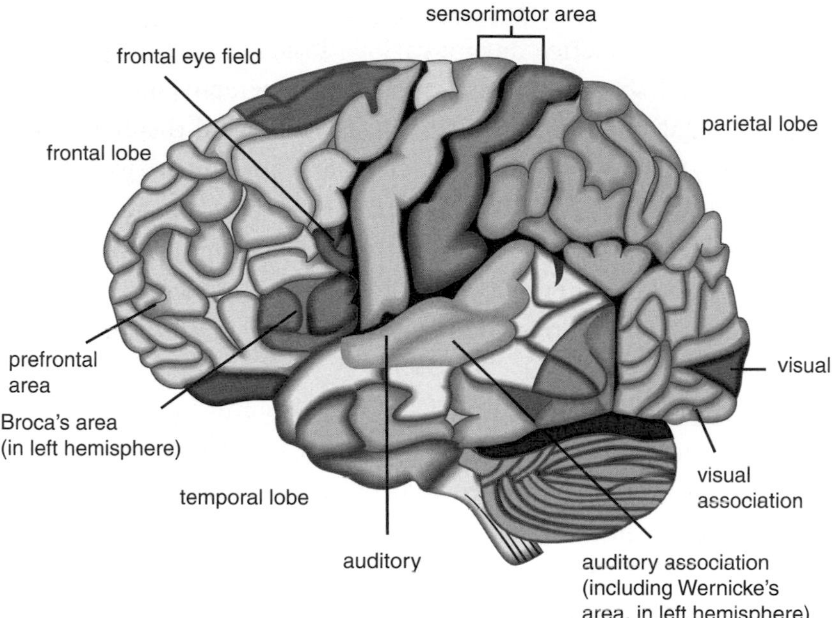


*Figure 3 Areas of the brain associated with WAIS indexes.*

1. *Verbal Comprehension: Broca's area (rear of frontal lobe) and Wernicke's area (mid-temporal lobe).* Aging: *The only regions of the brain to show prominent grey matter increase into adulthood.*
2. *Working Memory: The WAIS measures this using arithmetic (which involves remembered knowledge) and digit span (part of which involves simple recall), so several areas come into play.* Aging: *Areas too diverse to estimate.*
3. *Analytic or fluid intelligence: Prefrontal area.* Aging: *Earliest region to show age-related decline.*
4. *Processing Speed: Perhaps the central nervous system (associated with decline in motor function).* Aging: *Later than the prefrontal area.*

*Sources:* AFAR, 2009, p. 2; Resnick, Lamar, & Driscoll, 2007, p. 562; Sowell, Thompson, & Toga, 2004, p. 390.

It looks as if we can do a reasonable job of mapping for Analytic and Verbal Abilities. I do not know the potency of the technology available to survey the brain. I am told that MRI

(Magnetic Resonance Imaging) has great promise in determining which areas are active during various kinds of cognition. I am told that PET scans (Positron Emission Tomography) have shown age-related decline in the effects of dopamine and the condition of axons. Perhaps it is capable of discriminating between the rates of loss in neural plasticity and rates of myelin thinning of high-performing and average-performing subjects respectively, and can do so this for the analytic areas on the brain map. Others more sophisticated than I will know what is possible and what to look for.

Merely because there is a verbal bonus, we must not assume that we will find no physiological tendency for high-performing verbal brains to require more maintenance with age than low-performing verbal brains. It is possible that a growing verbal exercise gap between the bright and the average after retirement swamps a slight tendency in that direction. However, the analytic and verbal areas of the brain do show a different profile with age. As Figure 3 notes, the verbal areas are the only ones that show real grey matter increase into adulthood, and the analytic area is the first to show age-related decline.

Presumably, throughout human evolution, the main reason people survived past the age of procreation was because of the help they could give to their own grandchildren (thus perpetuating genes advantageous for longevity). Perhaps their child-minding roles required the persistence of Verbal Ability but placed little premium on Analytic Ability. If so, there would be little evolutionary pressure to eliminate a trade-off between high performance and high maintenance for Analytic Ability that manifests itself only in old age. It may even be that the less one analyzes one's lot when child-minding, the more chance there is of preserving one's sanity.

Whatever the role of environment and physiology, something seems to be levying a bright tax on our Analytic Ability:

intelligent minds do worse in the struggle against age. The ideas they create are another matter. If these tip the balance in favor of truth over falsehood, they bequeath an inheritance as timeless as our eternal adversary.

This chapter has been mainly a puzzles chapter rather than a progress chapter. But it would be very boring if sociology, psychology, and brain physiology had no new problems to solve. If the evidence stands up, the growing adult/child vocabulary gap and the bright tax will put a premium on expertise in all three.

# 6 Race and gender

Race and gender IQ differences arouse strong emotions and therefore I excluded them from *What Is Intelligence?* I did not want critical assessment of my views on intelligence lost in a welter of acrimonious debate. Look at what happened to *The Bell Curve*, which was 90 percent about other subjects and debated as if it were 90 percent about race.

I have offered my case that the black/white IQ gap is probably environmental in origin elsewhere (Flynn, 1980, 2008), and will not repeat it here. However, much of this book preaches the message that differences between Wechsler subtests are central to interpreting IQ trends. The following will, I hope, show that these subtest differences are not central to the race and IQ debate, at least not for the reasons given by thinkers such as Jensen and Rushton. As a bonus, we may enhance our understanding of why WISC subtests differ in a variety of ways: not only in the size of the black/white performance gap, but also in terms of their *g*-loadings, heritability, and sensitivity to inbreeding depression.

## The significance of *g*-loadings

Let us review what was said in Chapter 2. We posit a construct called *g* (the general intelligence factor) because people who excel on one cognitive task tend to excel on others. Subtests that are better predictors of how well you will do on cognitive tasks in general are assigned a high *g*-loading, while subtests that are worse predictors have a low *g*-loading. Thus, we can rank the ten subtests of the WISC or WAIS into a hierarchy from the subtest that has the largest *g*-loading to the subtest that has the smallest. The most important thing about the *g*-loading hierarchy is that it tallies with the cognitive complexity of the task a particular subtest involves.

When comparing groups, it is interesting to see how performance differences vary as *g*-loadings rise. Rarely will a "superior" group lose ground as *g*-loadings rise, but it can happen, as when females best males on mathematical problems of moderate difficulty yet fall behind on the most difficult problems. Usually it will be an "inferior" group that falls further behind as cognitive tasks become more complex. This allow us to distinguish two kinds of problem-solving gaps between groups: the Wechsler *IQ gap*, which treats the ten subtests as of equal weight; and the Wechsler *GQ gap*, which weights the subtest scores in accord with their *g*-loadings. For example, the latter gives vocabulary score differences between two groups double the weight of coding score differences. Vocabulary has about twice the *g*-loading of coding.

The GQ and IQ gaps between the races differ by no more than one point (SD = 15). This seems surprising until we note that with the exception of coding, the various Wechsler subtests differ little in terms of their *g*-loadings. All of them measure either cognitively complex tasks (fluid *g*) or things such as vocabulary, whose acquisition reflects the cognitive complexity of assimilating the meaning of words (crystallized *g*). The small gap between GQ and IQ is perfectly compatible with a moderate correlation between the size of group difference and the hierarchy of *g*-loadings.

Does the fact that the performance gap between the races is larger the more complex the task tell us anything about genes versus environment? Imagine that one group has better genes for height and reflex arc but suffers from a less rich basketball environment (less incentive, worse coaching, less play). The environmental disadvantage will expand the between-group performance gap as complexity rises, just as much as a genetic deficit would. I have not played basketball since high school. Recently, I found that I could still make nine out of ten layups. But I have fallen far behind on the more difficult shots: my attempts at a fadeaway jump shot from the edge of the circle are ludicrous. The skill gap between basketball "unchallenged" players and those still active will be more pronounced the more difficult the task. In sum, someone exposed to a poor environment hits what I call a "complexity ceiling." Clearly, the existence of this ceiling does not differentiate whether the performance gap is due to genes or environment.

Correlations showing that group gaps in basketball skills rise with complexity loading (*g*-loading), or rise with the heritability of the skill, or rise with how much the skill is affected by inbreeding depression make sense. Of course height and quickness are more important the more complex the skill, and of course these traits are heritable and adversely affected by inbreeding. But they do not decide the causal question.

## History of a debate

Originally, Jensen (1973) argued as follows: (1) the heritability of IQ within whites and probably within blacks was 0.80 and between-family factors accounted for only 0.12 of IQ variance – with only the latter relevant to group differences; (2) the square root of the percentage of variance explained gives the correlation between between-family environment and IQ, a correlation of about 0.33 (square root of 0.12 = 0.34); (3) if there is no genetic difference, blacks can be treated as a sample of the white population selected out by environmental inferiority; (4) enter regression to the mean – for blacks to score 1 SD below whites for IQ, they would have to be 3 SDs (3 × 0.33 = 1) below the white mean for quality of environment; (5) no sane person can believe that – it means the average black cognitive environment is below the bottom 0.2 percent of white environments; (6) evading this dilemma entails positing a fantastic "factor X," something that blights the environment of every black to the same degree (and thus does not reduce within-black heritability estimates), while being totally absent among whites (thus having no effect on within-white heritability estimates).

I used the Flynn effect to break this steel chain of ideas: (1) the heritability of IQ both within the present and the last generation may well be 0.80 with factors relevant to group differences at 0.12; (2) the correlation between IQ and relevant environment is then 0.33; (3) the present generation is analogous to a sample of the last selected out by a more enriched environment (a proposition I defend by denying a significant role to genetic enhancement); (4) enter regression to the mean – since the Dutch of 1982 scored 1.33 SDs higher than the Dutch of 1952 on Raven's Progressive Matrices, the latter would have needed to have a cognitive environment 4 SDs (4 × 0.33= 1.33) below the average environment of the former; (5) either there was a factor X that separated the generations (which I too dismiss as fantastic) or something was wrong with Jensen's case. When Bill Dickens and I developed our model, we knew what was wrong: the model shows how heritability estimates can be as high as you please without robbing environment of its potency to create huge IQ gains over time.

I never claimed that the Flynn effect had *causal* relevance for the black/white IQ gap. I claimed that it had *analytic* relevance. Jensen had argued that environment (at least between groups both located in a modern western society) was so feeble that an astronomical environmental difference had to be posited to explain a 1-SD IQ gap. The Dutch showed that the environmental difference in question was less than whatever environmental enhancement they had enjoyed over 30 years. The gap needed was dragged out of the stars down to earth. If black IQ gains were 0.3 points per year, the environmental lag between blacks and whites would only amount to 50 years ($0.30 \times 50 = 15$ IQ points). In a recent book (Flynn, 2008, Chapter 3), I proved that this was so. Scored against the whites of 1947–48, the blacks of 2002, some 54 years later, had a mean IQ of 104.31 and a GQ of 103.52.

## The Flynn effect mantra

Unfortunately, the general public has tended to think that the fact massive IQ gains over time have environmental causes somehow *shows* that the black/white IQ gap has environmental causes. Rushton and Jensen (2010) note the rise of such a notion and then trace its fall, that is, argue against it. Jensen (1998) complains that the Flynn effect is repeatedly thrown at him as a kind of mantra. My recent book (Flynn, 2008, p. 79) offers my sympathies: "Flynn himself ... does not believe that IQ gains show that blacks can match whites for IQ ... when environments are equal." From my point of view, there was no "rise and fall of the Flynn effect." It never rose: showing that something is possible is not the same as showing that something is true.

Today, I can say just why a causal explanation of IQ gains does not provide the key to the black/white IQ gap because I finally have a hypothesis about the former. Again see Chapter 2: the twentieth century saw people putting on scientific spectacles that gave them new "habits of mind." Rather than differentiating things to capitalize on their differential utility, people find it natural to classify things as a prerequisite to understanding. Rather than tying logic to the concrete, people find it natural to take the hypothetical seriously and use logic on the abstract. Thus the huge score gains on similarities (classification) and Raven's Progressive Matrices (logical sequences of symbols).

This hypothesis erases a preoccupation that affected an exchange with Rushton that took place some 12 years ago (Flynn,

1999a, 1999b). Gains on Raven's were so huge that I believed IQ gains must represent *fluid g* gains. Accordingly, I ranked the WISC subtests in terms of the magnitude of their correlations with Raven's, and found a modest correlation with the magnitude of IQ gains on each subtest. Today I would not be surprised or disturbed if a wider array of evidence negated this result. The significance of IQ gains rests on what they tell us about the evolution of our minds in the twentieth century, not on whether we have some kind of *g* advantage on our ancestors. And the new habits of mind are too diverse and complex to be captured by the concept of "enhanced fluid *g*."

## Status of the race and IQ debate

The fact that the GQ gap between blacks and whites is larger than the IQ gap has causal significance. If blacks did eliminate the IQ gap without eliminating the GQ gap, they would still be less able to solve the most complex cognitive problems, which might be deemed the most significant. Moreover, the fact that blacks have an unusual problem with complexity shows that an explanation of the IQ gap should look for aspects of the black environment that discourage cognitive challenge or, at least, downgrade its presence. I took upon myself the burden of offering a scenario of a succession of black environments from infancy to early adulthood based on the deprivation of complexity (Flynn, 2008). It is significant that when the racial IQ gap was eliminated among children fathered by black soldiers in postwar Germany, the GQ gap was gone. This is not to claim that this study settles the debate; rather it gives us confidence that if the IQ gap proves to be entirely environmental, the GQ gap will prove so as well.

American blacks are not in a time warp so that the environmental causes of their IQ gap with whites are identical to the environmental causes of the IQ gap between the generations. The race and IQ debate should focus on testing the relevant environmental hypotheses. The Flynn effect is no shortcut; the fact that the black/white performance gap expands with *g*-loadings or complexity is no shortcut. There are no shortcuts at all.

## Comments on Rushton and Jensen

Rushton and Jensen (2010) wrote a guest editorial for the prestigious journal *Intelligence* that summarized their latest views. I will comment on their points by numbered section, so as to allow readers to consult the original.

1. They assert that the Flynn sources listed give the FE as a reason for expecting the B/W gap to disappear. In fact, these give the FE as a reason for thinking that an environmental hypothesis is viable. I always turned to other kinds of evidence when testing its truth. In addition, I never said real intelligence levels were rising. For 20 years, I searched for something that would show that gains were neither artifacts nor in any simple sense intelligence gains.
2. The contention that "if population group differences are greater on the more *g*-loaded and more heritable subtests, it implies they have a genetic origin" (Rushton & Jensen, 2010, p. 214) is now seen to be false. All of the data from this methodology (whether called the "method of correlated vectors" or the "Jensen effect") is irrelevant. I am not sure but I suspect that *g* does have some root in brain physiology. Height is rooted in physiology but height differences between groups may be due to differences in diet. The assertion that "culture-only" theories predict a zero relationship between heritability and group differences is false.
3. I do not believe that outbreeding or any other genetic enhancement has caused recent IQ gains, but outbreeding

may have played a role in earlier times depending on the nation (see Chapter 3). My belief that the fact the *g* gap between black and white "tells us something about causes" (it tells us to look for whether environmental factors are friendly or unfriendly to cognitively demanding pursuits) does not reverse a past position but is a new insight.

4. Dickens and Flynn (2006a) published data showing that between 1972 and 2002, black Americans had gained 5.5 IQ points on whites and closed the *g* gap by 5.13 points. At both times, both in 1972 and 2002, blacks lost ground on whites as they aged (from ages 4 to 24) by about 12 points. The critical points Rushton and Jensen raise were answered in our rebuttal to their critique at the time. I urge readers to consult it (Dickens & Flynn, 2006b).

Box 28 sets out data that Rushton and Jensen present on black academic achievement. Note the tendency for blacks to lose ground with age at any given time: in 1966, they lost 5 points between ages 12 and 18; in 2008, they lost 8 points between ages 13 and 17 (1975 is an exception). If you average the three data sets, blacks lose 0.93 points per year between the ages of 13 and 17 for a total of 3.71 points. This is not far from the Dickens and Flynn (2006a) estimate of 2.40 IQ points lost between those ages. Note that the NAEP data (Nation's Report Card) show that blacks have made academic gains on whites between 1975 and 2008: 15 points at age 13; 6 points at age 17. The latter virtually matches the Dickens and Flynn estimate that blacks gained 5.5 IQ points between 1972 and 2002. On the other hand, I find the huge academic gain at age 13 implausible.

However, the data are deeply disturbing. Rushton, Jensen, and Flynn all think that black IQ is significant largely because it predicts academic achievement. Therefore, black IQ and the achievement values should be roughly the same. Compare 1 and

**Box 28**

Black academic achievement (whites set at 100)

| Place | Date | Ages | Score |
|---|---|---|---|
| 1. Georgia | 1954 | 14 | 86 |
| 2. US (Coleman Report) | 1966 | 12 | 87 |
| | 1966 | 15 | 84 |
| | 1966 | 18 | 82 |
| 3. US (Nation's Report Card) | 1975 | 13 | 70 |
| | 1975 | 17 | 71 |
| 4. US (Nation's Report Card) | 2008 | 13 | 85 |
| | 2008 | 17 | 77 |

2 in Box 28: does anyone really believe that blacks in Georgia in 1954 equaled black IQ nationwide in 1966? The Georgia value is too high: Jensen (1973) gives a much lower black value (80.7) for five Southeastern states including Georgia circa 1960. Compare 2, 3, and 4 in Box 28: does anyone really believe that the IQ of black 13-year-olds has been bounding all over the place, from about 84 to 87 in 1966, down to 70 in 1975, up to 85 in 2008? The value of 70 would be at least as low as blacks in sub-Saharan Africa.

Much of the academic achievement data is a mess. That is why Dickens and Flynn confined themselves to Wechsler and Stanford–Binet data to trace racial IQ trends from 1972 to 2002. It was quite consistent in yielding a gain of black on white of 5.5 IQ points over that period.

## Summary on race

(1) *g* would be of no interest were it not correlated with cognitive complexity. (2) Given a hierarchy of tasks, a worse performing group (whatever the cause of its deficit) will tend to hit a

"complexity ceiling" – fall further behind a better group the more complex the task. (3) Heritability of relevant traits will increase the more complex the task. (4) Thus, the fact that group performance gaps correlate with heritability gives no clue to the origin of group differences. (5) When a lower performing group gains on a higher performing one, their gains will tend to diminish the more complex the task. Thus, blacks have gained 5.50 IQ points on whites since 1972 but only 5.13 GQ points. (6) Recent achievement test data confirm these IQ gains but the data as a whole pose problems for the external validity of black IQ (discrepancies with academic achievement). (7) The Flynn effect is irrelevant to showing that the racial IQ gap is environmental, but it was historically valuable in clarifying the debate.

Some elaboration on the fifth point above: as the values imply, the black gains on whites since 1972, taken subtest by subtest, have a slight negative correlation with the *g*-loadings of those subtests. This does not mean that you can dismiss those score gains. In the case of each and every subtest, blacks gained on whites on tasks with high cognitive complexity. Imagine we ranked the tasks of basketball from easy to difficult: making layups, foul shots, jump shots from within the circle, jump shots outside the circle, and so on. If a team gains on another in terms of all of these skills, it has closed the shooting gap between them, despite the fact that it may close gaps less the more difficult the skill. When a worse performing group begins to gain on a better, their gains on less complex tasks will always tend to be greater than their gains on the more complex.

## *g* and gender

Although I do not identify fluid *g* with intelligence, it measures a component of intelligence, namely, mental acuity (Flynn, 2009c, p. 53) or the ability to solve problems on the spot. Some years ago, Lynn (1998b, 1998c), Mackintosh (1998), and Flynn (1998b)

**Box 29**

Lynn believes men have better genes for intelligence because of different work roles. During most of our past, men were doing conceptually demanding things, such as planning how to hunt and trap often-dangerous animals. Women were just raising children, which, as Lynn points out, even animals can do. Why women's intelligence rose above the level of animals seems mysterious. Perhaps they were fortunate in the sense that men wanted them to be bright enough to talk to (men later regretted this). Some women object that raising human children is more conceptually demanding than raising kittens.

were locked in a controversy about whether males and females differed for mean IQ. We agreed on Raven's Progressive Matrices as the best measure of IQ because of its virtues, whether they are described as a good measure of intelligence, or fluid *g*, or on-the-spot problem solving.

After an exhaustive review of the literature, Lynn and Irwing (2004) discovered what they saw as a trend by age. Females matured earlier than males but males went on maturing and eventually surpassed females. Therefore, while females might score higher than males on Raven's in childhood, males catch them at about age 14 and by 15, show a significant advantage, which escalates to about 5 IQ points by maturity. Lynn (1999) has supplied an evolutionary scenario as to why men have been more highly selected for intelligence than women (see Box 29).

Lynn's case is plausible if you merge all Raven's studies. But that means lumping the current generation of women with past generations, large and excellent samples with samples of convenience, and nonelite samples with elite samples (such as those composed of university students). I want to focus on the question that I find of greatest interest: whether there is a male advantage that suggests genetic superiority.

With this in mind, I will isolate Raven's data from five advanced nations in which women have enjoyed the effects of modernity, and which allow us to compare females with males both below and above the age of 14. Other criteria: the data must be recent and of high quality (large standardization samples). It is possible that every one of these nations has a cognitive environment that favors females; but that contention would give the holders of a genetic hypothesis a formidable case to argue.

I will also show that beginning at age 15, samples drawn from schools must allow for the fact that more males than females are school dropouts, which eliminates a low-scoring group from the male sample. And paradoxically, I will argue that the fact that university females have a lower mean IQ than males is evidence for genetic parity rather than male superiority.

## University samples

*Gender parity hypothesis:* In the general population of 17- to 22-year-olds, males and females have the same mean IQ (100) and SD (15). But the university IQ threshold for males is 100 and for females 95. If so, male university students would have a mean IQ of 111.97 (the bottom half of the curve is gone) and an SD of 9.04 (the missing half reduces the full curve's SD). Females would have a mean of 108.99 (the bottom 37 percent of the curve gone) and an SD of 9.97 (less than half of their curve is gone). The male mean would be 2.98 points higher (111.97 – 108.99); and the female SD would be 110 percent of the male (9.97 divided by 9.04).

I am sorry to introduce the mathematics but it is really not controversial. Think of it this way. If the university population is drawn from the upper 50 percent of males and the upper 63 percent of females, then of course the male sample is more elite and will have a higher mean IQ. And if the university population contains a larger portion of the full female IQ curve than the male, then of course the female sample is more complete and will come closer to their population SD than the male sample will.

*Male superiority hypothesis:* In the general population, males have a mean IQ of 100, females a mean of 95, and both an SD of 15. The IQ threshold for males and females is the same at 100. If so, male university students would still have a mean of 111.97 and an SD of 9.04. Females would have a mean of 110.30. The bottom 63 percent of the curve gone would raise the mean of the remainder by 1.02 SDs; and 1.02 × 15 = 15.30, which plus 95 = 110.30. Females would have an SD of 8.18 (with the bottom 63 percent gone). Therefore, the male mean would be 1.67 points higher (111.97–110.30); and the female SD would be just over 90 percent of the male SD (8.18 divided by 9.04).

It is interesting to note that the male superiority hypothesis predicts a male IQ advantage (among university students) smaller than that predicted by the gender parity hypothesis. If the mathematics is alien to you, take my word for it (actually take the word of the greatest mathematician that ever lived: Gauss). Everyone can see the effect of the male superiority hypothesis on SDs: the SD of university females would have to be lower than that of males (the upper half of males can get into university, but only the upper 37 percent of females). The equality hypothesis clearly predicts the opposite: a higher SD for university women. So keep your eye on the SDs.

## What does the data say?

I reviewed the university data collected by Irwing and Lynn (2005). My thesis of gender parity applies to the current generation in nations or groups where women enjoy modernity. Therefore, I set aside university data from 1964 to 1986 (in favor of that from 1998 to 2004), data from developing nations, and one set that did not specify the nature of the Raven's test. The data remaining cover 6,230 subjects from four nations.

Box 30 shows that the results confirm the gender parity hypothesis: males have an IQ advantage of 2.73 points (predicted 2.98); the female SD is 106 percent of the male (predicted 110). I suspect that the latter shortfall is because females do not quite have SD parity in the general population. Mathematics and science have a robust correlation with Raven's. Ceci and Williams (2010) found that while there was no difference between the genders at the mean on these tests, the male SD was larger. Between 2006 and 2010, there were 6.58 7th-grade males who got a perfect score on SAT-Mathematics for every female. Between 1990 and 2010, there were eight 7th-grade males who got a perfect score on the ACT-Science test, but only one female. Nai, Putallaz, and Makel (2010) studied the top 0.01 percent on a variety of standardized mathematics tests. From 1990–2010, there were two to four males for every female.

A perfect fit for the university data is achieved if you posit the following values for the general population: the genders equal for mean IQ at 100; the female SD at 14.62, slightly lower than male at 15; a female IQ threshold for university at 96, that is, 4 points lower than the male at 100 (see the discussion in Appendix IV).

In any event, the results are far from those predicted by the male advantage hypothesis, namely, a 1.67-point male advantage and a female SD at only 90 percent of male. The fact that the within-sample female SD is so much larger than the male is devastating. How could the female SD soar above the male SD among university students except as a result of a lower IQ threshold, one that allowed a larger proportion of females into university?

The alternative would be to assume that the general population SD for females was huge. If they have a mean IQ of 95 and only the top 37 percent qualify for university, the university sample SD would be only 0.5453 of the population SD. Yet

**Box 30 (see Table AIV1 in Appendix IV)**

There are nine recent university samples with adequate data. In each case, I give the nation, the date, the male advantage in IQ points, and the percentage you get when you divide the female SD by the male SD. Where the female SD is larger, it equals more than 100% of the male SD; where smaller, it equals less than 100%.

| | |
|---|---|
| Canada (1998) | 2.45 IQ points – 105% |
| Canada (2000) | 4.34 IQ points – 104% |
| South Africa (2000) | 2.19 IQ points – 82% |
| Spain (2002) | 2.81 IQ points – 110% |
| Spain (2004) | 2.47 IQ points – 102% |
| Spain (2004) | 2.72 IQ points – 109% |
| USA (1998) | 4.44 IQ points – 119% |
| USA (1998) | 2.13 IQ points – 97% |
| USA (2004) | 2.93 IQ points – 110% |
| Average: | 2.94 IQ points – 104% |
| **Weighted Average:** | **2.73 IQ points – 106%** |

it is 1.06 times the male SD. The male SD is the equivalent of 9 IQ points; so the female within-sample SD would be 9.54 points (1.06 x 9); and that divided by 0.5453 = 17.5 points as the female SD in the general population. In fact, the dilemma is far worse than this. If you assume a common IQ threshold for male and female university students, it is impossible to explain both the male IQ advantage and the larger SD for females we find in the university data. See the discussion in Appendix IV.

## Students at a magnet school

Thus far, I have made no case to suggest why females should be able to get into university with lower IQs than males. Before looking at the genders qualifying for university, I will look at those who qualified for a special school. Duckworth and Seligman (2006) studied 198 students (age 13.4 years) at a magnet school. They had qualified (three years earlier) on the basis of grades and standardized tests. On the Otis–Lennon, girls had a mean IQ of 106.94, which implies that the bottom 27.7 percent were missing; and a threshold of 91.1. The boys had 111.21, which implies that the bottom 46.8 percent were missing; and a threshold of 98.8. So for admission to this school, the female threshold was 7.7 IQ points lower.

After entry into the school, girls had a Grade Point Average (GPA) 0.6 male SDs higher than boys. However, the within-school SD is attenuated and should be corrected: 0.6 times 0.62 equals 0.372 population SDs or the equivalent of 5.6 IQ points. In other words, girls could spot boys 4.27 IQ points (111.21 – 106.94) and outperform them academically by 5.6 points. Using delay of gratification measures and estimates of self-control, Duckworth and Seligman concluded that the girls had more self-discipline.

On a standardized academic achievement test, girls scored 1.3 points above boys. Because universities emphasize SAT (Scholastic Aptitude Test) scores for admission, we would expect a lower female IQ threshold for university students amounting to at least 5 points (1.3 + 4.27 = 5.57).

## Students in general

Between 1990 and 2000, female high-school graduates in America had a GPA well above boys (Coates & Draves, 2006). The only values given for a GPA SD show that the female mean would be 0.342 to 0.402 SDs above the male. Gurian (2001) estimates that boys get 70 percent of the Ds and Fs and girls get 60 percent of the As. About 80 percent of high-school dropouts are boys. Coates and Draves find a similar pattern in the UK, Ireland, Scandinavia, Australia, New Zealand, and Canada. No advanced nation has as yet been found to be an exception.

**Box 31 (see Table AIV2 in Appendix IV)**

For each nation or group of nations, I give: the female reading advantage translated into an IQ-points metric (SD = 15); how much lower the female IQ threshold for university entrance would be, if university students were selected purely on the basis of reading; and the female IQ deficit (compared to males) that would result among university students (assuming gender parity in the general population).

| | |
|---|---|
| Western/Central Europe | 5.78 points (reading advantage); 2.89 (lower threshold); 1.97 (lower IQ) |
| USA | 6.60 points (reading advantage); 3.30 (lower threshold); 2.24 (lower IQ) |
| Argentina | 6.31 points (reading advantage); 3.15 (lower threshold); 2.14 (lower IQ) |
| Australia | 5.94 points (reading advantage); 2.97 (lower threshold); 2.02 (lower IQ) |
| Estonia | 8.30 points (reading advantage); 4.15 (lower threshold); 2.82 (lower IQ) |
| Israel | 4.99 points (reading advantage); 2.50 (lower threshold); 1.70 (lower IQ) |
| New Zealand | 5.27 points (reading advantage); 2.63 (lower threshold); 1.79 (lower IQ) |

The Organisation for Economic Co-operation and Development (OECD) published the results for 15-year-olds on a test of reading proficiency (PISA, 2006). In 57 nations, high-school girls outperformed boys. Box 31 gives results for nations and groups of nations that are of particular interest. It makes little difference whether we take results for the 15 nations of Western and Central Europe (including Iceland and Scandinavia), or the USA, or the median from five nations that will be closely analyzed soon. All values suggest that the female IQ threshold for university entrance is about 3 points below the male threshold, and that the mean IQ of female university students is about 2 points below males.

US data were not available from the OECD. However, the Nation's Report Card shows that the median for girls' reading proficiency was at the 67th percentile of the boys' curve (USDE, 2003). This means that the US gender gap is a bit high but comparable to nations such as Austria, Belgium, Germany, Italy, Norway, and Sweden. It should be noted that males do marginally better than females for mathematics (PISA, 2006, Table 6.2c). I assume that reading and good grades bolster confidence to go to university; and that lacking mathematics proficiency discourages few students. Rather they choose a nonscience major. The Nation's Report Card also shows that girls open up an even greater gap for written composition: their median was at the 75th percentile of the boy's curve.

I will state what I think is a judicious conclusion: until the possibility of different gender IQ thresholds is investigated, university samples are suspect. It can easily be done. Get a good sample of the entering class, and just observe whether men show a tendency to disappear at an IQ level of, say, 4 points above where women begin to disappear.

## Argentina

The Universidad Nacional of La Plata standardized Raven's between 1996 and 2000 on 1,695 students. They ranged from 13 to 30 years of age, and the sample was designed to simulate a random sample of the city's in-school population (Rossi-Casé, 2000). The samples appear to have achieved their objective of simulating randomness. The nearest census (1991) shows that among those aged from 15 to 24 years the in-school population was 50.81 percent female (Karmona, 2003). The sample is 50.56 percent female (573 males and 585 females), an almost perfect match (see Appendix IV).

**Box 32 (see Tables AIV3 and AIV4 in Appendix IV)**

For every age group, the male mean IQ has been set at 100. The first means given for females have not been adjusted for the fact that more low-scoring boys than girls are missing from the in-school sample. The second means have been adjusted where appropriate – see the discussion in the text.

| Ages | IQ | IQ adjusted |
|---|---|---|
| 13–14 | 100.12 | 100.12 |
| 15–19 | 100.17 | 100.79 |
| 20–24 | 99.95 | 100.39 |
| 25–29 | 100.13 | – |
| 30 | 100.31 | – |

Box 32 falsifies Lynn's hypothesis about gender maturity: boys do not pass girls at the age of 15 and begin to show an advantage that increases to 5 points at full maturity. Rather, at all ages from 13 to 30, females at least match males. This is true even when their mean IQ is not adjusted to allow for the fact that beginning at age 15, male in-school samples become more and more elite. The adjusted values reinforce the point. Girls actually better boys by about half of an IQ point beginning at 15.

Almost everyone is in school until 14. After that, an increasing number of low-scoring boys are no longer at school, easily more than absent girls. Since I will be adjusting school samples to compensate for the surplus of missing boys throughout, some detail is in order to illustrate the procedure. First, at all ages, we need a correlation between dropping out of school and IQ. Herrnstein and Murray (1994, pp. 145–146) give data that yield 0.60 as the correlation between IQ and staying in high school to get a diploma. Having no value for Argentina, I used 0.50 as a conservative estimate. Second, we need a Raven's SD for the Argentine population that has not been attenuated by missing people at the bottom of the curve. Because almost all Argentine children are still in school at ages 13–14, I selected the largest SD for those ages (the male SD of 6.26) as an estimate of unattenuated SD.

Returning to Box 32, let us now go by age. There is no adjustment for ages 13–14 because virtually everyone is still in school. The procedure for ages 15–19 is straightforward. To get the unadjusted female IQ: (1) take the female raw score advantage and divide it by the Raven's population SD (6.26 points); (2) multiplying that by 15 (and adding 100) gives the proper value. In this case, girls were 0.0112 SDs above boys, and that times 15 put them 0.17 IQ points above boys, for a mean IQ of 100.17.

Census data allow us to adjust for the male bias in the sample. For ages 15–19, 76.26 percent of all females were in secondary or tertiary institutions or had a secondary or tertiary qualification; but only 70.63 percent of all males matched them (INDEC, 2002; Karmona, 2003). Here we again use the mathematics of a normal curve. The bottom 29.37 percent of boys is missing, which would raise the mean of the remainder by 0.488 SDs. The bottom 23.74 percent of girls is missing, which would raise the mean by 0.405 SDs. The male bias is 0.083 SDs (0.488–0.405) and times 15 = 1.245 IQ points. However, that would only be true if the correlation between school absence and IQ were perfect. Since we have put the correlation at 0.5, that times 1.245 equals 0.62 IQ points as the real male bias. Therefore, we adjust the female mean IQ upward: 100.17 + 0.62 = 100.79 or the value given in Box 32.

The next age group from the census is ages 20–24. Here we are clearly dealing with those in universities and other tertiary institutions, and we know nothing about university IQ thresholds, so the adjustment at that age (female mean IQ of 99.95 adjusted to 100.39) must be taken with a grain of salt. The La Plata tertiary students are atypical in that they show no female deficit for IQ. There were peculiar local conditions.

High unemployment put secondary school graduates under great pressure to continue their education. The percentage of those in tertiary education is extraordinary, about 54 percent, midway between the secondary levels and the tertiary levels that prevail elsewhere. Whatever we make of the ages 20–24 values, there is no case for adjusting IQs at ages 25–29 and age 30. By then, the reasons for people being absent from in-education samples would be legion.

In any event, the La Plata standardization sample yields data for seven age categories ranging from 13–14 to 30. And even unadjusted values show that the largest female deficit at any age is 0.19 IQ points (see note to Table AIV4 in Appendix IV).

## New Zealand, Australia, and South Africa

The New Zealand and Australian data are from standardization samples tested in 1984 and 1986 (Reid & Gilmore, 1988; de Lemos, 1988). The South African data are from Lynn (2002b), who reports the results Owen (1992) got when he tried to derive South African norms for Raven's by tests administered between 1985 and 1988. Thus, these school samples are all from the mid- to late 1980s but they are the latest available.

Box 33 shows that New Zealand females may actually be a point or two better on Raven's than males at ages 15–16 or the ages at which Lynn posits the advent of a male advantage. Efforts to locate in-school data for the genders in New Zealand (circa 1984) failed, so no adjustment for male bias could be made. In Australia (circa 1986), the percentage of girls in school was 1.04 times that of boys (Lamb, 2003). If New Zealand were similar, a value corrected for bias would be about 101.70. The Australians administered Raven's both timed and untimed (all other administrations herein were untimed). At ages 14.5 to 16.5, timed gave females 99.78 rising to 100.11 (adjusted) and untimed 99.41 rising to 99.74.

**Box 33 (see Table AIV5 in Appendix IV)**

For each nation or ethnic group, I give ages covered, the unadjusted female IQ, and the adjusted female IQ (where census data make this possible). In every case, the male mean IQ has been set at 100. In all cases, Raven's was administered untimed with the exception of the values from Australia marked with a (T).

| | | |
|---|---|---|
| New Zealand (15–16) | 101.37 | – |
| Australia (14.5–16.5) | 99.78 (T) | 100.11 (T) |
| Australia (14.5–16.5) | 99.41 | 99.74 |
| White South Africa (15) | 100.38 | 100.80 |
| Indian South Africa (15) | 96.38 | – |
| Colored South Africa (15–16) | 97.36 | – |
| Black South Africa (16–17) | 95.29 | – |

Since New Zealand and Australia were tested at much the same time, the Raven's raw scores should have been the same. In fact, the NZ mean was 49.63 and the Australian was 47.67, a difference equivalent to about 4.5 IQ points. The scores demonstrate the superiority of New Zealanders to Australians, something the former have long suspected.

Box 33 shows White South Africans, at age 15, with female IQ rising from 100.38 to 100.80 (adjusted). Mrs. van Niekek and Mr. Zenzo provided unpublished data from the South Africa census of 1985, which allowed me to derive in-school gender ratios and make the adjustment. Since age 15 is the lowest age given for the supposed female IQ decline, this data might seem of little interest. It gains significance from the values for nonwhite ethnic groups in South Africa. Going from whites to Indian and colored to blacks, female IQ declines from almost 101 to 95. Females lose ground going from a group that resembles the women of advanced nations to groups in which their status is subordinate.

## Estonia

In 2000, Raven's was standardized in 27 Estonian-speaking schools (Lynn *et al.*, 2002b) on students aged 12–18 (1,250 males and 1,441 females). The samples for ages 16 to 18 show radically reduced SDs thanks to the elite character of those tested at those ages. Using a proper value for SD (6.71) shows that males aged 16–18 outscored females by 1.05 IQ points. Initially, the data seemed too flawed to use, for example, they showed girls aged 13 with a lower Raven's raw score than those aged 12, something that could not be true of the general population. However, I perceived sources of sample bias that accounted for such anomalies and devised corrections.

First, for grade 10 and above, the standardization included only students in academic secondary schools, that is, gymnasia and "keskkools" (schools just as academic as gymnasia). This means that the sample omits Estonian youth who drop out of the academic stream after the age of 15, youths I will call the "the nonacademic group." A majority of this group are not dropouts in the literal sense: almost 50 to 60 percent of them are in vocational high schools. Nonetheless the nonacademic group includes many genuine dropouts and many more males than females.

Second, they tested grades 6, 8, 10, and 12 rather than all grades. This affected sample quality from age to age. It is normal for students to reach their 12th birthday while in grade 6. If most of your 12-year-olds come from grade 6, you have only normal students and omit the slow students who are in grades 5 and below. Therefore, you get mean IQ *inflation* for that age. If most of your 13-year-olds also come from grade 6, you have mainly students who are one year behind. Therefore, you get mean IQ

**Box 34 (see Table AIV6 in Appendix IV)**

For each age, I give the unadjusted female IQ, the number of IQ points the biases were worth (– means they favored females, + means they favored males), and the adjusted female IQ. At all ages, the male mean IQ has been set at 100. I also give the percentage of males and females missing because they have "dropped out" of the academic stream.

| | | | | | |
|---|---|---|---|---|---|
| 12 | 107.40 | −0.48 | 106.92 | 1% (F) | 1% (M) |
| 13 | 104.38 | −1.27 | 103.11 | 1% (F) | 1% (M) |
| 14 | 100.18 | +0.58 | 100.76 | 2% (F) | 3% (M) |
| 15 | 102.79 | +0.27 | 103.06 | 5% (F) | 8% (M) |
| 16 | 98.14 | +2.26 | 100.40 | 12% (F) | 20% (M) |
| 17 | 99.15 | +0.97 | 100.12 | 21% (F) | 38% (M) |
| 18 | 99.55 | +1.22 | 100.77 | 35% (F) | 55% (M) |

*deflation* for that age. We have now solved our mystery. Going from ages 12 to 13, you are going from normal students to substandard students. In the case of girls, this produced the absurd result of a drop in the Raven's raw score with age.

This distortion can affect one gender more than the other, as you go from age to age, because girls go through school faster than boys. In Estonia, sample biases affected gender comparisons primarily at ages 13, 16, 17, and 18. To estimate the biases, I constructed 14 normal curves: one for each sex at each age from 12 to 18. These told me what percentiles were missing (always some low percentiles and often some high ones).

The results are shown in Box 34. Appendix IV gives a detailed discussion of its derivation. However, I think that Box 34 on its own will convince you that the adjustments make sense, if you look at the "dropouts" from the academic stream beginning at age 16. Prior to that age, not many are missing, but when the option of pursuing vocational training kicks in, the number of missing males rises from 20 percent (at age 16) to 55 percent (at age 18). The number of missing females is far less, rising from 12 percent (at age 16) to 35 percent (at age 18). Clearly, the academic stream of males is more elite than the academic stream of females. Superimposed on this pro-male bias are the helter-skelter effects of testing only every other grade.

Now let us look at both the unadjusted and the adjusted female IQs. Even the unadjusted values do not offer Lynn's thesis much support. Females do fall behind males at age 16 by about 2 points. But rather than then showing a steady decline toward their ultimate 5-point deficit at age 20, they start to gain on males, and by 18, are only 0.45 points behind. Using the proper or adjusted scores, females never fall behind males and by 18, are 0.77 points ahead of them.

My adjustments do not explain the high female IQ at age 12, which just seems odd. But after that, they average at 101.615 and vary around that figure by only 1.5 points. During the crucial ages of 15–18, when they are supposed to be in decline, they average at 101.09, which is a good match for where they are at age 18. Recall that Argentina showed women aged 15–19 at 100.79, and New Zealand showed women aged 15–16 at 101.37. For these three nations at least, the data suggest that women may be about one point above men on Raven's at maturity. The appendix to this section may seem daunting, so I will offer an inducement: it shows that Raven's performance and speed of progress through school are correlated (in Estonia) at about 0.70.

## Israel

Flynn (1998b) reports military data from Israel for 17-year-olds who took a shortened version of Raven's from 1976 to 1984. Men outscored women by the equivalent of 1.4 IQ points. The data are clearly from a past generation, but the circumstances that generated them may well persist. The female deficit is entirely due to the fact that about 20 percent of the women were primarily from Orthodox homes, usually of Eastern European origin. They had a mean IQ of about 90.6, about 10 points below the mainstream of Israeli women. They were sheltered from modernity, that is, either married at age 17 and a half, or were wards of their fathers until passed on to their husbands.

To generalize, I believe that whether or not women achieve Raven's parity with men is a good test of whether a society has achieved full modernity. Israel still has a huge minority that has successfully resisted its influence. I am aware that the Orthodox would say that this is indeed their objective and that it preserves their very identity. Whatever the weight of their success in the spiritual scales, Israel pays a heavy price in the unrealized potential of so many of its women for secular pursuits.

## Men and women and genes

Five advanced nations show gender parity on Raven's beyond age 14. Lynn (1994, 1999: Lynn & Irwing, 2004) has been consistent in naming 15 as the age at which males forge ahead, but this does not debar a hypothesis that the age of onset is 16 or 17. This would render inconclusive all data except those from Argentina and Estonia. But even two nations put a heavy burden on any hypothesis that women have inferior genes for general intelligence. It is possible that these two nations foster a cognitive environment that favors women over men, but the supporting evidence would have to go far beyond Raven's scores.

Moreover, age 17 edges into the university age range, and university data cannot be taken seriously until we evidence similar or dissimilar IQ thresholds. Nothing herein denies that women born prior to the current generation performed worse on Raven's; or that women in developing nations still do so. The full effect of modernity on women may be crucial.

## Hole to the center of the earth

I look forward to a world in which all are treated as individuals (and I know that Arthur Jensen and Richard Lynn share that vision). Spending years of my life on this kind of research has been about as welcome as being drafted to help dig a gigantic hole to the center of the earth. But there is always a bonus when science teaches us something about the real world, and that includes the origin of group differences. The search for the causes of the black/white IQ gap, still incomplete, has educated me about the problems of black Americans and possible solutions (Flynn, 2008). As for women, they are doing a good job of advancing their own cause. In old age, it is the one area about which I am certain that there has been progress in my own lifetime.

# 7 The sociological imagination

Some thirty-five years ago, I began my periodic visits to the field of psychology. Over time, I became uneasy about something that seemed both odd and crippling: the isolation of the study of intelligence from an awareness of the social context within which all human behavior occurs. Many psychologists are happy to infer the social consequences of what they learn about intelligence. But all the causal arrows tend to run one way: they do not infuse their study of intelligence with social awareness.

Over 50 years ago, C. Wright Mills (1959) published *The Sociological Imagination*. The sociological imagination is the ability to see people socially and take into account how they interact and influence each other. I will emphasize a facet of the sociological imagination: always asking what social behavior lies behind measurements and models. To illustrate what happens when social awareness recedes into the background, I will offer 14 examples.

## (1) The mystique of the brain

Students of intelligence look forward to the day when all cognitive behavior can be explained in terms of brain physiology. But if they become obsessed by that task, they forget that understanding brains is only part of understanding human intelligence. Jensen (2011) is worth quoting at some length.

"The term Flynn effect, however, will go down in history as a blind alley in psychometrics, viz., trying to answer a basic, nontrivial factual question using wholly inappropriate data." Preceding remarks make it clear that the factual question is whether there have been real cognitive gains over time, and that the reason the data are inappropriate is that higher IQ scores over time, in themselves, cannot distinguish real gains from test sophistication, particularly growing familiarity with mental tests.

> Suppose a study were performed on the secular trend in the mean height (measured in either centimeters or inches) of 10-year-old school children born and reared in a given locality over the past century. The result per se is not controversial and provides a valid basis for research on its causes ... Why? Because "height" can be defined objectively by describing the physical operations used to measure it. The problem with IQ tests and virtually all other scales of mental ability in popular use is that the scores they yield are only ordinal (i.e., rank-order) scales; they lack properties of true ratio scales, which are essential to the interpretation of the obtained measures.

This means that IQ is measured only on a comparative scale. Someone gets more items right or wrong than the average person (who has an IQ of 100 by definition). We then give them a percentile rank for their age (if they are at the 84th percentile, they get an IQ of 115). But we can measure height on an absolute scale. Someone is six feet tall even if they are the only person alive. If people are six inches taller today than formerly, the gain is real. If people get more questions right today, even on the same IQ test, we can always ask why, and suspect that the reasons have nothing to do with cognitive gains.

Jensen's solution to the problem is Reaction Times (RTs): how long it takes someone to release a button when they see a light go on. This is because RTs can be measured on an absolute scale: either people are quicker today than some years ago or they are not. And he proposes a theory that links RTs to a physiological definition of intelligence: "Intelligence is the periodicity of neural oscillation in the action potentials of the brain and central nervous system."

In fact, RTs as a measure of neural speed and efficiency raise the same problems as IQ gains over time. They may be contaminated by factors irrelevant to intelligence. Flynn (1991b) argues that RTs are influenced by cross-cultural differences in temperament and strategy that have nothing to do with neural speed. But I want to set that question aside because my main point is that Jensen's reasoning is flawed even if we had a physiological measure of intelligence that was both reliable and used an absolute scale (say from MRI scans of the brain).

The flaws can be described as follows: (1) a mistaken definition of intelligence; (2) ignoring that all human behavior requires at least three levels of explanation; (3) ignoring the significance of comparative measurements; and (4) ignoring the fact that social science methodology can eliminate the possibility of confounding variables without reference to brain physiology.

Jensen defines intelligence in terms of events in the brain and nervous system. This is no more sensible than defining extroversion in terms of physiological events. There may be a physiological description that explains who is extroverted. But the only reason we are aware of that is because it correlates with extroversion defined as being outgoing in your interaction with other people. To say that brain events exhaust what we mean by the word "extroversion" would render such correlations irrelevant. We could only say that the brain events in question correlate with themselves, which would be meaningless because they are identical. Jensen does not stick to his definition. To justify certain brain states as the physiological basis of intelligence, he refers to nonphysiological behavior that he considers intelligent behavior, and therefore, relevant; for example, that a certain brain physiology correlates with who learns better and faster.

The flawed definition would be a merely verbal mistake the reader could set aside, if it did not lead to the next mistake. But as so often, reductionism leads to mistaken beliefs about significance and explanation. No matter how successful physiology is, no human behavior can be explained purely in physiological terms. A basketball player with one second to go takes a three-point shot beyond the circle and makes a basket. Assume a perfect knowledge of physiology: we can predict all of the movements of his body and of the ball as it goes through the air. But to understand the behavior, sociology must tell us that there is a game called basketball without which no one would be doing something so trivial as throwing balls through hoops; and individual differences must tell us that he is the best shot on the team and therefore was designated to make the crucial (potentially winning) shot. No doubt physiology can tell us the effects of playing basketball on the body and what physical traits make him the best shot. Good – but it could never give a Martian a real understanding of the behavior.

Note that nonphysiological information is often the only conceivable way of predicting human behavior. Even if it were possible for brain data on 100 million people to predict how each person intends to vote, a public opinion poll will be the most parsimonious device. And when we get to the sociological significance of the fact we use elections rather than guns to select rulers, what will brain data have to say about that? It may isolate the physiology of the authoritarian personality, but it will not predict the penalty people will pay for a Stalin.

Jensen makes dismissive comments about IQ tests and cognitive trends over time as evidence that could inform us about group differences. IQ tests may offer only a relative (comparative) measure of intelligence but much of what people want to know about intelligence is comparative. Will blacks someday have the cognitive skills they need to compete on equal terms with whites? If blacks do catch whites for IQ, and IQ keeps its external validity for academic achievement, is Jensen saying that this lacks significance until grounded in brain physiology? That would be heroic reductionism. Parents want comparative information: is my child bright enough (compared to other children) so that he or she can outcompete them to get into medical school?

An eye chart gives only a comparative measure. If you have 20/20 vision, you see at 20 feet what most people see at 20 feet. Before we had much knowledge of the physiology of the eye, people could tell that their vision was better with spectacles than without them. We have no absolute measure of the war-making behavior of the Allies and Axis powers during World War II, and certainly cannot reduce their behavior to the physiological level, but we know who won. I cannot give an absolute measure of the ability to classify or use logic on the hypothetical, but I can say we are much better at both today than our ancestors were in 1900.

The possibility of confounding variables afflicts all levels of explanation, and science can often deal with them level by level. Do larger brains signal that intelligence has increased or that people have just got bigger? The first step is to calculate a brain-size-to-body-mass ratio and see if that correlates with IQ. Is it possible that more exposure to tests causes IQ gains over time? Find out if IQ gains go on at the same rate even after (for political reasons) testing is less frequent. Is it possible that one of my children scores higher on IQ tests than the other because he is more hyperactive than she is? Give them tests that are not affected by that factor.

In sum, there is no logic to reducing intelligence to talking about brain states, or the causes of intelligence to explanations in terms of brain states. Brain physiology has a fascination that tempts us to forget all we know about human behavior on the personal and social level. We need a BIDS theory of intelligence that integrates what we know about the brain, about individual differences, and about society (see Box 35).

**Box 35**

The fact that some sciences are more advanced than others sets up a pecking order that leads to bad science overall. The physiologist looks down on the psychologist because of his "inferior" methodology and both look down upon the sociologist. However, just because a discipline is not as advanced as we would like does not mean it can be ignored. Better a contribution from sociology that is a mix of science and mere historical generalization than no contribution at all.

The sad thing is when a discipline tries to upgrade its scientific credentials by annexing concepts from more exact disciplines. When I was a student, I was assigned a book (I cannot locate it now) that applied Einstein's theory of relativity to politics. Over some 400 pages, it said that everything was relative. Even the great Quincy Wright (1955) tried to render the study of international relation more rigorous by using matrices. We were advised to conceive of nations as if they were maggots crawling through a 16-dimensional semi-opaque cheese.

## (2) The mystique of *g*

For a third time: *g* is of interest because when we rank tests (say the ten Wechsler subtests) by their *g*-loadings, we find that we are also ranking them for cognitive complexity. The link with cognitive complexity is eternal because it lends significance to the construct on the level on which intelligent behavior takes place: the level of conscious solution of problems. No evidence that *g* has an underlying stratum in the brain can break the link, any more than finding that a measure of spatial mapping has a substratum in the hippocampus can break the link with how well we map in everyday life. A measure of mapping ability is significant only if the taxi drivers who do best on it are best at finding their way about London.

Once the link is clear, we can focus on what affects our ability to deal with cognitively complex tasks in everyday life. Once we think in those terms, we are immediately led to construct a social scenario. And when we do that, we see that *either* environmental deprivation *or* genetic deficiency can cause one person (or group) to fall further behind another person (or group) as we climb the complexity ladder (even in basketball). It was this, constructing a social scenario about people actually performing tasks of increasing complexity, that made us immune to the notion that a "wider performance gap with *g*-loading pattern" between two groups eliminates environmental hypotheses. And it was this that kept us from being hypnotized by the fact that *g* is heritable or inversely associated with inbreeding and so forth.

## (3) The mystique of measurement

Once you realize that *g* is interesting only because it measures cognitive complexity, you also realize that the fact that IQ gains are not positively correlated with *g* means no more than this: our minds have not altered over time purely in terms of more complex cognition becoming easier for us.

Why should they? Acquiring vocabulary is a cognitively complex task. But if society does not make greater demands on the vocabulary schoolchildren use with one another in everyday life, they will make only minor gains on a vocabulary subtest. Classification may be less cognitively complex than amassing a large vocabulary. But if society imposes tasks that require classifying things as a prerequisite to understanding, rather than always differentiating things to exploit their different uses, people will show large gains on the similarities subtest. The relative cognitive complexity of the tasks (or their relative *g*-loadings) is beside the point. If you do not care about anything but finding an absolute measure of our ability to deal with cognitive complexity, an absolute measure of intelligence if you will, you will not be interested. Since you cannot correlate IQ gains with *g*, you dismiss them as "hollow" (Jensen, 1998). But that is only because you have been blinded to social significance by psychometric obsessions.

I will make a final attempt to try to convince *g*-men to alter their thinking. The behavior of an individual is unified by a mind. Therefore, when you compare the performance of two individuals on IQ tests, you are comparing two minds. If one person has a better mind than another, they are likely to do better on all or most of a wide range of cognitive tasks. That creates the "positive manifold," which is the origin of *g*. When you compare group performances on a wide range of cognitive tasks, you are comparing two collections of minds. There can be on average a *g* difference between the two, if their performance varies systematically with the complexity of tasks. There can even be a "better brain" difference if one generation profits from hybrid vigor or better nutrition.

However, and this is the key, setting those possibilities aside, there are still interesting things to investigate. Generations do not each have a group mind to unify things. If there has been a significant shift in the cognitive demands society makes, you may not be comparing a worse mind with a better one, but rather people whose minds were adapted to one cognitive environment with those whose minds are adapted to another cognitive environment.

You may well believe the new environment represents a higher stage of civilization. Perhaps you are correct (I am no cultural relativist). But whether or not this is true will be decided by cultural criteria, and not by the criterion of whether there is a *g* difference between the two populations. The new demands may be stronger for skills that are moderately complex (classification), weaker for those highly complex (vocabulary). In one sentence: the evolution of cognitive skills between generations is interesting (for most of us) despite the possibility that the sacred *g* lacks relevance. The presence or absence of a unifying mind delineates psychology from sociology. The boundary should not become a chasm excavated by different paradigms.

## (4) The tale of the twins

The fact that kinship studies produced high heritability estimates crippled understanding of the impact of environment on IQ and of how environment could produce large IQ differences between groups. See Jensen (1973, 1980, 1998) and Herrnstein and Murray (1994, pp. 298–299).

That is because we did not look behind the fact that identical twins, even when raised apart, attain adult IQs far more alike than randomly selected individuals. We did not ask what sort of social dynamics might produce this result. By default, we assumed that these twins had no more in common in terms of environment than randomly selected individuals. And finally, we assumed that what heritability studies told us about the role of environment in the context of individual differences set limits on the dynamic role of environment as society evolves over time.

It all seemed so plausible. If genes dominated IQ variance between individuals, environment must be feeble. And if much the same environmental factors both separate groups and separate individuals within groups, how could the former be potent if the latter were feeble? If an environmental factor were potent between groups, perhaps SES, surely it would be potent between individuals as well. But that conflicted with the evidence: the twins showed that *no* environmental factor was potent between individuals.

The only way out of this bind seemed to be the concept of a ridiculous factor X. There would have to be an environmental factor that varied between groups but that was utterly uniform within groups. It would have to be a sort of blindfold that afflicted every black equally and was totally absent among whites. Then it could explain the IQ gap between black and white but would not register in twin studies. Whenever two black families raised black twins, there would never be a case in which one of them did not impose the handicap. Whenever two white families raised white twins, there would never be a case in which one of them did impose the handicap. How absurd!

The Dickens–Flynn model added a sociological dimension. Having described it in detail in the past (Flynn, 2009c), I will be brief here.

A pair of identical twins have the same genes and therefore, both are taller and quicker than average. Although raised apart, both will tend to play basketball often, make their grade-school team, make their high-school team, and get professional coaching. If their identical genes accessed identical basketball environments, they would have the same BAQ (basketball ability quotient) when they reach 18. And even though environmental factors are very powerful (imagine the effect on two short twins of getting no practice, no team play, no coaching), their potency would be missed in twin studies.

Heritability is estimated purely on the basis of the tendency of the twins to get the same IQ, ignoring the fact that their identical genes for intelligence have allowed them to benefit from environments for intelligence whose quality is highly similar. The potency of doing homework, getting good feedback, liking school, getting into an honors stream, getting the best teachers is entirely missed. Genetic differences small at birth begin beneficial/baneful feedback loops that vastly expand performance differences with age.

The Dickens–Flynn model calls these loops the *individual multiplier*. It is encouraging to note that Haworth *et al.* (2010) endorse the concept of an individual multiplier to explain (as does the model) the rise of heritability with age. They studied 11,000 pairs of twins and found that the genetic proportion of IQ variance rose from 0.41 at age 9 to 0.66 at age 17. To quote

(p. 1112): "We suggest that the answer lies with genotype–environment correlation: as children grow up, they increasingly select, modify and even create their own experiences in part based on their genetic propensities."

The Dickens–Flynn model also included the concept of a *social multiplier*. It dispelled the illusion that only an impossible factor X could explain how environment could cause large IQ differences between groups. TV is invented and hugely expands interest in basketball. There is an initial rise in average performance that becomes self-fueling. First, the level of passing and shooting rises, and every player is influenced to match it so as not to fall behind. Then someone steals an advantage by passing with either hand, which impels every player to do that. Then someone steals an advantage by shooting with either hand and everyone has to learn to do that. There is an enormous escalation in basketball performance in one generation, even though there has been no change in genes for height and quickness.

But these causal interactions are not, of course, like a factor X. They do not affect every person equally within either the old or new generation. Within both, genetic differences are active, dictating who will gain most from the new standard of play that prevails (the individual multipliers keep spinning). Some people are still taller than others, some less injury prone, some more naturally ambidextrous. It is the same with IQ. The growth of the scientific ethos, the complexity of the modern world, expanded formal education, will raise the mean IQ between generations even though they have no uniform effect within a generation.

If our minds had not been gridlocked in a way that exiled all we knew about society, we would never have been confused. Everyone knew that the expansion of tertiary education (an environmental factor that separates the generations) had produced huge between-generation difference in adult active vocabulary. But tertiary education does not have to be wholly absent in one generation and universal in the next to do this.

And it need not affect heritability estimates of how much genes affect vocabulary within a generation. It may well be that genes are equally influential (thanks to being matched to quality of environment) in determining who goes to university (and who gets a vocabulary bonus) within both the present and the last generation.

The factor X dilemma reigned for 30 years (1969 to 1999). The twin studies convinced a whole generation of psychologists that environmental hypotheses about large between-group IQ differences were suspect. Would it have troubled us for even five years, had not the psychology of individual differences and social psychology occupied separate residences in our minds?

## (5) The triumph of the elite

*The Bell Curve* provoked much debate about race, but almost nothing about a far more profound challenge to humane-egalitarian ideals. I refer to the meritocracy thesis.

The meritocracy thesis contends that when we seek social justice, our ideals self-destruct in practice. The three-step argument: (1) assume we make progress toward the equalization of environments – to the degree that occurs, all remaining talent differences between people will be a result of differences in genes for talent; (2) assume we make progress toward the abolition of privilege – to the degree that occurs, there will be a social mobility that brings all of the good genes to the top and allows all bad genes to sink to the bottom; (3) therefore, the upper classes will become a genetic elite whose children inherit their status because of superior merit, while the lower classes become a self-perpetuating genetic dump, too stupid to be of use in the modern world, an underclass that is underemployed, criminal, and prone to drugs and illegitimacy.

In fact, it is not humane-egalitarian ideals but the argument itself that self-destructs. Let us look at its psychological and sociological assumptions: (1) that obsession with money and status is a constant rather than a psychology that may evolve or alter; (2) that such a psychology is consistent with sacrifice of money and status to promote equality; (3) that people can be immiserated and yet provide their children with a beneficial environment. The fact that these improbable assumptions have gone unstated is the best example of a failure of the sociological imagination.

Many of us have been forced to participate in the annual school cross-country race. It did not rank us for genes for even the very limited talent of distance running because most students did not care or try. With the rise in affluence, do middle-class Americans care about the prestigious and high-paying professions as much as in the past? That is not self-evident. Already the shine has faded on the professions of doctor and lawyer, work after all not intrinsically interesting to many, and many of my best students see the corporate world as riddled with compromises they find repugnant. Research scientist retains its limited appeal to those with special traits, but the training is hard work, so that America at least has to make good a shortfall with foreigners.

Affluence means that you will not be banished from the middle classes if you follow your own star: everyone who is a real human being feels a tension between what the market will pay them to do and what they would ideally like to do to develop a talent or for enjoyment. In New York, there are legions that choose fringe success in the arts over becoming a cost accountant. If the best and the brightest go in a thousand different directions, money and prestige will not rank for genes for talent (even entrepreneurial talent) any more than the school race.

In *The Mind–Body Problem*, Rebecca Goldstein (1983) says that each person has a mattering map. To my father what mattered was enough money to maintain his family in decency but beyond that, real life was sociability and arguing politics at the local pub. Those I grew up with were much the same. Their sense of a day well spent ranged from playing decent softball with their workmates, to some carpentry, to a sing-along at a pub, to cards at the firehouse. To the more idealistic what matters is the old Platonic ideal of doing work that gives you a sense of self-worth and also contributes to a better society. I do not deny that some will always remain obsessed with shaking the last dollar out of the money tree, but they represent our failure to create the psychological prerequisites of a humane and diverse society, not some deep-seated flaw at the heart of humane ideals.

What are the prerequisites for the abolition of privilege and the equalization of environments? Certainly redistribution of resources through progressive taxation and the welfare state, so that all have a decent chance in life. Even if you define this in terms of a negative income tax, it takes money out of the pockets of the wealthy and gives it to the less fortunate. The meritocracy thesis posits a people obsessed with personal wealth and advantaging one's own children, yet happy to make sacrifices to abolish privilege and equalize opportunity. Is that a coherent psychology? Finally, how can an underclass whose children are doomed from birth be allowed to develop? The dynamics of the meritocracy thesis yields not a meritocracy but a social order with unequal environments and privilege rampant. To sustain an egalitarian society in existence, huge resources must be allocated not according to "merit" (market success) but according to need.

A class-stratified meritocracy requires something improbable: a population both money drunk and justice drunk. The thesis sucks us into a narrow world delineated by what partitions trait variance: the smaller environmental differences, the greater the role of genes; the greater the role of genes, the more genetic differences dictate behavior. This kind of isolation from social analysis begets illusion: a model floating above our heads without a plausible social scenario to keep it aloft.

Perhaps the best demonstration of my point is the fact that Herrnstein and Murray could even state the meritocracy thesis without a barrage of criticism from social scientists on purely evidential grounds. The thesis is supposed to be a serious hypothesis about the effects of egalitarian policies. Therefore, when I read it, I expected it to be supplemented by a list of all advanced nations ranked in terms of how far they had carried the equalization of environments; and those same nations ranked by the size of their demoralized underclass. As everyone knows, these two hierarchies would correlate not positively but negatively: the Scandinavian nations (Sweden, Norway, Finland) would stand near the top in terms of their welfare states, but near the bottom in terms of the percentage of their demoralized citizens.

No doubt Herrnstein and Murray would have arguments as to why the correlation is negative "thus far." That would be the beginning of a serious debate; for example, we might debate whether the skills requirements of an advanced society can render useless a sizable percentage of their population, or whether people have an intrinsic utility that will be expressed in the expansion of service work. The further such a debate proceeds the more the meritocracy thesis will be ignored in favor of serious social analysis.

## (6) The history of nutrition in Britain

It has been 30 years since Lynn (1982, 1990) began to argue that improved nutrition among the lower classes has been a potent force behind IQ gains over the last two generations. And yet, no one has done the obvious. No one has consulted dieticians to determine the following: whether nutrition has improved since 1950 (some think that junk food and the obesity epidemic signal a worse diet); if so, where has it improved and among what sectors of the population; and whether the dietary history of various nations matches IQ trends nation by nation, with particular attention to class and ethnicity.

The reader knows why I am not ready to devote the time to exhaust this agenda. But certainly, those who take the nutritional hypothesis seriously should do so. It is not clear whether the inhibition is the amount of work involved, or the failure to appreciate that they need a social reality that legitimizes their assumptions.

## (7) The history of urbanization in Turkey

I want to return to a study whose authors did show an awareness of sociology. When studying cognitive change in developing nations, we must not make mechanical use of that old workhorse socioeconomic status (SES). Class comparisons (how much IQ has risen among the middle class) assume a modicum of stability over time for the class in question. When a developing nation undergoes rapid industrialization and urbanization, "class" comparisons may be virtually meaningless.

Recall the analysis of IQ gains on the Draw-a-Person Test in Turkey (Kagitcibasi, & Biricik, 2011). It reported results from the city of Bursa and surrounding villages.

During the 33 years in question, Bursa grew from a town of 100,000 to a large city of 2.55 million. Its middle class grew from something like 30,000 to 600,000. Clearly the children of the original middle class were about one-twentieth of the new middle class. The concepts central here are less class and more geography. A small city became a huge city and essentially *created* the middle class as a significant component of the region's population. People from largely rural backgrounds migrated to the city and their children attained white-collar or professional or small-business jobs.

The authors rightly presented an analysis in terms of the effects of urbanization and modernity. Part of the story is the saga of those who remained in remote villages. Over time conditions were revolutionized. The villages now have better schools, better roads connecting them to the city, and perhaps most important, their isolation has been mitigated by exposure to the mass media. The rest of the story is the dynamics of the growth of the city of Bursa: how did it manage to absorb this huge number of rural migrants and give so many of them economic opportunity? The development of the automotive industry was important but there had to be more to it than this.

Even if there are higher incomes among the new middle class, I suspect that the main causes of the IQ gains are the other effects of modernity. Not only in the remote villages but also in Bursa itself modern schools manufactured scientific spectacles, the media promoted a visual culture, the modern world demanded faster information processing, and the teaching of the basics improved. Since Turkey is a developing nation, better health and nutrition may have boosted IQ. But the point is that comparing the IQs of the old and new classes tells us nothing except that urbanization in Turkey has been a success story.

## (8) The history of teenage subculture

I have speculated that the evolution of teenage subculture in America explains the emergence of a huge gap between the active vocabularies of adults and their children. Whether this is true or not, the social trends at work are bound to be significant. The test scores are less important in themselves than because they pose a sociological puzzle.

## (9) Intelligence and intelligences

Gardner (1983) advanced the notion of seven intelligences: linguistic, logical-mathematical, musical, spatial, bodily-kinesthetic, self-oriented personal, and other-directed personal.

Whether it makes sense to call all of these by the same name should have been a strictly scientific question of interest mainly to researchers. Perhaps we have overlooked the fact that a Mozart integrates a wide variety of musical "ideas" into a composition rather like Einstein integrated a wide range of spatial and temporal concepts into the theory of relativity. If so, musical and logical-mathematical ability might have more in common than we had thought. Perhaps we have ignored the mental dimension of the behavior of a ballet dancer who gives a wonderful performance. If these commonalities exist, and have gone unrecognized, calling them all intelligences would be a rhetorically effective way of giving them notoriety.

But few treated the question in that way (Gardner is not of course to blame for all the excesses of his converts). The issue of whether the seven abilities should all be called "intelligences" became equivalent to the ethical question of whether children who had one rather than another (were good at sport but not at their studies) were equally worthy of regard. And by extension, whether someone who was not particularly good at any of them should be valued for whatever he or she could do.

My answer to the ethical questions would be yes; but I feel compelled to add that you do not change social reality by playing with words. The social realities of America are these. Being at the 90th percentile for the kind of "intelligences" that get professional credentials opens up a thousand doors; being at the 90th percentile for softball does not. Every parent knows this. They will not forget what they know when told that their children rank high (although not particularly high) on "bodily-kinesthetic intelligence" but not on anything else.

## (10) Intelligence is not *über alles*

Weyl (1966) called Chinese- and Japanese-Americans "the American natural aristocracy." By the 1980s, the achievements of young people whose parents had come from East Asia made a powerful impression on the public imagination. They were about 2% of the population, but 14% of those at Harvard, 16% at Stanford, 20% at MIT, 21% at Cal Tech, 25% at Berkeley (Flynn, 1991a). When journalists approached Arthur Jensen for an explanation, he said they did so well because they are smarter (Brand, 1987).

Anyone who dines at a Chinese restaurant and sees a child sleeping over his school books wake up, stretch, and pick up a book knows that something other than intelligence causes the academic achievements of Chinese-Americans. Flynn (1991a) analyzed the class that graduated from high school in 1966. During their senior year, the Coleman Report confirmed that they had no higher IQs than their white counterparts. However, they could concede whites 4.5 IQ points and match them on the SAT, and concede them almost 7 IQ points and match them for high-school grades. This meant that they could secure entry to the same universities as whites despite lower IQs. In the fall of 1966, Chinese entering Berkeley had an IQ threshold 7 points below whites.

Their lower IQ threshold partially explains why they were vastly overrepresented at universities. In addition, 78 percent of those who could qualify actually went, while among whites it was only 60 percent. In other words, it was not higher IQ scores but sociology of the family that explains the remarkable academic achievements of Chinese-Americans. Their parents create children atypical of the larger society; that is, children who accept cognitive challenge and have a passion for educational excellence. When Chinese tell other Chinese that their child has failed, the first question is, "a fail or a Chinese fail"? The latter usually means they did not top the class.

## (11) The intellectual inferiority of university women

As we have seen, just as Chinese-Americans can spot whites 7 IQ points and match them for qualifying for university, so women can spot men 4 or 5 points. Most parents are well aware that their children go to schools in which girls dominate the honor roll and get better grades than boys. Why was it not obvious that the lower mean IQ of university women might be due to a lower IQ threshold for university entrance, rather than representing IQ inferiority in the general population? Yet, Irwing and Lynn (2005) assumed the latter. The fact that the lower threshold for females was signaled by greater IQ variance among female university students was also taken as representative of the general population. University students were analyzed as if they were born at university rather than arriving as social products.

## (12) The "psychotic" attitude of black women toward marriage

Mills (1959) says that the sociological imagination connects personal troubles with social circumstances. The black women of America have been castigated for bearing children out of wedlock, as if their social circumstances were identical to those of white women.

For every 100 American non-Hispanic white women of marriageable age, there are 86 promising spouses, that is, men who are alive, not in jail, and worked at least half-time over the previous 12 months. For every 100 Hispanic white women, there are 96 promising spouses, as a result of a huge (and partially illegal) influx of males from South America. For every 100 black women, there are 57 promising spouses, which is to say that almost half of them must either go childless or have a child by a man unpromising as a permanent partner (Flynn, 2008).

Their dilemma is also the product of limited racial intermarriage. In 1900, when Irish-American women found half of Irish-American males dysfunctional, they could marry Swedes, Italians, and even Englishmen. The fact that they could marry out gave them a huge pool of promising partners. Black women are trapped. Indeed, they are net losers from what interracial marriage exists: five black men leave the pool of potential spouses to partner nonblack women, while only two black women find a long-term spouse outside their race (Flynn, 2008). Every generation of black American women face a marriage market worse than that of Russian women after World War II, which left 70 Russian men alive for every 100 women. The USSR accepted that there would be many solo-mother homes. Black American women are given lectures. Their president advises them "not to lie down with any fool," as if there were enough nonfools to go around.

Lynn (2002a) asserts that the fact that black American women have a more negative attitude toward marriage is a sign of psychosis. Their attitudes are not symptoms of mental illness but recognition of their social circumstances. We may see their plight as a collection of "personal problems," but that says more about us than about them.

## (13) The dull are violent

Deary, Weiss, and Batty (2011) have made sensible recommendations as to how medical practitioners should tailor prescriptions to the cognitive ability of their patients. One of their findings is that in Sweden, there is a correlation between low IQ and hospitalization for violence-inflicted injury, even when SES is taken into account. This correlation calls for analysis of what social circumstances might lie behind it.

I was reared in a gang-organized area where gangs were staffed by ethnicity: blacks versus an alliance of nonblack Catholics (Irish, Italian, Puerto Rican, Filipino). The culture was one of defense of honor and territory by fighting. Teenagers challenged other teenagers to fight: the path between IQ and injury was not a matter of being too unintelligent to have mediation or coping skills. If challenged, resort to such was proof of cowardice, and the sanctions were to be outcast and bullied. If you won, you might have the high status of the best street fighter in your group; if you lost honorably, you were a member of the group in good standing. Gangs challenged each other. Failure to fight and risk injury meant having no place to "play" and low self-esteem. Pub culture was a major leisure-time amusement and going to a pub was likely to lead to challenges. Football (gridiron) was a leisure sport that led to challenges.

In sum, fighting for honor and territory was not a behavioral manifestation of low IQ. Yet as a group we undoubtedly had a lower mean IQ than Washington DC as a whole. But our culture rather than low IQ was the active factor.

It might seem that allowing for lower SES would capture this etiology. Not entirely: Jewish boys in our neighborhood simply did not go out on the street after school and socialized through the Synagogue. They avoided risk because their self-esteem did not include honor as we defined it. We thought they were cowards but they did not care. I doubt Swedish data would pick up any of this. I suspect that US data would show an even stronger correlation than Sweden, even after SES is allowed for. But it would be wrong to conclude that the extra is a result of cognitive rather than ethnic or cultural factors.

It is one thing to help people close the gap between functional and dysfunctional intelligence. It is another thing to ask people to alter behavior that for them defines personal self-esteem and a full life. If a physician wants to preserve his or her patients from injury, an IQ score might do some good. If they suffer from accidents around the home, a pamphlet that spells out the dangers and how to avoid them is recommended.

But as far as avoiding interpersonal violence is concerned, it makes more sense to consult a social worker or social psychologist who knows something about their circumstances.

**Box 36**

The silliest piece of social science I have seen was not in psychology but in politics: a thesis on nonvoting in the Washington metropolitan area. The candidate was unaware that the Hatch Act banned the residents of the city proper, the District of Columbia, from voting in Congressional elections. As mainly federal government employees, they were thought subject to pressure or bias. They constituted one-fourth of those sampled. The supervisor's attempt to defend the merits of the thesis was fascinating.

## (14) The dull drive cars

Sometimes blindness to social reality is too egregious to be taken as characteristic of a discipline. I recall a paper in which the author concluded that what leisure activities Maryland 8th graders chose was indicative of their intelligence. Those who rode horses had high IQs and those who drove cars had low IQs. In Maryland at that time, no one rode horses that did not come from a family of elite SES. You had to be 16 to get a driver's license. Anyone who was still in the 8th grade at age 16 was at least two years older than the norm for that grade (see Box 36).

## There are people there

Some of the examples are important and some idiosyncratic. But a common thread runs through them all: failure of the sociological imagination. Behind correlations and IQ curves, behind heritability estimates and the stratification of genes by class, behind who goes to university and who achieves, behind who drives a car and who suffers from violence, behind who marries and who does not, there are real people living out their lives. I do not understand why many psychologists have not developed the habit of always constructing a social scenario to explain their results. They do not have to journey outside their field. They need not take sociology courses – their own discipline includes social psychology. I recommend that courses in social psychology give students a list of errors they will be prone to make if they do not take society seriously.

# 8 Progress and puzzles

First, let us celebrate progress. We now know that over the last century, America really did alter its priorities concerning what kind of mind schoolchildren should develop. We are less concerned that they have a large fund of socially valuable information than that they have a better understanding of complex relationships between concepts (Genovese, 2002). Has the fact that Americans have put on scientific spectacles during the twentieth century made thinking about moral and political issues more sophisticated? There is a prima facie case that it has enhanced the quality of moral debate but no evidence. The evidence about political debate hints at more sophisticated thinking (Rosenau & Fagan, 1997), but shows reluctance on the part of presidential candidates to transcend rhetoric when they address a mass audience (Gorton & Diels, 2010). Fortunately, Gorton and Diels intend to examine political debate in depth.

Recent data about IQ trends show that the twenty-first century may hold some surprises. The demise of IQ gains in Scandinavian countries may not be replicated in other developed nations, at least not until the century is well advanced. Why there is this difference is one of our new puzzles. Data on cognitive trends in developing nations are beginning to accumulate. If we can only integrate these trends with social developments, we may know which nations are likely to eliminate the IQ gap between the developed and developing world, and which will not. One thing is certain: developing nations are not frozen at their current level of problem solving.

Progress in charting the evolutionary history of human groups (e.g. whose ancestors were where during the Ice Ages) promises to falsify scenarios about racial differences based on climate. The challenge is to develop new, more detailed, more potent scenarios that explain group differences that may be genetic in origin: the apparent advantage of East Asians for spatial visualization, gender differences for this cognitive skill, to say nothing of the spatial deficit of Jewish Americans (Flynn, 1991a).

There is strong evidence that females match males on Raven's Progressive Matrices even at maturity, unless their societies have not undergone modernity (as in developing nations) or women have been shielded from the effects of modernity (like Orthodox women in Israel). The fact that university women tend to have lower mean IQs than university men appears to be a social phenomenon with roots in the fact that women are better adapted to formal education. However, there is a simple way to establish whether this is true: testing freshmen to see whether females have a lower IQ threshold for university entry than males.

Despite spurious appeals to traditional rules of evidence, more judges are beginning to understand the relevance of obsolete norms to the IQ scores of offenders in capital cases. Solid data now reveal grave discrepancies between the two tests recommended for capital cases: the Wechsler tests (particularly the WAIS-III) give much higher IQs in the retardate range than the Stanford–Binet (Silverman *et al.*, 2010).

This must be addressed immediately. In addition, we are now aware that a whole range of clinical measuring instruments, certainly memory tests, are also suspect because of obsolete norms (Baxendale, 2010; Rönnlunda & Nilsson, 2009). We must give high priority to determining which are deceptive and by how much. It is depressing that the literature, even in journals devoted to mental retardation, shows a lack of awareness of the information needed to interpret IQ scores: what test, when it was normed, when it was sat, what rate of obsolescence, whether it is really adequate at low-IQ levels (Liu *et al.*, 2012); and if relevant, what national differences may exist (Roivainen, 2009).

Analysis of WAIS trends with age reveals a differential pattern for the four kinds of cognitive skills the test measures. Here puzzles begin to overshadow progress. Cross-sectional analysis reveals a bright tax for both analytic and information processing skills: the brighter the person (at any age up to 65) the more sharp the downward curve in old age. Whether this is because of the physiology of the aging brain, or an environmental shift at retirement, or a combination of the two is unknown. The same analysis reveals a bright bonus for verbal skills, and that working memory is bright neutral. These trends must be confirmed by longitudinal studies of individuals as they age.

But I will be surprised if they do not reveal the same pattern. My simulation of a longitudinal study compares those who were 65 in 1995 (WAIS-III) with those who were 75 in 2006 (WAIS-IV). That is a pretty good match. They are of course not being compared to one another directly, but only to the 35-year-olds who were the contemporaries of each group. So even the simulation is a mix of longitudinal and cross-sectional data. In addition, the simulation compares some people who are alive at 65 with a group from which they, at 75, would be absent (because they were deceased). But that would be true of the comparisons for all IQ levels. How likely is it that the brightest people from the highest IQ level have tended to die more often that the brightest people at low IQ levels? It is certainly worth a ten-year longitudinal study to verify whether the bright tax is real or an artifact. Thus far no takers.

Herein I have tried to make amends for not doing a task I should have done years ago: compare trends on WISC subtests with trends on WAIS subtests. The two most interesting trends pertain to a convergence and a divergence.

Adult gains on WAIS arithmetic are only slightly larger than the modest gains of schoolchildren on the WISC. The spread of tertiary education to half the population has made little difference. This failure of tertiary education is even more shocking than the failure of primary and secondary education. To produce enhanced performance, the latter needed to upgrade their quality, which is always difficult. Tertiary education is an add-on that was largely nonexistent before 1950. It merely had to do more good than no tertiary education. Signs of improved performance among young children are deceptive. They fade away when the mechanics of arithmetic gives way to being able to think with numbers. We are missing something here. All we know is that teaching small children to solve Raven's-type problems is not the answer.

The spread of tertiary education and more cognitively complex work roles have done something. They have dramatically enhanced the everyday vocabularies of adult Americans since 1950. Work appears more potent than university by a ratio of about three to one. But here we confront the greatest puzzle of them all. Comparing WISC vocabulary trends to WAIS trends, adults show gains for active vocabulary that are almost 0.90 of a standard deviation larger than the modest gains of schoolchildren. And yet adults raise and socialize their children. My hypothesis that teenage subculture has become more potent in insulating young people from their "natural" speech community does little more than restate the problem. But it does suggest a focus for study. In passing, we should recall that something similar may be going on in Britain that affects IQ gains in general. The gains over time we see among schoolchildren on Raven's turn into small losses for 14- to 15-year-olds.

I believe that progress in the intelligence area is impeded by lack of the sociological imagination. Somehow, psychologists have developed the habit of ignoring social scenarios that explain their results, in favor of psychological models that are deceptive because they have no social dimension. In so far as they attempt to integrate the psychology of human intelligence with another layer of analysis, they choose brain physiology. The danger here is that rather than integrating the two, they become reductionists. They wish to not only reduce the psychology of intelligence to brain behavior (which is a worthy objective) but also liquidate the psychology of human intelligence (despite the fact that problem solving is done by human minds). This approach would impoverish the discipline further: we would ignore both sociology and psychology in favor of physiology.

I do not know whether psychology in general, as distinct from the study of human intelligence, lacks social sophistication. No doubt sociologists will be only too happy to inform me on this point.

There is a growing awareness that it is crippling to make *g* the measure of everything to do with cognitive abilities. First, its utility should not seduce us into forgetting what the social sophistication of Sternberg and Heckman and Seligman and Duckworth has taught us: that analytic intelligence does not exhaust the range of cognitive skills or personal traits that contribute to the achievements our society values.

Second, in understanding the history of cognitive trends over time, it plays a very tangential role. Never forget what stands behind the significance of *g*: that it is a measure of cognitive complexity. There is simply no reason why growing modernity should not enhance a number of relatively autonomous mental attributes, without there being some grand design such that the *degree* of cognitive complexity determines which attributes progress. If that were true, IQ gains would equal *g* gains; but why should the developing needs of society (concerning which problems it most wants solved) have such a strange design? As this implies, IQ gains can have socially significant effects without being *g* gains.

Third, it has no unique contribution to make in understanding racial differences in IQ. The method of correlated vectors, the fact that racial differences in IQ expand as subtest *g*-loadings rise, does not settle whether those differences are genetic or environmental in origin. Environmental deprivation also predicts that group differences will expand with the complexity of the task.

Having made explicit the limitations of *g*, I want to praise its virtues. After reading the manuscript of this book, a colleague asked me why *g* had any significance at all. Does it really add anything to the concept of Wechsler Full Scale IQ?

It is true that if you weight the various Wechsler subtests in terms of the size of their *g*-loadings, rather than treating them as equally significant, the GQ you get is not much different from Full Scale IQ. For example the 15-point IQ gap between black and white Americans (at age 21) becomes a GQ gap of about 16 points. However, this is true only because the pioneers who designed IQ tests were sleepwalking their way to subtests with high *g*-loadings. Setting aside items designed to measure things such as memory, they intuitively welcomed items that posed problems of ascending cognitive complexity (block design) or learning that could not occur without cognitive complexity (vocabulary).

To this it may be said why not just jettison *g* for the concept of cognitive complexity? Well, it is one thing to have a heuristic, an abstract concept that suggests a focus, and another thing to have a way of measuring it, so that tasks can be compared and ranked with some precision. We may feel that one day is warmer than the last, but a thermometer can do better than that. We may know intuitively that vocabulary (assuming equal opportunity) ranks minds for the cognitive complexity of the concepts they can absorb, but that it is more *g*-loaded than picture completion is something we cannot intuit. Yes, yes, I know that *g* differs if you derive it from a basket of mainly verbal tests, or from another basket, or from Raven's. But if the baskets all contain a really wide range of cognitive skills what emerges from one to the next is pretty similar.

The construct of *g* confirms that David Wechsler was on the right track, and that is something very good to know. It provides a theoretical foundation for the best instruments we have for measuring individual differences concerning the kind of analytic intelligence at a premium in the developed world. That is my world and the world to which almost all of the nations on this earth aspire. It even ranks individuals for analytic intelligence in societies in which it is much less valued. Sociologists should be glad they have the concept of SES (socioeconomic status) even though it does not have much relevance to the people of Tierra del Fuego. Psychologists should thank Jensen for pursuing his life-long mission, against great odds, to clarify the concept of *g*. In addition to intellectual eminence, he had the courage to face down opposition often political rather than scientific. If I have made a significant contribution to the literature, virtually every endeavor was in response to a problem set by Arthur Jensen.

Read John Stuart Mill. When you suppress an idea, you suppress every debate it may inspire for all time. Step forward, those who believe they have the omniscience to censor the content of the intellectual history of humankind.

# Appendix I: Tables and comments on IQ trends (see Chapter 3)

Box 6 in Chapter 3 gives estimates for gains over time on certain WISC and WAIS subtests and projects those gains into the future (up to 2012). It is derived from four tables.

(1) Table AI1 gives WISC gains on all subtests from the WISC (1947.5) to the WISC-IV (2001.75). Table AII3 in Appendix II adds detail on the calculations.

(2) Table AI2 uses past trends to project the gain from the WISC-IV to the "WISC-V" on the assumption that the latter will be normed in 2012. This entails pro-rating all subsequent trends over the interval of 24.5 years that separated the norming of the WISC and WISC-R. All calculations are explained at the bottom of the table. The final column gives what I think the actual Scaled Score gains (SD = 3) will bc from the WISC-IV to the WISC-V, just for fun. To get the modern age values in Box 6, average the four Modern world values numbered (1) to (4) respectively.

(3) Table AI3 gives WAIS gains on all subtests from the WAIS to the WAIS-IV. Table AII2 in Appendix II adds detail on both scores and calculations.

(4) Table AI4 uses past trends to project the gain from the WAIS-IV to the "WAIS-V" on the assumption that the latter will be normed in 2016. This entails projecting all subsequent trends over the interval of 24.5 years that separated the norming of the WAIS and WAIS-R. All calculations are explained at the bottom of the table. The final column gives what I think the actual Scaled Score gains (SD = 3) will be from the WAIS-IV to the WAIS-V, just for fun. To get the modern age values in Box 6, average the four Modern World values numbered (1) to (4) respectively.

Table AI1 WISC subtest gains: 1947 to 2002

| | WISC to WISC-R 1947.5–72 | WISC-R to WISC-III 1972–89 | WISC-III to WISC-IV 1989–2001.75 | WISC to WISC-IV 1947.5–2001.75 | WISC to WISC-IV 1947.5–2001.75 |
|---|---|---|---|---|---|
| | Gain 24.5 yrs. (SD = 3) | Gain 17 yrs. (SD = 3) | Gain 12.75 yrs. (SD = 3) | Gain 54.25 yrs. (SD = 3) | IQ Gain 54.25 yrs. (SD = 15) |
| Information | 0.43 | −0.3 | 0.3 | 0.43 | 2.15 |
| Arithmetic | 0.36 | 0.3 | −0.2 | 0.46 | 2.30 |
| Vocabulary | 0.38 | 0.4 | 0.1 | 0.88 | 4.40 |
| Comprehension | 1.20 | 0.6 | 0.4 | 2.20 | 11.00 |
| Picture completion | 0.74 | 0.9 | 0.7 | 2.34 | 11.70 |
| Block design | 1.28 | 0.9 | 1.0 | 3.18 | 15.90 |
| Object assembly | 1.34 | 1.2 | [0.93] | [3.47] | [17.35] |
| Coding | 2.20 | 0.7 | 0.7 | 3.60 | 18.00 |
| Picture arrangement | 0.93 | 1.9 | [1.47] | [4.30] | [21.50] |
| Similarities | 2.77 | 1.3 | 0.7 | 4.77 | 23.85 |

*Note:* The expanded paperback edition of 2009 has typographical errors (omits minus signs) that distort its Table 1.

*Source:* Adapted from J. R. Flynn, *What Is Intelligence? Beyond the Flynn Effect*, Cambridge University Press, 2007, Table 1 with permission of the Syndics of the Cambridge University Press. See that table for sources and a description of the derivation of the estimates.

Table AI2 Using subtest trends to predict gains from the WISC-IV to WISC-V (assuming: normed 10 years apart; and Full Scale IQ gains continue at 0.30 points per year)

| | (1) W–WR (SD = 15) | (2) WR–W3 pro-rated (SD = 15) | (2)/(1) | (3) W3–W4 pro-rated (SD = 15) | (3)/(2) | (4) W4–W5 pro-rated (SD = 15) | (4+) W4–W5 actual (SD = 3) |
|---|---|---|---|---|---|---|---|
| *Basics* | | | | | | | |
| Information | 2.15 | −2.16 | – | 2.88 | – | 0.96 | 0.08 |
| Arithmetic | 1.80 | 2.16 | – | −1.92 | – | 0.68 | 0.06 |
| Vocabulary | 1.90 | 2.88 | – | 0.96 | – | 1.91 | 0.16 |
| *Modern world* | | | | | | | |
| Comprehension | 6.00 | 4.32 | 72% | 3.84 | 89% | 3.42 | 0.28 |
| Picture completion | 3.70 | 6.48 | 175% | 6.72 | 104% | 6.99 | 0.57 |
| Block design | 6.40 | 6.48 | 101% | 9.60 | 148% | 14.21 | 1.16 |
| Coding | 11.00 | 5.04 | 46% | 6.72 | 133% | 8.94 | 0.73 |
| *Spectacles* | | | | | | | |
| Similarities | 13.85 | 9.36 | 68% | 6.72 | 72% | 4.84 | 0.39 |

*Notes:*

Pro-rating: All later gains are pro-rated to match the 24.5 years of the early WISC–WISC-R period. For example: the WISC-III to WISC-IV period is only 12.75 years; therefore, I multiplied all of its gains by 1.92 (24.5/12.75 = 1.92). Therefore, the 0.40 gain for Comprehension in Table AI1 becomes: (1) 0.40 × 5 = 2.00 (so SD will = 15 rather than 3); (2) 2.00 × 1.92 = 3.84, which the value shown in this table.

Prediction of WISC-IV–WISC-V gains – examples of calculations

Comprehension: (1) gain in W3–W4 period pro-rated over 24.5 years = 3.84; (2) assume that gain will fall to 89% of its rate – thus 3.84 × 0.89 = 3.42; (3) reduce it to what would be gained over 10 years by multiplying by 0.408 (10/24.5 = 0.408) – thus 3.42 × 0.408 = 1.39; (4) reduce from SD = 15 to SD = 3 – thus 1.39/5 = 0.28.

Similarities: (1) gain in W3–W4 period pro-rated over 24.5 years = 6.72; (2) assume that gain will fall to 72% of its rate – thus 6.72 × 0.72 = 4.84; (3) reduce it to what would be gained over 10 years by multiplying by 0.408 – thus 4.84 × 0.408 = 1.97; (4) reduce from SD = 15 to SD = 3 – thus 1.97/5 = 0.39.

The Basics subtests: These show no obvious trend, so the predictions are just the average of the earlier rates of gain.

*Source:* Table AI1.

Table AI3 WAIS subtest gains: from 1954 to 2006

| | WAIS to WAIS-R (1953.5–78) | WAIS-R to WAIS-III (1978–95) | WAIS-III to WAIS-IV (1995–2006) | WAIS to WAIS-IV (1953.5–2006) | WAIS to WAIS-IV (1953.5–2006) |
|---|---|---|---|---|---|
| | Gain 24.5 yrs. (SD = 3) | Gain 17 yrs. (SD = 3) | Gain 11 yrs. (SD = 3) | Gain 52.5 yrs. (SD = 3) | IQ Gain 52.5 yrs. (SD = 15) |
| Information | 1.1 | 0.0 | 0.5 | 1.6 | 8.0 |
| Arithmetic | 1.0 | −0.3 | 0.0 | 0.7 | 3.5 |
| Vocabulary | 1.8 | 0.6 | 1.0 | 3.4 | 17.0 |
| Comprehension | 1.8 | 0.5 | 0.4 | 2.7 | 13.5 |
| Picture completion | 1.8 | 0.4 | 0.9 | 3.1 | 15.5 |
| Block design | 1.0 | 0.7 | 0.3 | 2.0 | 10.0 |
| Object assembly | 1.3 | 0.9 | – | – | – |
| DS-Coding | 1.8 | 1.2 | 0.2 | 3.2 | 16.0 |
| Picture arrangement | 0.8 | 0.6 | 0.9 | 2.3 | 11.5 |
| Similarities | 2.2 | 0.9 | 0.7 | 3.8 | 19.0 |

*Source:* Adapted from Flynn, 2009b, Table 2 – with permission of publishers of *Applied Neuropsychology*. See that table for sources and derivation of the estimates.

Table AI4 Using subtest trends to predict gains from the WAIS-IV to WAIS-V (assuming: normed 10 years apart; Full Scale IQ gains continue at 0.30 points per year)

| | (1) W–WR | (2) WR–W3 pro-rated | (2)/(1) | (3) W3–W4 pro-rated | (3)/(2) | (4) W4–W5 pro-rated | (4+) W4–W5 SD = 3 |
|---|---|---|---|---|---|---|---|
| *Basics* | | | | | | | |
| Information | 5.50 | 0.00 | – | 5.57 | – | 3.69 | 0.30 |
| Arithmetic | 5.00 | −2.16 | – | 0.00 | – | 0.95 | 0.08 |
| Vocabulary | 9.00 | 4.32 | – | 11.14 | – | 8.15 | 0.67 |
| *Modern world* | | | | | | | |
| Comprehension | 9.00 | 3.60 | 40% | 4.45 | 124% | 5.52 | 0.45 |
| Picture completion | 9.00 | 2.88 | 32% | 10.02 | 348% | (12.00) | 0.98 |
| Block design | 5.00 | 5.04 | 101% | 3.34 | 66% | 2.20 | 0.18 |
| DS-Coding | 9.00 | 8.64 | 96% | 2.23 | 26% | 0.58 | 0.05 |
| *Spectacles* | | | | | | | |
| Similarities | 11.00 | 6.48 | 59% | 7.80 | 120% | 9.36 | 0.76 |

Pro-rating: All later gains are pro-rated to match the 24.5 years of the early WAIS–WAIS-R period. For example: the WAIS-III to WAIS-IV period is only 11 years; therefore, I multiplied all of its gains by 2.227 (24.5/11.0 = 2.227). Therefore, the 0.40 gain for Comprehension in the pervious table becomes: (1) 0.40 × 5 = 2.00 (so SD will = 15 rather than 3); (2) 2.00 × 2.227 = 4.45, which is the value shown in this table.

Prediction of WAIS-IV–WAIS-V gains – examples of calculations

Comprehension: (1) gain in W3–W4 period pro-rated over 24.5 years = 4.45; (2) assume that gain will rise to 124% of its rate – thus 4.45 × 1.24 = 5.52; (3) reduce it to what would be gained over 10 years by multiplying by 0.408 (10/24.5=0.408) – thus 5.52 × 0.408 = 2.25; (4) reduce from SD = 15 to SD = 3 – thus 2.25/5 = 0.45.

Picture arrangement: If you use the latest trend to calculate a prediction for this subtest, you get a nonsense result (10.02 × 3.48 = a projected gain equivalent to 34.87 IQ points!). Therefore I capped the estimate at 12.00, which is one point higher than any rate of gain that has been registered thus far.

Similarities: (1) gain in W3–W4 period pro-rated over 24.5 years = 7.80; (2) assume that gain will rise to 120% of its rate – thus 7.80 × 1.20 = 9.36; (3) reduce it to what would be gained over 10 years by multiplying by 0.408 – thus 9.36 × 0.408 = 3.82; (4) reduce from SD = 15 to SD = 3 – thus 3.82/5 = 0.76.

The Basics subtests: These show no obvious trend, so the predictions are just the average of the earlier rates of gain.

*Source:* Table AI3.

Table AI5 Coloured Progressive Matrices IQ gains by age in Britain from 1947 to 1982 and 1982 to 2007. Gains over the top half and bottom half of the curve compared where possible (age in years)

| Age | 5.5 | 6.0 | 6.5 | 7.0 | 7.5 | 8.0 | 8.5 | 9.0 | 9.5 | 10.0 | 10.5 | 11.0 | 11.5 |
|---|---|---|---|---|---|---|---|---|---|---|---|---|---|
| 1947–1982 | 5.04 | 2.82 | 4.23 | 5.73 | 7.83 | 9.40 | 8.11 | 6.41 | 4.70 | 5.69 | 5.69 | 5.46 | – |
| Top half | 8.82 | 5.76 | 7.40 | 8.43 | 11.61 | 13.51 | 11.51 | 8.65 | 5.73 | 7.35 | 6.15 | – | – |
| Bottom half | 1.27 | −0.12 | 1.06 | 3.04 | 4.06 | 5.28 | 4.72 | 4.17 | 3.67 | 4.03 | 5.23 | 5.46 | – |
| | | | | | (7.25) | | | | | | | | |
| 1982–2007 | 10.32 | 10.81 | 11.75 | | 10.89 | 14.53 | 13.58 | 11.22 | 8.22 | 6.37 | 5.46 | 6.37 | 6.37 |
| Top half | 11.69 | 13.00 | 14.83 | | 12.34 | – | – | – | – | – | – | – | – |
| Bottom half | 8.95 | 8.62 | 8.66 | | 9.44 | – | – | – | – | – | – | – | – |

| | Average gain all ages | Average rate all ages |
|---|---|---|
| 1947–1982 | 5.93 points | 0.170 points per year |
| Top half | 8.63 points | 0.247 points per year |
| Bottom half | 3.49 points | c.100 points per year |
| 1982–2007 | 9.66 points | 0.386 points per year |
| Top half (ages 5.5–7.25) | (12.97 points) | – |
| Bottom half (ages 5.5–7.25) | (8.92 points) | – |
| 1947–2007 | 15.59 points | 0.260 points per year |

Box 7 in Chapter 3 summarizes results from the standardizations of the Coloured Progressive Matrices (CPM) in Britain. Table AI5 (above) gives estimates of IQ gains for every age group. These are based on the SDs from the various 1982 age distributions. The 1982 distributions provide the best metric because their data are common to all comparisons and they are at the mid-point in time. Table AI5 is based on its subsidiary tables (below), which show how the raw data was analyzed age by age.

Some prefatory comment on the subsidiary tables may be helpful. For each percentile we have the raw score (for the CPM out of 30) that is the cutting line for that percentile. The difference between the raw scores for the two years of testing is divided by the chosen SD to convert it into standard deviation units – then multiplied by 15 to convert it into IQ points. These are averaged to get the gain over the whole curve. Then they are averaged over the top and bottom halves of the curve with the 50th percentile included in both (given dual weight because it is surrounded by the most subjects). Finally, the top and bottom estimates are weighted to tally with the overall average gain. As the ceiling effect begins to bite, difficulties arise that are described under the relevant data sets.

Comparing 1947 and 1982 (using SD from 1982)

Age: 5.5 years (those from 5 years 3 months to 5 years 8 months; subsequent samples all have a similar 6 months' range)

| Percentiles | 1982 | 1947 | Dif./SD | SDUs | IQ points |
|---|---|---|---|---|---|
| 95 | 22 | 19 | 3/4.255 | 0.705 | 10.58 |
| 90 | 20 | 17 | 3/4.255 | 0.705 | 10.58 |
| 75 | 18 | 15 | 3/4.255 | 0.705 | 10.58 |
| 50 | 15 | 14 | 1/4.355 | 0.235 | 3.53 |
| 25 | 12 | 12 | 0/4.255 | 0.000 | 0.00 |
| 10 | 10 | (10) | 0/4.255 | 0.000 | 0.00 |
| 5 | 8 | (8) | 0/4.255 | 0.000 | 0.00 |

Average gain = 5.04 points Rate: 5.04/35 = 0.144 points per year
The top vs. bottom half: 8.82 & 1.27

Bracketed values were invented to allow a comparison over the whole curve that represents the fact that there are no gains at the 25th percentile. The estimated gain over the bottom half of the curve assumes a gain between the 50th and 25th percentiles.

Age: 6.0 years

| Percentiles | 1982 | 1947 | Dif./SD | SDUs | IQ points |
|---|---|---|---|---|---|
| 95 | 24 | 21 | 3/4.559 | 0.658 | 9.87 |
| 90 | 21 | 20 | 1/4.559 | 0.219 | 3.29 |
| 75 | 19 | 17 | 2/4.559 | 0.439 | 6.58 |
| 50 | 16 | 15 | 1/4.559 | 0.219 | 3.29 |
| 25 | 13 | 13 | 0/4.559 | 0.000 | 0.00 |
| 10 | 11 | 12 | −1/4.559 | −0.219 | −3.29 |
| 5 | 9 | (9) | 0/4.559 | 0.000 | 0.00 |

Average gain = 2.82 points Rate: 2.82/35 = 0.081 points per year

The top vs. bottom half: 5.76 & −0.12

Age: 6.5 years

| Percentiles | 1982 | 1947 | Dif./SD | SDUs | IQ points |
|---|---|---|---|---|---|
| 95 | 26 | 23 | 3/4.559 | 0.658 | 9.87 |
| 90 | 23 | 21 | 2/4.559 | 0.439 | 6.58 |
| 75 | 20 | 18 | 2/4.559 | 0.439 | 6.58 |
| 50 | 17 | 15 | 2/4.559 | 0.439 | 6.58 |
| 25 | 14 | 14 | 0/4.559 | 0.000 | 0.00 |
| 10 | 12 | 12 | 0/4.559 | 0.000 | 0.00 |
| 5 | 11 | (11) | 0/4.559 | 0.000 | 0.00 |

Average gain = 4.23 points

Rate: 4.23/35 = 0.121 points per year

The top vs. bottom half: 7.40 & 1.06

Age: 7.0 years

| Percentiles | 1982 | 1947 | Dif./SD | SDUs | IQ points |
|---|---|---|---|---|---|
| 95 | 28 | 24 | 4/4.863 | 0.823 | 12.34 |
| 90 | 25 | 22 | 3/4.863 | 0.617 | 9.25 |
| 75 | 21 | 19 | 2/4.863 | 0.411 | 6.17 |
| 50 | 18 | 16 | 2/4.863 | 0.411 | 6.17 |
| 25 | 16 | 14 | 2/4.863 | 0.411 | 6.17 |
| 10 | 13 | 13 | 0/4.863 | 0.000 | 0.00 |
| 5 | 12 | 12 | 0/4.863 | 0.000 | 0.00 |

Average gain = 5.73 points

Rate: 5.73/35 = 0.164 points per year

The top vs. bottom half: 8.43 & 3.04

Age: 7.5 years

| Percentiles | 1982 | 1947 | Dif./SD | SDUs | IQ points |
|---|---|---|---|---|---|
| 95 | 31 | 25 | 6/5.471 | 1.097 | 16.45 |
| 90 | 28 | 23 | 5/5.471 | 0.914 | 13.71 |
| 75 | 23 | 20 | 3/5.471 | 0.548 | 8.23 |
| 50 | 20 | 17 | 3/5.471 | 0.548 | 8.23 |
| 25 | 17 | 15 | 2/5.471 | 0.366 | 5.48 |
| 10 | 14 | 14 | 0/5.471 | 0.000 | 0.00 |
| 5 | 13 | 12 | 1/5.471 | 0.183 | 2.74 |

Average gain = 7.83 points

Rate: 7.83/35 = 0.224 points per year

The top vs. bottom half: 11.61 & 4.06

Age: 8.0 years

| Percentiles | 1982 | 1947 | Dif./SD | SDUs | IQ points |
|---|---|---|---|---|---|
| 95 | 32 | 26 | 6/5.471 | 1.097 | 16.45 |
| 90 | 30 | 24 | 6/5.471 | 1.097 | 16.45 |
| 75 | 25 | 21 | 4/5.471 | 0.731 | 10.97 |
| 50 | 22 | 18 | 4/5.471 | 0.731 | 10.97 |
| 25 | 18 | 16 | 2/5.471 | 0.366 | 5.48 |
| 10 | 15 | 14 | 1/5.471 | 0.183 | 2.74 |
| 5 | 14 | 13 | 1/5.471 | 0.183 | 2.74 |

Average gain = 9.40 points

Rate: 9.40/35 = 0.269 points per year

The top vs. bottom half: 13.51 & 5.28

Age: 8.5 years

| Percentiles | 1982 | 1947 | Dif./SD | SDUs | IQ points |
|---|---|---|---|---|---|
| 95 | 33 | 28 | 5/6.079+ | 0.823 | 12.34 |
| 90 | 32 | 26 | 6/6.079 | 0.987 | 14.81 |
| 75 | 27 | 23 | 4/6.079 | 0.658 | 9.87 |
| 50 | 24 | 20 | 4/6.079 | 0.987 | 9.87 |
| 25 | 20 | 17 | 3/6.079 | 0.494 | 7.40 |
| 10 | 16 | 15 | 1/6.079 | 0.165 | 2.47 |
| 5 | 14 | 14 | 0/6.079 | 0.000 | 0.00 |

Average gain = 8.11 points

Rate: 8.11/35 = 0.232 points per year

The top vs. bottom half: 11.51 & 4.72

+ Hitherto the entire 1982 curve has been used to derive a value for the SD. Now the 1982 distribution begins to show a ceiling effect above the 90th percentile. To avoid an overestimate of gains, the bottom half is used to estimate the SD over the whole curve. This calculation for the SD will be used through age 10.5.

Age: 9.0 years

| Percentiles | 1982 | 1947 | Dif./SD | SDUs | IQ points |
|---|---|---|---|---|---|
| 95 | 34 | 30 | 4/6.687 | 0.598 | 8.97 |
| 90 | 33 | 28 | 5/6.687 | 0.748 | 11.22 |
| 75 | 29 | 26 | 3/6.687 | 0.449 | 6.73 |
| 50 | 26 | 22 | 4/6.687 | 0.598 | 8.97 |
| 25 | 22 | 19 | 3/6.687 | 0.449 | 6.73 |
| 10 | 17 | 16 | 1/6.687 | 0.150 | 2.24 |
| 5 | 15 | 15 | 0/6.687 | 0.000 | 0.00 |

Average gain I = 6.41 points Rate I: 6.41/35 = 0.183 points per year

The top vs. bottom half I: 8.65 & 4.17

Average gain II = 7.30 points Rate II: 7.30/35 = 0.209 points per year

The top vs. bottom half II: 10.43 (estimated) & 4.17

Beginning at age 9, the top half of the 1982 curve is depressed by the ceiling effect and gives an underestimate (labeled "gain I"). If we assume that the ratio of top half to bottom half gains was the same as the ratio of ages 8.0–8.5 (2.5/1), we get a larger estimate (labeled "gain II"). Despite this, I will use gain I in my analysis because it gives actual values for top and bottom and that is the main point of the analysis.

Age: 9.5 years

| Percentiles | 1982 | 1947 | Dif./SD | SDUs | IQ points |
|---|---|---|---|---|---|
| 95 | 35 | 32 | 3/7.295 | 0.411 | 6.17 |
| 90 | 33 | 31 | 2/7.295 | 0.274 | 4.11 |
| 75 | 31 | 28 | 3/7.295 | 0.411 | 6.17 |
| 50 | 28 | 24 | 4/7.295 | 0.548 | 8.22 |
| 25 | 24 | 21 | 3/7.295 | 0.411 | 6.17 |
| 10 | 19 | 18 | 1/7.295 | 0.137 | 2.06 |
| 5 | 16 | 16 | 0/7.295 | 0.000 | 0.00 |

Average gain I = 4.70 points Rate I: 4.70/35 = 0.134 points per year

The top vs. bottom half I: 5.73 & 3.67

Average gain II = 6.42 points Rate II: 6.42/35 = 0.183 points per year

The top vs. bottom half II: 9.18 (estimated) & 3.67

Age: 10.0 years

| Percentiles | 1982 | 1947 | Dif./SD | SDUs | IQ points |
|---|---|---|---|---|---|
| 95 | 35 | 32 | 3/7.903 | 0.380 | 5.69 |
| 90 | 33 | 31 | 2/7.903 | 0.253 | 3.80 |
| 75 | 32 | 26 | 6/7.903 | 0.759 | 11.39 |
| 50 | 30 | 24 | 6/7.903 | 0.759 | 11.39 |
| 25 | 25 | 22 | 3/7.903 | 0.380 | 5.69 |
| 10 | 21 | 20 | 1/7.903 | 0.127 | 1.90 |
| 5 | 17 | 17 | 0/7.903 | 0.000 | 0.00 |

Average gain I = 5.69 points Rate I: 5.69/35 = 0.163 points per year

The top vs. bottom half I: 7.35 & 4.03

Average gain II = 7.05 points Rate II: 7.05/35 = 0.202 points per year

The top vs. bottom half II: 10.08 (estimated) & 4.03

Age: 10.5 years

| Percentiles | 1982 | 1947 | Dif./SD | SDUs | IQ points |
|---|---|---|---|---|---|
| 95 | 35 | 33 | 2/7.903 | 0.253 | 3.80 |
| 90 | 34 | 31 | 3/7.903 | 0.380 | 5.69 |
| 75 | 33 | 29 | 4/7.903 | 0.506 | 7.59 |
| 50 | 31 | 26 | 5/7.903 | 0.606 | 9.09 |
| 25 | 26 | 22 | 4/7.903 | 0.506 | 7.59 |
| 10 | 22 | 20 | 2/7.903 | 0.253 | 3.80 |
| 5 | 18 | 17 | 1/7.903 | 0.127 | 1.90 |

Average gain I = 5.69 points Rate I: 5.69/35 = 0.163 points per year

The top vs. bottom half I: 6.15 & 5.23

Average gain II = 9.15 points Rate II: 9.15/35 = 0.261 points per year

The top vs. bottom half II: 13.07 (estimated) & 5.23

Age: 11.0 years

| Percentiles | 1982 | 1947 | Dif./SD | SDUs | IQ points |
|---|---|---|---|---|---|
| 95 | 35 | 35 | 0* | – | – |
| 90 | 35 | 34 | 1* | – | – |
| 75 | 33 | 31 | 2* | – | – |
| 50 | 31 | 28 | 3/8.247++ | 0.364 | 5.46 |
| 25 | 28 | 24 | 4/8.247 | 0.485 | 7.28 |
| 10 | 23 | 21 | 2/8.247 | 0.243 | 3.64 |
| 5 | 20 | 17 | 3/8.247 | 0.364 | 5.46 |

Average gain I = 5.46 points Rate I: 5.46/35 = 0.156 points per year

The top vs. bottom half I: – & 5.46

Average gain II = 9.56 points Rate II: 9.56/35 = 0.273 points per year

The top vs. bottom half II: 13.65 (estimated) & 5.46

* These values are not used because the 1982 distribution now shows a large negative skew due to a ceiling effect. Note that only 4 raw score points separate the 50th and 95th percentiles, while 11 points separate the 50th and 5th percentiles.

++ Since even the 50th percentile shows some evidence of the ceiling effect, the SD has been calculated over the bottom 25 percent of the curve.

Comparing 1982 and 2007 (using SD from 1982)

The same introduction (look back to comparing 1947 and 1982) applies here.

Age: 5.5 years (years/months of samples below)

| Percentiles | 1982 (5/3–5/8) | 2007 (5/0–5/11) | Dif./SD | SDUs | IQ points |
|---|---|---|---|---|---|
| 95 | 22 | 25.5 | 3.5/4.255 | 0.823 | 12.34 |
| 90 | 20 | 24.5 | 4.5/4.255 | 1.058 | 15.86 |
| 75 | 18 | 20.5 | 2.5/4.255 | 0.589 | 8.81 |
| 50 | 15 | 17.5 | 2.5/4/255 | 0.589 | 8.81 |
| 25 | 12 | 14.5 | 2.5/4.255 | 0.589 | 8.81 |
| 10 | 10 | 12.0 | 2.0/4.255 | 0.470 | 7.05 |
| 5 | 8 | 11.0 | 3.0/4.255 | 0.705 | 10.58 |

Average gain = 10.32 points Rate: 10.32/25 = 0.413 points per year

Top vs. bottom half: 11.69 & 8.95

Age: 6.0 years (years/months of samples below)

| Percentiles | 1982 (5/9–6/2) | 2007 (5/6–6/5) | Dif./SD | SDUs | IQ points |
|---|---|---|---|---|---|
| 95 | 24 | 27.5 | 3.5/4.559 | 0.768 | 11.52 |
| 90 | 21 | 26.5 | 5.5/4.559 | 1.206 | 18.10 |
| 75 | 19 | 22.5 | 3.5/4.559 | 0.768 | 11.52 |
| 50 | 16 | 19.5 | 3.5/4.559 | 0.768 | 11.52 |
| 25 | 13 | 16.0 | 3.0/4.559 | 0.658 | 9.87 |
| 10 | 11 | 12.5 | 1.5/4.559 | 0.329 | 4.94 |
| 5 | 9 | 11.5 | 2.5/4.559 | 0.548 | 8.23 |

Average gain = 10.81 points Rate: 10.81/25 = 0.432 points per year

Top vs. bottom half: 13.00 & 8.62

Age: 6.5 years (years/months of samples below)

| Percentiles | 1982 (6/3–6/8) | 2007 (6/0–6/11) | Dif./SD | SDUs | IQ points |
|---|---|---|---|---|---|
| 95 | 26 | 29.5 | 3.5/4.559 | 0.768 | 11.52 |
| 90 | 23 | 28.5 | 5.5/4.559 | 1.206 | 18.10 |
| 75 | 20 | 25.0 | 5.0/4.559 | 1.097 | 16.45 |
| 50 | 17 | 21.5 | 4.5/4.559 | 0.987 | 14.81 |
| 25 | 14 | 17.5 | 3.5/4.559 | 0.768 | 11.52 |
| 10 | 12 | 13.5 | 1.5/4.559 | 0.329 | 4.94 |
| 5 | 11 | 12.5 | 1.5/4.559 | 0.329 | 4.94 |

Average gain = 11.75 points Rate: 11.75/25 = 0.470 points per year

Top vs. bottom half: 14.83 & 8.66

Age: 7.25 years (years/months of samples below)

| Percentiles | 1982 (6/9–7/8) | 2007 (6/6–7/11) | Dif./SD | SDUs | IQ points |
|---|---|---|---|---|---|
| 95 | 29.5 | 31.5 | 2.0* | – | – |
| 90 | 26.5 | 30.5 | 4.0/5.167 | 0.774 | 11.61 |
| 75 | 22.0 | 27.5 | 5.5/5.167 | 1.064 | 15.97 |
| 50 | 19.0 | 24.0 | 5.0/5.167 | 0.968 | 14.52 |
| 25 | 16.5 | 20.0 | 3.5/5.167 | 0.677 | 10.16 |
| 10 | 13.5 | 16.0 | 2.5/5.167 | 0.484 | 7.26 |
| 5 | 12.5 | 14.5 | 2.0/5.167 | 0.387 | 5.81 |

Average gain = 10.89 points Rate: 10.89/25 = 0.436 points per year

The top vs. bottom half: 12.34 & 9.44

* This value is not used because the 2007 distribution now shows a negative skew due to a ceiling effect. Note that only 7.5 raw score points separate the 50th and 95th percentiles, while 9.5 points separate the 50th and 5th percentiles. This effect is exaggerated with agc, that is, by age 11, the ratio is 4 points to 8. Perhaps more to the point, the raw score at the 95th percentile has gone above 30. Note Jensen, cited in the text, on the fact that scores above 30 may be underestimates of the child's ability due to a ceiling effect. From here on, comparisons at the top of the curve are progressively dropped and further comparisons between the top and bottom halves are impossible.

Age: 8.0 years (years/months of samples below)

| Percentiles | 1982 (7/9–8/2) | 2007 (7/0–8/11) | Dif./SD | SDUs | IQ points |
|---|---|---|---|---|---|
| 95 | 32 | 33.0 | 1.0 | – | – |
| 90 | 30 | 32.0 | 2.0 | – | – |
| 75 | 25 | 29.5 | 4.5/5.471 | 0.823 | 12.34 |
| 50 | 22 | 27.0 | 5.0/5.471 | 0.914 | 13.71 |
| 25 | 18 | 24.0 | 6.0/5.471 | 1.097 | 16.45 |
| 10 | 15 | 20.0 | 5.0/5.471 | 0.914 | 13.71 |
| 5 | 14 | 18.0 | 6.0/5.471 | 1.097 | 16.45 |

Average gain = 14.53 points Rate: 14.53/25 = 0.582 points per year

(Bottom = 15.08)

Age: 8.5 years (years/months of samples below)

| Percentiles | 1982 (8/3–8/8) | 2007 (8/0–8/11) | Dif./SD | SDUs | IQ points |
|---|---|---|---|---|---|
| 95 | 33 | 33.0 | 0.0 | – | – |
| 90 | 32 | 32.0 | 0.0 | – | – |
| 75 | 27 | 30.0 | 3.0 | – | – |
| 50 | 24 | 28.0 | 4.0/6.079+ | 0.658 | 9.87 |
| 25 | 20 | 26.0 | 6.0/6.079 | 0.987 | 14.81 |
| 10 | 16 | 22.0 | 6.0/6.079 | 0.987 | 14.81 |
| 5 | 14 | 20.0 | 6.0/6.079 | 0.987 | 14.81 |

Average gain = 13.58 points Rate: 13.48/25 = 0.539 points per year

+ Hitherto the entire 1982 curve has been used to derive a value for the SD. Now the 1982 distribution begins to show a ceiling effect so only the bottom half is used. No estimate for gains over the bottom half is offered because the 2007 distribution now begins to be depressed even near the median.

Age: 9.0 years (years/months of samples below)

| Percentiles | 1982 (8/9–9/2) | 2007 (8/0–9/11) | Dif./SD | SDUs | IQ points |
|---|---|---|---|---|---|
| 95 | 34 | 34.0 | 0.0 | – | – |
| 90 | 33 | 33.0 | 0.0 | – | – |
| 75 | 29 | 31.0 | 2.0 | – | – |
| 50 | 26 | 28.5 | 2.5 | – | – |
| 25 | 22 | 26.5 | 4.5/6.687 | 0.673 | 10.09 |
| 10 | 17 | 22.5 | 5.5/6.687 | 0.822 | 12.34 |
| 5 | 15 | 20.0 | 5.0/6.687 | 0.748 | 11.22 |

Average gain = 11.22 points Rate: 11.22/25 = 0.449 points per year

Age: 9.5 years (years/months of samples below)

| Percentiles | 1982 (9/3–9/8) | 2007 (9/0–9/11) | Dif./SD | SDUs | IQ points |
|---|---|---|---|---|---|
| 95 | 35 | 35.0 | 0.0 | – | – |
| 90 | 33 | 34.0 | 1.0 | – | – |
| 75 | 31 | 32.0 | 1.0 | – | – |
| 50 | 28 | 29.0 | 1.0 | – | – |
| 25 | 24 | 27.0 | 3.0/7.295 | 0.411 | 6.17 |
| 10 | 19 | 23.0 | 4.0/7.295 | 0.548 | 8.22 |
| 5 | 16 | 21.0 | 5.0/7.295 | 0.685 | 10.28 |

Average gain = 8.22 points Rate: 8.22/25 = 0.329 points per year

Age: 10.0 years (years/months of samples below)

| Percentiles | 1982 (9/9–10/3) | 2007 (9/0–10/11) | Dif./SD | SDUs | IQ points |
|---|---|---|---|---|---|
| 95 | 35 | 35.5 | 0.5 | – | – |
| 90 | 33 | 34.5 | 1.5 | – | – |
| 75 | 32 | 32.5 | 0.5 | – | – |
| 50 | 30 | 30.0 | 0.0 | – | – |
| 25 | 25 | 27.5 | 2.5 | – | – |
| 10 | 21 | 23.5 | 2.5/8.247 | 0.303 | 4.55 |
| 5 | 17 | 21.5 | 4.5/8.247 | 0.546 | 8.18 |

Average gain = 6.37 points Rate: 6.37/25 = 0.255 points per year

At this point, ceiling effects become so large that the SD is calculated using only the bottom fourth of the curve.

Age: 10.5 years (years/months of samples below)

| Percentiles | 1982 (10/3–10/8) | 2007 (10/0–10/11) | Dif./SD | SDUs | IQ points |
|---|---|---|---|---|---|
| 95 | 35 | 36.0 | 1.0 | – | – |
| 90 | 34 | 35.0 | 1.0 | – | – |
| 75 | 33 | 33.0 | 0.0 | – | – |
| 50 | 31 | 31.0 | 0.0 | – | – |
| 25 | 26 | 28.0 | 2.0 | – | – |
| 10 | 22 | 24.0 | 2.0/8.247 | 0.243 | 3.64 |
| 5 | 18 | 22.0 | 4.0/8.247 | 0.485 | 7.28 |

Average gain = 5.46 points Rate: 5.46/25 = 0.218 points per year

Age: 11.0 years (years/months of samples below)

| Percentiles | 1982 (10/9–11/3) | 2007 (10/0–11/11) | Dif./SD | SDUs | IQ points |
|---|---|---|---|---|---|
| 95 | 35 | 36.0 | 1.0 | – | – |
| 90 | 35 | 35.5 | 0.5 | – | – |
| 75 | 33 | 33.5 | 0.5 | – | – |
| 50 | 31 | 32.0 | 1.0 | – | – |
| 25 | 28 | 29.0 | 1.0 | – | – |
| 10 | 23 | 26.0 | 3.0/8.247 | 0.364 | 5.46 |
| 5 | 20 | 24.0 | 4.0/8.247 | 0.485 | 7.28 |

Average gain = 6.37 points Rate: 6.37/25 = 0.255 points per year

Age: 11.5 years (years/months of samples below)

| Percentiles | 1982 (11/3–11/8) | 2007 (11/0–11/11) | Dif./SD | SDUs | IQ points |
|---|---|---|---|---|---|
| 95 | 35 | 36.0 | 1.0 | – | – |
| 90 | 35 | 36.0 | 1.0 | – | – |
| 75 | 34 | 34.0 | 0.0 | – | – |
| 50 | 32 | 33.0 | 1.0 | – | – |
| 25 | 30 | 30.0 | 0.0 | – | – |
| 10 | 25 | 28.0 | 3.0/8.247 | 0.364 | 5.46 |
| 5 | 22 | 26.0 | 4.0/8.247 | 0.485 | 7.28 |

Average gain = 6.37 points Rate: 6.37/25 = 0.255 points per year

Box 8 in Chapter 3 summarizes results from the standardizations of the Standard Progressive Matrices (SPM) in Britain. Table AI6 gives estimates of IQ gains for every age group. These are based on the SDs from the various 1979 age distributions. The 1979 distributions provide the best metric because their data is common to all comparisons and they are at the mid-point in time. Table AI6 is followed by its subsidiary tables, which show how the raw data was analyzed age by age.

Some prefatory comment on the subsidiary tables may be helpful. For each percentile we have the raw score (for the SPM out of 60) that is the cutting line for that percentile. The difference between the raw scores for the two years of testing is divided by the chosen SD to convert it into standard deviation units, and then multiplied by 15 to convert it into IQ points. These are averaged to get the gain over the whole curve. Then they are averaged over the top and bottom halves of the curve with the 50th percentile included in both (given dual weight because it is surrounded by the most subjects). Finally, the top and bottom estimates are weighted to tally with the overall average gain. As the ceiling effect begins to bite, difficulties arise that are described under the relevant data sets.

Table AI6 Standard Progressive Matrices IQ gains by age in Britain from 1938 to 1979 and 1979 to 2008. Gains over the top half and bottom half of the curve compared where possible (age in years)

| Age | 7.5 | 8.0 | 8.5 | 9.0 | 9.5 | 10.0 | 10.5 | 11.0 | 11.5 | 12.0 | 12.5 | 13.0 | 13.5 | 14.0 | 14.5 | 15.5 |
|---|---|---|---|---|---|---|---|---|---|---|---|---|---|---|---|---|
| 1938–79 | – | 9.69 | 10.89 | 10.20 | 9.33 | 9.21 | 11.68 | 12.08 | 11.41 | 9.30 | 7.87 | 6.80 | 6.80 | 6.80 | – | – |
| Top half | – | 9.69 | 10.21 | 9.05 | 7.95 | less | less | less | less | less | less | less | less | less | – | – |
| Bottom half | – | – | – | – | 10.71 | more | more | more | more | more | more | more | more | more | – | – |
| 1979–2008 | 11.86 | – | 10.70 | – | 8.48 | – | 6.07 | – | 1.30 | – | 2.50 | – | 1.15 | – | −2.24 | −1.51 |
| Top half | 10.96 | – | 9.23 | – | 5.12 | – | 3.43 | – | −0.69 | – | −0.30 | – | −2.79 | – | −6.29 | −5.61 |
| Bottom half | 12.76 | – | 12.17 | – | 11.83 | – | 8.70 | – | 3.29 | – | 5.30 | – | 5.09 | – | 1.82 | 2.59 |

| | Average gain all ages | Average rate all ages |
|---|---|---|
| 1938–1979 | 9.39 points | 0.229 points per year |
| Top half | less | less |
| Bottom half | more | more |
| 1979–2008 | 4.26 points | 0.147 points per year |
| Top half | 2.07 points | 0.072 points per year |
| Bottom half | 7.06 points | 0.243 points per year |
| 1938–2008 | 13.65 points | 0.195 points per year |

## Comparing 1938 and 1979 (using SD from 1979)

Age: 8.0 years

| Percentiles | 1979 | 1938 | Dif./SD | SDUs | IQ points |
|---|---|---|---|---|---|
| 95 | 40 | 38 | 2/8.511 | 0.235 | 3.52 |
| 90 | 38 | 34 | 4/8.511 | 0.470 | 7.05 |
| 75 | 33 | 24 | 9/8.511 | 1.057 | 15.86 |
| 50 | 25 | 18 | 7/8.511 | 0.822 | 12.34 |
| 25 | 17 | – | – | – | – |
| 10 | 14 | – | – | – | – |
| 5 | 12 | – | – | – | – |

Average gain = 9.69 points Rate: 9.69/41 = 0.236 points per year

The top vs. bottom half: 9.69 & unknown

Age: 8.5 years

| Percentiles | 1979 | 1938 | Dif./SD | SDUs | IQ points |
|---|---|---|---|---|---|
| 95 | 42 | 39 | 3/8.815 | 0.340 | 5.10 |
| 90 | 40 | 36 | 4/8.815 | 0.454 | 6.81 |
| 75 | 36 | 29 | 7/8.815 | 0.794 | 11.91 |
| 50 | 31 | 21 | 10/8.815 | 1.134 | 17.02 |
| 25 | 22 | 14 | 8/8.815 | 0.908 | 13.61 |
| 10 | 16 | – | – | – | – |
| 5 | 13 | – | – | – | – |

Average gain = 10.89 points Rate: 10.89/41 = 0.266 points per year

The top vs. bottom half: 10.21 & unknown

Age: 9.0 years

| Percentiles | 1979 | 1938 | Dif./SD | SDUs | IQ points |
|---|---|---|---|---|---|
| 95 | 44 | 41 | 3/9.119 | 0.329 | 4.93 |
| 90 | 42 | 38 | 4/9.119 | 0.439 | 6.58 |
| 75 | 38 | 32 | 6/9.119 | 0.658 | 9.87 |
| 50 | 33 | 24 | 9/9.119 | 0.987 | 14.80 |
| 25 | 25 | 16 | 9/9.119 | 0.987 | 14.80 |
| 10 | 17 | – | – | – | – |
| 5 | 14 | – | – | – | – |

Average gain = 10.20 points    Rate: 10.20/41 = 0.249 points per year

The top vs. bottom half: 9.05 & unknown

Age: 9.5 years

| Percentiles | 1979 | 1938 | Dif./SD | SDUs | IQ points |
|---|---|---|---|---|---|
| 95 | 46 | 43 | 3/9.422 | 0.318 | 4.78 |
| 90 | 44 | 41 | 3/9.422 | 0.318 | 4.78 |
| 75 | 41 | 34 | 7/9.422 | 0.743 | 11.14 |
| 50 | 36 | 28 | 8/9.422 | 0.849 | 12.74 |
| 25 | 28 | 18 | 10/9.422 | 1.061 | 15.92 |
| 10 | 19 | 13 | 6/9.422 | 0.637 | 9.55 |
| 5 | 15 | (11) | 4/9.422 | 0.425 | 6.37 |

Average gain = 9.33 points

Rate: 9.33/41 = 0.227 points per year

Top & bottom half: 7.95 & 10.71

The ratio favors the bottom half of the curve over the top half of by 0.74 to 1. But the spread over the top and bottom halves of the 1979 curve gives an even lower ratio of 0.48 to 1. Nonetheless, gains over the bottom half have begun to equal the gains over the top half at younger ages, which probably signals an emerging trend for larger gains over the bottom half. The bracketed value was invented (based on older ages groups) so that this emerging trend could be recorded.

Age: 10.0 years

| Percentiles | 1979 | 1938 | Dif./SD | SDUs | IQ points |
|---|---|---|---|---|---|
| 95 | 48 | 45 | – | – | – |
| 90 | 46 | 43 | – | – | – |
| 75 | 42 | 37 | – | – | – |
| 50 | 38 | 30 | 8/12.766 | 0.627 | 9.40 |
| 25 | 32 | 20 | 12/12.766 | 0.940 | 14.10 |
| 10 | 23 | 13 | 10/12.766 | 0.783 | 11.75 |
| 5 | 17 | (11) | 6/12.766 | 0.470 | 7.05 |

Average gain = 10.58 × 0.87 = 9.21 points
Rate: 9.21/41= 0.225 points per year

The gain over the bottom half of the curve is now larger than any recorded over the top half, so the fact of greater gains at lower IQ levels is almost certain. However, since a ceiling effect is clearly lowering gains over the top half of the curve to a substantial degree, and also lowering variance over the whole curve, the estimate of gains will be calculated as follows: (1) raw score gains over the bottom half will be divided by the SD over the bottom half; (2) that estimate cannot be allowed to stand for the whole curve because to do that would be to assume that gains over the top half of the curve were as great as over the bottom half, which is false and would produce an inflated estimate; (3) the only age that allows a real comparison of bottom and top halves is age 9.5, which showed a ratio of 0.74 to 1; (4) since 1.74/2 = 0.87, I will discount gains over the bottom half by that to get the best possible estimate for the whole curve. That method will be followed both here and for all older ages.

Age: 10.5 years

| Percentiles | 1979 | 1938 | Dif./SD | SDUs | IQ points |
|---|---|---|---|---|---|
| 95 | 49 | 48 | – | – | – |
| 90 | 47 | 45 | – | – | – |
| 75 | 43 | 39 | – | – | – |
| 50 | 39 | 33 | 6/10.334 | 0.581 | 8.71 |
| 25 | 33 | 23 | 10/10.334 | 0.968 | 14.52 |
| 10 | 27 | 15 | 12/10.334 | 1.161 | 17.42 |
| 5 | 22 | 13 | 9/10.334 | 0.871 | 13.06 |

Average gain = 13.43 × 0.87 = 11.68 points
Rate: 11.68/41 = 0.285 points per year

Age: 11.0 years

| Percentiles | 1979 | 1938 | Dif./SD | SDUs | IQ points |
|---|---|---|---|---|---|
| 95 | 50 | 50 | – | – | – |
| 90 | 48 | 47 | – | – | – |
| 75 | 44 | 41 | – | – | – |
| 50 | 40 | 35 | 5/9.726 | 0.514 | 7.71 |
| 25 | 34 | 26 | 8/9.726 | 0.823 | 12.34 |
| 10 | 29 | 16 | 13/9.726 | 1.337 | 20.05 |
| 5 | 24 | 14 | 10/9.726 | 1.028 | 15.42 |

Average gain = 13.88 × 0.87 = 12.08 points
Rate: 12.08/41 = 0.295 points per year

Age: 11.5 years

| Percentiles | 1979 | 1938 | Dif./SD | SDUs | IQ points |
|---|---|---|---|---|---|
| 95 | 51 | 51 | – | – | – |
| 90 | 49 | 49 | – | – | – |
| 75 | 45 | 43 | – | – | – |
| 50 | 41 | 37 | 4/9.726 | 0.411 | 6.17 |
| 25 | 36 | 29 | 7/9.726 | 0.720 | 10.80 |
| 10 | 31 | 18 | 13/9.726 | 1.337 | 20.05 |
| 5 | 25 | 15 | 10/9.726 | 1.028 | 15.42 |

Average gain = 13.11 × 0.87 = 11.41 points
Rate: 11.41/41 = 0.278 points per year

Age: 12.0 years

| Percentiles | 1979 | 1938 | Dif./SD | SDUs | IQ points |
|---|---|---|---|---|---|
| 95 | 52 | 51 | – | – | – |
| 90 | 50 | 49 | – | – | – |
| 75 | 46 | 45 | – | – | – |
| 50 | 41 | 39 | 2/9.119 | 0.219 | 3.29 |
| 25 | 37 | 32 | 5/9.119 | 0.548 | 8.22 |
| 10 | 31 | 22 | 9/9.119 | 0.987 | 14.80 |
| 5 | 26 | 16 | 10/9.119 | 1.097 | 16.45 |

Average gain = 10.69 × 0.87 = 9.30 points
Rate: 9.30/41 = 0.227 points per year

Age: 12.5 years

| Percentiles | 1979 | 1938 | Dif./SD | SDUs | IQ points |
|---|---|---|---|---|---|
| 95 | 53 | 52 | – | – | – |
| 90 | 51 | 50 | – | – | – |
| 75 | 47 | 46 | – | – | – |
| 50 | 42 | 41 | 1/9.119 | 0.110 | 1.65 |
| 25 | 38 | 34 | 4/9.119 | 0.439 | 6.58 |
| 10 | 32 | 25 | 7/9.119 | 0.768 | 11.51 |
| 5 | 27 | 17 | 10/9.119 | 1.097 | 16.45 |

Average gain = 9.05 × 0.87 = 7.87 points
Rate: 7.87/41 = 0.192 points per year

Age: 13.0 years

| Percentiles | 1979 | 1938 | Dif./SD | SDUs | IQ points |
|---|---|---|---|---|---|
| 95 | 54 | 52 | – | – | – |
| 90 | 52 | 50 | – | – | – |
| 75 | 49 | 47 | – | – | – |
| 50 | 43 | 43 | 0/9.119 | 0.000 | 0.00 |
| 25 | 39 | 35 | 4/9.119 | 0.439 | 6.58 |
| 10 | 33 | 27 | 6/9.119 | 0.658 | 9.87 |
| 5 | 28 | 19 | 9/9.119 | 0.987 | 14.80 |

Average gain = 7.81 × 0.87 = 6.80 points
Rate: 6.80/41 = 0.166 points per year

Age: 13.5 years

| Percentiles | 1979 | 1938 | Dif./SD | SDUs | IQ points |
|---|---|---|---|---|---|
| 95 | 54 | 53 | – | – | – |
| 90 | 53 | 51 | – | – | – |
| 75 | 49 | 48 | – | – | – |
| 50 | 44 | 44 | 0/9.119 | 0.000 | 0.00 |
| 25 | 41 | 37 | 4/9.119 | 0.439 | 6.58 |
| 10 | 35 | 28 | 7/9.119 | 0.768 | 11.51 |
| 5 | 29 | 21 | 8/9.119 | 0.877 | 13.16 |

Average gain = 7.81 × 0.87 = 6.80 points
Rate: 6.80/41 = 0.166 points per year

Age: 14.0 years

| Percentiles | 1979 | 1938 | Dif./SD | SDUs | IQ points |
|---|---|---|---|---|---|
| 95 | 55 | 53 | – | – | – |
| 90 | 54 | 52 | – | – | – |
| 75 | 50 | 48 | – | – | – |
| 50 | 45 | 44 | 1/9.119 | 0.110 | 1.65 |
| 25 | 42 | 38 | 4/9.119 | 0.439 | 6.58 |
| 10 | 36 | 28 | 8/9.119 | 0.877 | 13.16 |
| 5 | 30 | 23 | 7/9.119 | 0.768 | 11.51 |

Average gain = 7.81 × 0.87 = 6.80 points
Rate: 6.80/41 = 0.166 points per year

## Comparing 1979 and 2008 (using SDs from 1979)

The same introduction (look back to comparing 1938 and 1979) applies here with a complication. In 2008, the new SPM PLUS was used and a table provided that allows one to translate the 1979 SPM scores into their 2008 SPM PLUS equivalents – or to do the reverse (2008 scores into 1979 scores). I decided to do both for each age group in turn. As we shall see, this allows a partial check on the reliability of the translation table.

Age: 7.5 years (2008 to 1979)

| Percentiles | 1979 | 2008 | Dif./SD | SDUs | IQ points |
|---|---|---|---|---|---|
| 95 | 37 | 41.5 | 4.5/7.903 | 0.569 | 8.54 |
| 90 | 35 | 39.8 | 4.8/7.903 | 0.607 | 9.11 |
| 75 | 30 | 35.5 | 5.5/7.903 | 0.696 | 10.44 |
| 50 | 22 | 30.5 | 8.5/7.903 | 1.076 | 16.13 |
| 25 | 15 | 24.5 | 9.5/7.903 | 1.202 | 18.03 |
| 10 | 12 | 18.4 | 6.4/7.903 | 0.810 | 12.15 |
| 5 | 11 | 14.5 | 3.5/7.903 | 0.443 | 6.64 |

Average gain = 11.31 points Rate: 11.31/29 = 0.390 points per year

The top vs. bottom half: 10.22 & 12.40

Note that from age 7.5 years on, gains over the bottom half are larger than gains over the top half. This contrasts with the pattern on Coloured Matrices (from 1982 to 2007) at age 7.25. However, the Coloured Matrices data yield no comparisons above that age, so no conflict can be assumed.

Age: 7.5 years (1979 to 2008)

| Percentiles | 1979 | 2008 | Dif./SD | SDUs | IQ points |
|---|---|---|---|---|---|
| 95 | 27.0 | 31.0 | 4.0/5.562 | 0.719 | 10.79 |
| 90 | 26.0 | 29.8 | 3.8/5.562 | 0.683 | 10.25 |
| 75 | 22.0 | 26.5 | 4.5/5.562 | 0.809 | 12.14 |
| 50 | 17.0 | 22.5 | 5.5/5.562 | 0.989 | 14.83 |
| 25 | 12.0 | 18.5 | 6.5/5.562 | 1.169 | 17.53 |
| 10 | 9.3 | 14.4 | 5.1/5.562 | 0.917 | 13.75 |
| 5 | 8.7 | 11.5 | 2.8/5.562 | 0.503 | 7.55 |

Average gain = 12.41 points Rate: 12.41/29 = 0.428 points per year

The top vs. bottom half: 11.70 & 13.12

Age: 8.5 years (2008 to 1979)

| Percentiles | 1979 | 2008 | Dif./SD | SDUs | IQ points |
|---|---|---|---|---|---|
| 95 | 42 | 47.5 | 5.5/8.815 | 0.624 | 9.36 |
| 90 | 40 | 45.2 | 5.2/8.815 | 0.590 | 8.85 |
| 75 | 36 | 40.5 | 4.5/8.815 | 0.510 | 7.66 |
| 50 | 31 | 35.5 | 4.5/8.815 | 0.510 | 7.66 |
| 25 | 22 | 30.5 | 8.5/8.815 | 0.964 | 14.46 |
| 10 | 16 | 24.4 | 8.4/8.815 | 0.953 | 14.29 |
| 5 | 13 | 19.0 | 6.0/8.815 | 0.681 | 10.21 |

Average gain = 10.11 points Rate: 10.11/29 = 0.349 points per year

The top vs. bottom half: 8.26 & 11.96

Age: 8.5 years (1979 to 2008)

| Percentiles | 1979 | 2008 | Dif./SD | SDUs | IQ points |
|---|---|---|---|---|---|
| 95 | 31 | 36.5 | 5.5/6.383 | 0.862 | 12.92 |
| 90 | 30 | 34.2 | 4.2/6.383 | 0.658 | 9.87 |
| 75 | 27 | 30.5 | 3.5/6.383 | 0.548 | 8.22 |
| 50 | 23 | 26.5 | 3.5/6.383 | 0.548 | 8.22 |
| 25 | 17 | 22.5 | 5.5/6.383 | 0.862 | 12.92 |
| 10 | 12 | 18.4 | 6.4/6.383 | 1.003 | 15.04 |
| 5 | 10 | 15.0 | 5.0/6.383 | 0.783 | 11.75 |

Average gain = 11.28 points Rate: 11.28/29 = 0.389 points per year

The top vs. bottom half: 10.19 & 12.37

Age: 9.5 years (2008 to 1979)

| Percentiles | 1979 | 2008 | Dif./SD | SDUs | IQ points |
|---|---|---|---|---|---|
| 95 | 46 | 48.0 | 2.0/9.422 | 0.212 | 3.18 |
| 90 | 44 | 46.3 | 2.3/9.422 | 0.244 | 3.66 |
| 75 | 41 | 44.0 | 3.0/9.422 | 0.318 | 4.78 |
| 50 | 36 | 40.5 | 4.5/9.422 | 0.478 | 7.16 |
| 25 | 28 | 35.5 | 7.5/9.422 | 0.796 | 11.94 |
| 10 | 19 | 28.4 | 9.4/9.422 | 0.998 | 14.96 |
| 5 | 15 | 23.5 | 8.5/9.422 | 0.902 | 13.53 |

Average gain = 8.46 points Rate: 8.46/29 = 0.292 points per year
Top & bottom half: 4.86 & 12.06

Suddenly, the ratio favors the bottom half of the curve by 0.40 to 1. But this is not due to a greater gain over the bottom half of the curve – the one for this age is typical of younger ages. It is entirely due to a drop of gains over the top half to 53 percent of that of younger ages. A possibility: 33 SPM PLUS score = 44 SPM score. Perhaps at this level and above, the conversion table should give SPM PLUS scores a higher equivalent.

Age: 9.5 years (1979 to 2008)

| Percentiles | 1979 | 2008 | Dif./SD | SDUs | IQ points |
|---|---|---|---|---|---|
| 95 | 35 | 37.0 | 2.0/6.991 | 0.286 | 4.29 |
| 90 | 33 | 35.3 | 2.3/6.991 | 0.329 | 4.93 |
| 75 | 31 | 33.0 | 2.0/6.991 | 0.286 | 4.29 |
| 50 | 27 | 30.5 | 3.5/6.991 | 0.501 | 7.51 |
| 25 | 21 | 26.5 | 5.5/6.991 | 0.787 | 11.80 |
| 10 | 15 | 21.4 | 6.4/6.991 | 0.915 | 13.73 |
| 5 | 12 | 18.0 | 6.0/6.991 | 0.858 | 12.87 |

Average gain = 8.49 points Rate: 8.49/29 = 0.293 points per year
Top & bottom half: 5.38 & 11.60

The ratio between top and bottom at this age is little affected by using the conversion table in reverse. Therefore, since a low ratio of upper half gains to lower half gains is favorable to a hypothesis I reject (the nutrition hypothesis), I will continue to count the upper half of the curve but with growing skepticism.

Age: 10.5 years (2008 to 1979)

| Percentiles | 1979 | 2008 | Dif./SD | SDUs | IQ points |
|---|---|---|---|---|---|
| 95 | 49 | 49.0 | 0.0/8.207 | 0.000 | 0.00 |
| 90 | 47 | 47.9 | 0.9/8.207 | 0.110 | 1.64 |
| 75 | 43 | 45.5 | 2.5/8.207 | 0.305 | 4.57 |
| 50 | 39 | 43.0 | 4.0/8.207 | 0.487 | 7.31 |
| 25 | 33 | 38.0 | 5.0/8.207 | 0.609 | 9.14 |
| 10 | 27 | 31.8 | 4.8/8.207 | 0.585 | 8.77 |
| 5 | 22 | 28.5 | 6.5/8.207 | 0.792 | 11.88 |

Average gain = 6.19 points Rate: 6.19/29 = 0.213 points per year

Top & bottom half: 3.24 & 9.14

The trend for the estimates to favor the bottom half of the curve accelerates.

Age: 10.5 years (1979 to 2008)

| Percentiles | 1979 | 2008 | Dif./SD | SDUs | IQ points |
|---|---|---|---|---|---|
| 95 | 38 | 38.0 | 0.0/6.383 | 0.000 | 0.00 |
| 90 | 36 | 36.9 | 0.9/6.383 | 0.141 | 2.11 |
| 75 | 32 | 34.5 | 2.5/6.383 | 0.392 | 5.87 |
| 50 | 29 | 32.0 | 3.0/6.383 | 0.470 | 7.05 |
| 25 | 25 | 28.0 | 3.0/6.383 | 0.470 | 7.05 |
| 10 | 20 | 23.8 | 3.8/6.383 | 0.595 | 8.93 |
| 5 | 17 | 21.5 | 4.5/6.383 | 0.705 | 10.57 |

Average gain = 5.94 points Rate: 5.94/29 = 0.205 points per year

Top & bottom half: 3.62 & 8.26

The reverse conversion reduces the ratio between top and bottom by a bit.

Age: 11.5 years (2008 to 1979)

| Percentiles | 1979 | 2008 | Dif./SD | SDUs | IQ points |
|---|---|---|---|---|---|
| 95 | 51 | 49.0 | −2.0/7.903 | −0.253 | −3.80 |
| 90 | 49 | 47.9 | −1.1/7−903 | −0.139 | −2.09 |
| 75 | 45 | 46.0 | 1.0/7.903 | 0.127 | 1.90 |
| 50 | 41 | 43.5 | 2.5/7.903 | 0.316 | 4.75 |
| 25 | 36 | 38.0 | 2.0/7.903 | 0.253 | 3.80 |
| 10 | 31 | 31.8 | 0.8/7.903 | 0.101 | 1.52 |
| 5 | 25 | 28.5 | 3.5/7.903 | 0.443 | 6.64 |

Average gain = 1.55 IQ points Rate: 1.55/29 = 0.053 points per year

Top & bottom half: −0.45 & 3.55

It seems incredible that 11.5-year-olds in 2008 score hardly better than 10.5-year-olds.

Age: 11.5 years (1979 to 2008)

| Percentiles | 1979 | 2008 | Dif./SD | SDUs | IQ points |
|---|---|---|---|---|---|
| 95 | 40.5 | 38.0 | −2.5/6.535 | −0.383 | −5.74 |
| 90 | 38.0 | 36.9 | −1.1/6.535 | −0.168 | −2.52 |
| 75 | 34.0 | 35.0 | 1.0/6.535 | 0.153 | 2.30 |
| 50 | 31.0 | 32.5 | 1.5/6.535 | 0.230 | 3.44 |
| 25 | 27.0 | 28.0 | 1.0/6.535 | 0.153 | 2.30 |
| 10 | 23.0 | 23.8 | 0.8/6.535 | 0.122 | 1.84 |
| 5 | 19.0 | 21.5 | 2.5/6.535 | 0.383 | 5.74 |

Average gain = 1.05 IQ points Rate: 1.05/29 = 0.036 points per year

Top & bottom half: −0.93 & 3.03

Suddenly this cohort seems to have had little "nutritional advantage." Was there some huge downturn in nutrition between those born in 1967–68 (11.5-year-olds) and those born in 1971–72 (7.5-year-olds) worth over 10 IQ points?

Age: 12.5 years (2008 to 1979)

| Percentiles | 1979 | 2008 | Dif./SD | SDUs | IQ points |
|---|---|---|---|---|---|
| 95 | 53 | 51.5 | −1.5/7.903 | −0.190 | −2.85 |
| 90 | 51 | 50.3 | −0.7/7.903 | −0.089 | −1.33 |
| 75 | 47 | 47.5 | 0.5/7.903 | 0.063 | 0.95 |
| 50 | 42 | 44.0 | 2.0/7.903 | 0.253 | 3.80 |
| 25 | 38 | 40.5 | 2.5/7.903 | 0.352 | 5.29 |
| 10 | 32 | 34.9 | 2.9/7.903 | 0.367 | 5.50 |
| 5 | 27 | 31.5 | 4.5/7.903 | 0.569 | 8.54 |

Average gain = 2.84 IQ points　　Rate: 2.84/29 = 0.098 points per year

Top & bottom half: 0.02 & 5.66

Age: 12.5 years (1979 to 2008)

| Percentiles | 1979 | 2008 | Dif/SD | SDUs | IQ points |
|---|---|---|---|---|---|
| 95 | 43.5 | 41.5 | −2.0/7.143 | −0.280 | −4.20 |
| 90 | 40.5 | 39.3 | −1.2/7.143 | −0.168 | −2.52 |
| 75 | 36.0 | 36.5 | 0.5/7.143 | 0.070 | 1.05 |
| 50 | 31.0 | 33.0 | 2.0/7.143 | 0.280 | 4.20 |
| 25 | 28.0 | 30.5 | 2.5/7.143 | 0.350 | 5.25 |
| 10 | 24.0 | 25.9 | 1.9/7.143 | 0.266 | 3.99 |
| 5 | 20.0 | 23.5 | 3.5/7.143 | 0.490 | 7.35 |

Average gain = 2.16 IQ points　　Rate: 2.16/29 = 0.074 points per year

Top & bottom half: −0.62 & 4.94

Age: 13.5 years (2008 to 1979)

| Percentiles | 1979 | 2008 | Dif./SD | SDUs | IQ points |
|---|---|---|---|---|---|
| 95 | 54 | 51.5 | −2.5/7.599 | −0.329 | −4.93 |
| 90 | 53 | 50.9 | −1.1/7.599 | −0.145 | −2.17 |
| 75 | 49 | 48.5 | −0.5/7.599 | −0.066 | −0.99 |
| 50 | 44 | 45.5 | 1.5/7.599 | 0.197 | 2.96 |
| 25 | 41 | 42.5 | 1.5/7.599 | 0.197 | 2.96 |
| 10 | 35 | 38.7 | 3.7/7.599 | 0.487 | 7.30 |
| 5 | 29 | 35.0 | 6.0/7.599 | 0.790 | 11.84 |

Average gain = 2.42 IQ points Rate: 2.42/29 = 0.084 points per year

Top & bottom half: −1.35 & 6.19

Age: 13.5 years (1979 to 2008)

| Percentiles | 1979 | 2008 | Dif./SD | SDUs | IQ points |
|---|---|---|---|---|---|
| 95 | 45.0 | 41.5 | −3.5/6.991 | −0.501 | −7.51 |
| 90 | 43.5 | 39.9 | −3.6/6.991 | −0.515 | −7.72 |
| 75 | 38.0 | 37.5 | −0.5/6.991 | −0.072 | −1.07 |
| 50 | 33.0 | 34.5 | 1.5/6.991 | 0.215 | 3.22 |
| 25 | 31.5 | 31.5 | 0.0/6.991 | 0.000 | 0.00 |
| 10 | 26.0 | 28.7 | 2.7/6.991 | 0.386 | 5.79 |
| 5 | 22.0 | 26.0 | 4.0/6.991 | 0.572 | 8.58 |

Average gain = −0.12 IQ points Rate: −0.12/29 = −0.004 points per year

Top & bottom half: −4.22 & 3.98

The reverse conversion gives us a cohort where there was a redistribution of food from the upper to the lower classes.

Age: 14.5 years (2008 to 1979)

| Percentiles | 1979 | 2008 | Dif./SD | SDUs | IQ points |
|---|---|---|---|---|---|
| 95 | 56 | 51.5 | −4.5/6.991 | −0.644 | −9.66 |
| 90 | 54 | 50.9 | −3.1/6.991 | −0.443 | −6.65 |
| 75 | 50 | 48.5 | −1.5/6.991 | −0.215 | −3.22 |
| 50 | 46 | 45.5 | −0.5/6.991 | −0.072 | −1.07 |
| 25 | 42 | 42.5 | 0.5/6.991 | 0.072 | 1.07 |
| 10 | 36 | 38.7 | 2.7/6.991 | 0.386 | 5.79 |
| 5 | 33 | 35.0 | 2.0/6.991 | 0.286 | 4.29 |

Average gain = −1.35 IQ points  Rate: −1.35/29 = −0.047 points per year

Top & bottom half: −5.185 & 2.485

The nonreverse conversion adds another "redistributive" cohort and a radical deterioration in the nutrition of the upper classes.

Age: 14.5 years (1979 to 2008)

| Percentiles | 1979 | 2008 | Dif./SD | SDUs | IQ points |
|---|---|---|---|---|---|
| 95 | 48.5 | 41.5 | -7.0/7.143 | −0.980 | −14.70 |
| 90 | 45.0 | 39.9 | −5.1/7.143 | −0.714 | −10.71 |
| 75 | 39.0 | 37.5 | −1.5/7.143 | −0.210 | −3.15 |
| 50 | 35.0 | 34.5 | −0.5/7.143 | −0.070 | −1.05 |
| 25 | 31.0 | 31.5 | 0.5/7.143 | 0.070 | 1.05 |
| 10 | 27.0 | 28.7 | 1.7/7.143 | 0.238 | 3.57 |
| 5 | 25.0 | 26.0 | 1.0/7.143 | 0.140 | 2.10 |

Average gain = −3.12 IQ points  Rate: −3.12/29 = −0.108 points per year

Top & bottom half: -7.40 & 1.16

The reverse conversion lessens "redistribution" but shows an even more radical deterioration in the nutrition of the upper classes.

Age: 15.5 years (2008 to 1979)

| Percentiles | 1979 | 2008 | Dif./SD | SDUs | IQ points |
|---|---|---|---|---|---|
| 95 | 57 | 53.0 | −4.0/7.295 | −0.548 | −8.22 |
| 90 | 55 | 51.8 | −3.2/7.295 | −0.439 | −6.58 |
| 75 | 51 | 50.0 | −1.0/7.295 | −0.137 | −2.06 |
| 50 | 47 | 46.5 | −0.5/7.295 | −0.069 | −1.03 |
| 25 | 42 | 43.5 | 1.5/7.295 | 0.206 | 3.08 |
| 10 | 36 | 38.8 | 2.8/7.295 | 0.384 | 5.76 |
| 5 | 33 | 35.5 | 2.5/7.295 | 0.343 | 5.14 |

Average gain = −0.56 IQ points Rate: −0.56/29 = −0.019 points per year

Top & bottom half: −4.41 & 3.29

Yet again, the nonreverse conversion adds another "redistributive" cohort and a radical deterioration in the nutrition of the upper classes.

Age: 15.5 years (1979 to 2008)

| Percentiles | 1979 | 2008 | Dif./SD | SDUs | IQ points |
|---|---|---|---|---|---|
| 95 | 50.5 | 43.5 | −7.0/7.751 | −0.903 | −13.55 |
| 90 | 46.5 | 41.8 | −4.7/7.751 | −0.606 | −9.10 |
| 75 | 40.5 | 39.0 | −1.5/7.751 | −0.194 | −2.90 |
| 50 | 36.0 | 35.5 | −0.5/7.751 | −0.065 | −0.97 |
| 25 | 31.0 | 32.5 | 1.5/7.751 | 0.194 | 2.90 |
| 10 | 27.0 | 28.8 | 1.8/7.751 | 0.232 | 3.48 |
| 5 | 25.0 | 26.5 | 1.5/7.751 | 0.194 | 2.90 |

Average gain = −2.46 IQ points Rate: −2.46/29 = −0.085 points per year

Top & bottom half: −6.81 & 1.89

And yet again, the reverse conversion lessens "redistribution" but shows an even more radical deterioration in the nutrition of the upper classes.

An interlude: Given its role, it is worth testing the reliability of the conversion table, the table that converts the Raven's PLUS scores of 2008 into equivalent scores on the Raven's Progressive Matrices used in earlier years. A partial test is that it should give consistent results when one compares the two conversions (1979 to 2008 scores; and 2008 to 1979 scores). This is very nearly the case as will emerge in the following discussion.

The conversion table gives Raven's scores from 30 to 42 the equivalents of 22 to 31 on Raven's PLUS. A preliminary comparison of the age tables in which both conversions were used made me suspect that it should be 21.5 to 30.5. In sum, I suspect Raven's PLUS scores should get not a bonus of 8 rising to 11 points (as the table gives), but rather a bonus of 8.5 rising to 11.5 points. But within that score range ONLY. This would iron out the discrepancies I found when using the conversion table both ways.

(1) Assume I am correct. Then converting Raven's (1979) to R+ (2008) scores will inflate gains over the top half of the curve compared to the bottom half (too generous); and converting R+ (2008) to R scores (1979) will deflate gains over the top half compared to the bottom half (too miserly).

(2) A difference of 0.5 raw score points added/subtracted to/from the top half is equivalent to about 1 IQ point (SD = 7.5). So as an experiment, let us alter a data set (8.5 years old) whose 1979 scores are entirely within the range that is suspect. The alteration: the 2008–1979 conversion gets 1 point added to its gains for the top four percentile groups; and the 1979–2008 conversion gets 1 point deducted, so:

| | 2008–1979 adjusted | 1979–2008 adjusted | Averaging the two (whether adjusted or not) |
|---|---|---|---|
| Percentiles | Gain IQ points | Gain IQ points | Gain IQ points |
| 95 | 10.36 | 11.92 | 11.14 |
| 90 | 9.85 | 8.87 | 9.36 |
| 75 | 6.96 | 7.22 | 7.09 |
| 50 | 8.66 | 7.22 | 7.94 |
| 25 | 14.46 | 12.92 | 13.69 |
| 10 | 14.29 | 15.04 | 14.66 |
| 5 | 10.21 | 11.75 | 10.98 |
| Ave. gain | 10.68 | 10.71 | 10.70 |
| Top gain | 9.21 | 9.25 | 9.23 |
| Bot. gain | 12.15 | 12.17 | 12.16 |
| Top–Bot. | −2.94 | −2.92 | −2.93 |

(3) The adjustment brings the comparisons of the top and bottom halves of the curves nicely into line and all values are now within about 1.5 points. There is nothing to choose between the two conversions, so I average them. For example:

15.5-year-olds from the SPM (see above) give two sets of values:

| | | | |
|---|---|---|---|
| 2008–1979: | −0.56 (overall) | −4.41 (top) | +3.29 (bot.) |
| 1979–2008: | −2.46 (overall) | −6.81(top) | +1.89 (bot.) |
| Average: | −1.51(overall) | −5.61 (top) | +2.59 (bot.) |

The last values are those you will find in Table AI6.

Box 9 in Chapter 3 shows that when the CPM and the SPM are compared over the ages they have in common, results from the two tests roughly tally. This is demonstrated in Table AI7, which reproduces the relevant age groups from Tables AI5 and AI6.

Table AI7 CPM and SPM IQ gains by age in Britain when the two tests are compared over the same ages and roughly the same periods

| Ages | 7.0 | 7.5 | 8.0 | 8.5 | 9.0 | 9.5 | 10.0 | 10.5 | 11.0 | Ave. | Rate |
|---|---|---|---|---|---|---|---|---|---|---|---|
| *Coloured Progressive Matrices* | | | | | | | | | | | |
| 1947–1982 | 5.73 | 7.83 | 9.40 | 8.11 | 6.41 | 4.70 | 5.69 | 5.69 | 5.46 | 6.56 | 0.187/yr. |
| 1982–2007 | | 10.89 | 14.53 | 13.58 | 11.22 | 8.22 | 6.37 | 5.46 | 6.37 | 9.58 | 0.382/yr. |
| *Raven's Progressive Matrices* | | | | | | | | | | | |
| 1938–1979 | – | – | 9.69 | 10.89 | 10.20 | 9.33 | 9.21 | 11.68 | 12.08 | 10.44 | 0.255/yr. |
| 1979–2008 | – | 11.86 | – | 10.70 | – | 8.48 | – | 6.07 | – | 9.28 | 0.320/yr. |

Box 10 in Chapter 3 merges the CPM and SPM data to get gaps between the gains over the top and bottom halves of the curve by birth date. The first step is to calculate Table AI8, which gives merged results by age and time of testing (see page 232).

The gap between the top and bottom halves is the difference between the rates per year times the number of years: 0.255 – 0.073 = 0.182; 0.182 × 37 years = a gap of 6.734 points.

The other values in Box 10 are derived in the same way and they are repeated here for convenience.

**Box 10**

This box shows how much the gap between the top and bottom halves closed or widened between those born in certain years. A –sign means the gap closed, a + sign means it widened.

| Ages | | | Born | Top/Bot. Gap |
|---|---|---|---|---|
| **Rates 1943–1980** | | | | |
| 5.5–8.25 | 0.255 (top half) | 0.073 (bot. half) | 1936 & 1973 | +6.7 pts. |
| 9.25 | 0.208 (top half) | 0.200 (bot. half) | 1934 & 1971 | +0.3 pts. |
| 10.25 | 0.193 (top half) | 0.227 (bot. half) | 1933 & 1970 | –1.3 pts. |
| 11.21–12.37 | lower (top half) | higher (bot. half) | 1932 & 1969 | (closed) |
| **Rates 1980–2008** | | | | |
| 5.5–6.25 | 0.513 (top half) | 0.352 (bot. half) | 1974 & 2002 | +4.5 pts. |
| 7.37 | 0.430 (top half) | 0.416 (bot. half) | 1973 & 2001 | +0.4 pts. |
| 8.25 | 0.318 (top half) | 0.488 (bot. half) | 1972 & 2000 | –4.8 pts. |
| 9.25–15.5 | –0.035 (top half) | 0.206 (bot. half) | 1968 & 1996 | –6.7 pts. |

Table AI8 Raven's gains by age from 1943 to 2008 (CPM & SPM merged) (gains over top and bottom halves of the curve compared wherever possible)

| | Rate 1943–1980 | | | Rate 1980–2008 | | | Rate 1943–2008 | | | Average IQ gains | | |
|---|---|---|---|---|---|---|---|---|---|---|---|---|
| Age | Ave. | Top | Bot. | Ave. | Top | Bot. | Ave. | Top | Bot. | 1943–1980 | 1980–2008 | 1943–2008 |
| 5.50 | .144 | .252 | .036 | .413 | .468 | .358 | .260 | .345 | .175 | 5.33 | 11.56 | 16.89 |
| 6.25 | .101 | .188 | .013 | .451 | .557 | .346 | .252 | .347 | .156 | 3.74 | 12.63 | 16.37 |
| 7.37 | .194 | .286 | .101 | .423 | .430 | .416 | .293 | .376 | .237 | 7.18 | 11.84 | 19.02 |
| 8.25 | .252 | .293 | .143 | .454 | .318 | .488 | .354 | .304 | .292 | 9.32 | 13.66 | 22.98 |
| 9.25 | .206 | .208 | .200 | .335 | .177 | .402 | .262 | .195 | .287 | 7.62 | 9.38 | 17.00 |
| 10.25 | .217 | .193 | .227 | .222 | .118 | .274 | .219 | .161 | .247 | 8.03 | 6.22 | 14.25 |
| 11.21 | .233 | – | .258 | .135 | –.024 | .255 | .191 | – | .257 | 8.62 | 3.78 | 12.40 |
| 12.37 | .209 | – | .241 | .086 | –.010 | .183 | .156 | – | .216 | 7.73 | 2.41 | 10.14 |
| 13.33 | .166 | – | .166 | .040 | –.096 | .176 | .112 | – | .170 | 6.14 | 1.12 | 7.26 |
| 14.25 | .166 | – | .166 | –.077 | –.217 | .063 | .061 | – | .122 | 6.14 | –2.16 | 3.98 |
| 15.50 | – | – | – | –.052 | –.193 | .089 | – | – | – | – | –1.92 | – |
| All | .189 | – | .155 | .221 | .139 | .277 | .216 | – | .216 | 6.99 | 6.23 | 14.03 |

*Notes:*
(1) See below under step 3 as to how the CPM and SPM results were merged.

(2) Averaging top and bottom will not always give the average for the whole curve. At some ages, all data sets gave results for all of these categories; but at other ages, one or more gave none for at least one category. The blanks designate where either data was missing or was inadequate to give an estimate.

(3) Pro-rating the rates for the two periods 1943–80 and 1980–2008 does not quite give the rate of gain for the whole 65 years – because the latter omits the 15.5-year-olds that appear in the second period but not in the first. For the same reason, adding the gains of the two periods is less than the total gain for the whole 65 years. If you drop the loss for 15.5-year-olds for 1980–2008, you will get the right total. A dummy value for that age of 6.38 gives: 6.93 + 6.23 = 13.16.

The second step is to derive the summary results in Box 10 from the above table. For example, ages 5.50 to 8.25 all show a clear advantage in favor of gains over the top half of the curve. Therefore, they have been averaged to give: 5.5–8.25 (ages); 0.255 (top); 0.073 (bot.).

The median age is 7 so this has been subtracted from 1943 to get a birth date of 1936; and it has been subtracted from 1980 to get a birth date of 1973. Thus the first line of Box 10 in the text:

5.5–8.25 (ages) 0.255 (top half) 0.073 (bot. half) 1936 & 1973 (born).

The third step is to show how the merged results in Table AI8 (merged CPM & SPM) were derived from Tables AI5 (CPM) and AI6 (SPM). The two earlier periods are 1947 to 1982 (CPM) and 1938 to 1979 (SPM) respectively, so I grouped them as applying to approximately 1943 to 1980. The two later periods are 1982 to 2007 (CPM) and 1979 to 2008 (SPM), which became 1980 to 2008. For each age, I average the CPM results. For example: I average the gains for ages 8 and 8.5 to get a value for age 8.25. Then I average the SPM results in the same way. Finally, after pro-rating them both, I average the two, which gives an overall value for each age.

As an example of merging for the "period" 1943 to 1980:

(1) From Table AI5, note the CPM overall gains for age 8 (9.40 points) and age 8.5 (8.11 points). These average at 8.755 for "age" 8.25.
(2) From Table AI6, note the SPM overall gains for age 8 (9.69 points) and age 8.5 (10.89 points). These average at 10.29 points for age 8.25.
(3) Now to pro-rate:

The CPM gains cover 35 years, so 35 × 8.755 = 306.425.
The SPM gains cover 41 years, so 41 × 10.29 = 421.89.
Add the two products; 306.425 + 421.89 = 728.315

Table AI9 Normative data for the SPM PLUS 2008

| Age in years | 7.5 | 8.5 | 9.5 | 10.5 | 11.5 | 12.5 | 13.5 | 14.5 | 15.5 |
|---|---|---|---|---|---|---|---|---|---|
| 95 | 31.0 | 36.5 | 37.0 | 38.0 | 38.0 | 41.5 | 41.5 | 41.5 | 43.5 |
| 90 | 29.8 | 34.2 | 35.3 | 36.9 | 36.9 | 39.3 | 39.9 | 39.9 | 41.8 |
| 75 | 26.5 | 30.5 | 33.0 | 34.5 | 35.0 | 36.5 | 37.5 | 37.5 | 39.0 |
| 50 | 22.5 | 26.5 | 30.5 | 32.0 | 32.5 | 33.0 | 34.5 | 34.5 | 35.5 |
| 25 | 18.5 | 22.5 | 26.5 | 28.0 | 28.0 | 30.5 | 31.5 | 31.5 | 32.5 |
| 10 | 14.4 | 18.4 | 21.4 | 23.8 | 23.8 | 25.9 | 28.7 | 28.7 | 28.8 |
| 5 | 11.5 | 15.0 | 18.0 | 21.5 | 21.5 | 23.5 | 26.0 | 26.0 | 26.5 |

Divide by the sum of the two periods (76): 728.315 divided by 76 = 9.583

Divide by the average of the two periods (38): 9.583 divided by 38 = 0.252 as the rate of gain of the merged data.

(4) In Table AI8, under age 8.25, average gain (earlier period), you will see 0.252.

Other promised tables from Chapter 3. The published normative data from the 2008 standardization the SPM PLUS are not given in a convenient form. Therefore, I offer a conventional Raven's presentation by age and percentile (Table AI9).

Finally, I promised a more detailed account of how the pattern of Raven's gains in Britain cannot be squared with a coherent nutritional history of Britain. It uses merged data organized by birth date to show how the IQ gaps between the top and bottom halves of the curve have been wildly fluctuating, which means of course that any nutritional history that tried to explain them would be equally chaotic (Table AI10).

Table AI10 A dietary history of Britain from 1925 to 1977

| Year | Upper class | Lower class | Class gap |
|---|---|---|---|
| 1925 | unknown | hugely worse | unknown |
| 1926 | unknown | hugely worse | unknown |
| 1927 | unknown | massively worse | unknown |
| 1928 | unknown | massively worse | unknown |
| 1929 | hugely worse | massively worse | greater |
| 1930 | massively worse | unknown | unknown |
| (1931–35) | NO DATA | | |
| 1936 | unknown | hugely worse | unknown |
| 1937 | unknown | hugely worse | unknown |
| 1938 | unknown | hugely worse | unknown |
| 1939 | unknown | massively worse | unknown |
| 1940 | massively worse | hugely worse | less |
| 1941 | massively worse | much worse | less |
| 1942 | massively worse | hugely worse | less |
| (1943–63) | NO DATA | | |
| 1964 | much better | worse | greater |
| 1965 | much better | comparable | greater |
| 1966 | better | much worse | greater |
| 1967 | comparable | much worse | greater |
| 1968 | comparable | worse | greater |
| 1969 | worse | much worse | greater |
| 1970 | much worse | hugely worse | greater |
| 1971 | much worse | hugely worse | greater |
| 1972 | hugely worse | hugely worse | same |
| 1973 | unknown | hugely/much worse | unknown |
| 1974 | unknown | hugely worse | unknown |
| 1975 | hugely worse | much worse | less |
| 1976 | hugely worse | much worse | less |
| 1977 | hugely worse | much worse | less |

*Criteria for labels*

| | |
|---|---|
| Massively worse: | a deficit of 15.0–25.0 IQ points |
| Hugely worse: | a deficit of 10.0–14.9 IQ points |
| Much worse: | a deficit of 5.0–9.9 points |
| Worse: | a deficit of 2.1–4.9 points |
| Comparable: | a deficit of 2 points to an advantage of 2 points |
| Better: | an advantage of 2.1 –4.9 points |
| Much better: | an advantage of 5.0 –9.9 points |

# Appendix II: Tables and comments relevant to capital cases and comparing the WAIS-III IQs of various nations (see Chapter 4)

Box 13 in Chapter 4 gives estimates for American IQ gains for 14 periods all post-1972. It is derived from Table AII1.

This table is useful for analyzing whether the norms of a given test seem eccentric. For example, if a test has substandard norms, it will inflate estimates when paired with a later test and deflate estimates when paired with an earlier test.

Use the Ideal vs. real column to assess the WAIS-III: (1) it is paired with a later test in (1), (3), and (7) and these show deviations of 3.70, 1.07, and 0.07 toward too many points gained; (2) it is paired with an earlier test in (9) and (14) and these show deviations of 0.90 and 2.50 toward too few points gained; (3) the sum of the deviations is 8.24 and divided by 5 equals 1.65, as the number of points by which the WAIS-III inflated IQ scores even at the time it was standardized.

Box 15 in Chapter 4 gives American IQ gains for both the WISC and WAIS from one standardization sample to the next. It is derived from Tables AII2 and AII3.

Box 16 in Chapter 4 adjusts the results from Roivainen (2009) to get comparisons between European nations and America on the WAIS-III. She used the raw score performances of these nations and the US WAIS-III norms to derive IQs, with an IQ above 100 showing that the nation has surpassed the US performance, and

Table AII1 Fourteen estimates of recent IQ gains over time

| Tests compared | Gains | Period (years) | Rate | Ideal gain | Ideal vs. real |
|---|---|---|---|---|---|
| (1) WAIS-III (1995) & SB-5 (2001) | +5.50 | 6 | +0.917 | 1.80 | 3.70 |
| (2) WAIS-R (1978) & SB-4 (1985) | +3.42 | 7 | +0.489 | 2.10 | 1.32 |
| (3) WAIS-III (1995) & WISC-IV (2001.75) | +3.10 | 6.75 | +0.459 | 2.03 | 1.07 |
| (4) WISC-III (1989) & SB-5 (2001) | +5.00 | 12 | +0.417 | 3.60 | 1.40 |
| **(5) WISC-III (1989) & WISC-IV (2001.75)** | +4.23 | 12.75 | **+0.332** | 3.83 | **0.40** |
| **(6) WISC-R (1972) & WISC-III (1989)** | +5.30 | 17 | **+0.312** | 5.10 | **0.20** |
| **(7) WAIS-III (1995) & WAIS-IV (2006)** | +3.37 | 11 | **+0.306** | 3.30 | **0.07** |
| (8) WISC-IV (2001.75) & WAIS-IV (2006) | +1.20 | 4.25 | +0.282 | 1.28 | 0.08 |
| **(9) WAIS-R (1978) & WAIS-III (1995)** | +4.20 | 17 | **+0.247** | 5.10 | **0.90** |
| (10) WISC-R (1972) & SB-4 (1985) | +2.95 | 13 | +0.227 | 3.90 | 0.95 |
| (11) SB-4 (1985) & SB-5 (2001) | +2.77 | 16 | +0.173 | 4.80 | 2.03 |
| (12) SB-LM (1972) & SB-4 (1985) | +2.16 | 13 | +0.166 | 3.90 | 1.74 |
| (13) WISC-R (1972) & WAIS-R (1978) | +0.90 | 6 | +0.150 | 1.80 | 0.90 |
| (14) WISC-III (1989) & WAIS-III (1995) | −0.70 | 6 | −0.117 | 1.80 | 2.50 |

| | | |
|---|---|---|
| Average of all 14 comparisons | +0.311 | 1.23 |
| Average of 4 WISC/WISC & WAIS/WAIS comparisons | **+0.299** | **0.39** |

*Test names and sources:*

(1) Wechsler Adult Intelligence Scale – 3rd edn. & Stanford–Binet 5: Roid (2003), Table 4.7.

(2) WAIS – Revised & SB-4: Thorndike *et al.* (1986), Table 6.9.

(3) WAIS-III & Wechsler Intelligence Scale for Children – 4th edn.: Wechsler (2003), Table 5.12.

(4) WISC – 3rd edn. & SB-5: Roid (2003), Table 4.6.

(5) WISC-III & WISC-III/IV (see Flynn & Weiss, 2007). The estimate given is the mid-point of the range of estimates for this pair of tests.

(6) WISC – Revised & WISC-III: Flynn (1998c), Table 1.

(7) WAIS-III & WAIS-IV: Wechsler (2008a), Table 5.5 (see Chapter 4 for detail).

(8) WISC-IV & WAIS-IV: Wechsler (2008a), Table 5.9.

(9) WAIS-R & WAIS-III: Wechsler (1997a), Table 4.

(10) WISC-R & SB-4: Thorndike *et al.* (1986), Table 6.7.

(11) SB-4 & SB-5: Roid (2003), Table 4.1.

(12) Stanford–Binet LM & SB-4: Thorndike *et al.* (1986), Table 6.6.

(13) WISC-R & WAIS-R: Wechsler (1981), Table 18.

(14) WISC-III & WAIS-III: Wechsler (1997a), Table 4.3.

*Note:* Stanford–Binet SDs of 16 must be allowed for in estimating gains.

Table AII2 Gains from the WAIS (1953–54) to WAIS-R (1978) to WAIS-III (1995) to WAIS-IV (2006)

| Subtest | W | W-R | Gain | W-R | W-III | Gain | W-III | W-IV | Gain | TG |
|---|---|---|---|---|---|---|---|---|---|---|
| Vocabulary | 11.9 | 10.1 | 1.8 | 10.8 | 10.2 | 0.6 | 11.0 | 10.0 | 1.0 | 3.4 |
| Similarities | 11.9 | 9.7 | 2.2 | 11.3 | 10.4 | 0.9 | 11.0 | 10.3 | 0.7 | 3.8 |
| Arithmetic | 11.3 | 10.3 | 1.0 | 10.1 | 10.4 | −0.3 | 9.7 | 9.7 | 0.0 | 0.7 |
| Digit span | 10.4 | 9.8 | 0.6 | 10.4 | 10.3 | 0.1 | 10.4 | 10.1 | 0.3 | 1.0 |
| Information | 11.4 | 10.3 | 1.1 | 10.5 | 10.5 | 0.0 | 10.4 | 9.9 | 0.5 | 1.6 |
| Comprehension | 12.0 | 10.2 | 1.8 | 11.0 | 10.5 | 0.5 | 10.5 | 10.1 | 0.4 | 2.7 |
| Pict. completion | 11.2 | 9.4 | 1.8 | 11.1 | 10.7 | 0.4 | 10.6 | 9.7 | 0.9 | 3.1 |
| DS-Coding | 11.6 | 9.8 | 1.8 | 11.8 | 10.6 | 1.2 | 10.0 | 9.8 | 0.2 | 3.2 |
| Block design | 10.9 | 9.9 | 1.0 | 11.4 | 10.7 | 0.7 | 10.5 | 10.2 | 0.3 | 2.0 |
| Pict. arrangement | 11.1 | 10.3 | 0.8 | 11.1 | 10.5 | 0.6 | 10.6 | 9.7 | 0.9 | 2.3 |
| Object assembly | 11.5 | 10.2 | 1.3 | 11.3 | 10.4 | 0.9 | – | – | – | – |
| Matrix reasoning | – | – | – | – | – | – | 10.9 | 10.3 | 0.6 | – |
| Sum SS | 125.2 | 110.0 | 15.2 | 120.8 | 115.2 | 5.6 | 115.6 | 109.8 | 5.8 | |

Full Scale IQ gains:

(1) Comparing 111.3 (WAIS) & 103.8 (WAIS-R) = 7.5/24.5 years = 0.306

(2) Comparing 105.8 (WAIS-R) & 101.6 (WAIS-III) = 4.2/17 years = 0.247

(3) Comparing 102.9 (WAIS-III) & 99.53 (WAIS-IV) = 3.37/11years = 0.306

Average rate from 1953–54 to 2006: 15.07/52.5 = 0.287 IQ points per year

Examples of calculations for WAIS-R and WAIS-III at ages 20 to 34

(1) Ages 20–24: WAIS-R SS = 120.8 = IQ 106.8; WAIS-III SS = 115.2 = IQ 102.2 (Wechsler, 1981, p. 97). Difference = 4.6 IQ points.

(2) Ages 25–34: WAIS-R SS = 120.8 = IQ 103.8; WAIS-III SS = 115.2 = IQ 100.2 (Wechsler, 1981. p. 99). Difference = 3.6 IQ points – and so forth.

Calculations for WAIS-III and WAIS-IV – all ages (Wechsler, 1997a, pp. 197–198)

(1) The conversions that surround (+/−10 points) the WAIS-IV raw score total of 109.8 are 100SS = 94IQ and 120SS = 105IQ. Therefore, a range of 20SS = 11 IQ points. 9.8/20 = 0.49 × 11 = 5.39 IQ points; and 94.0 + 5.39 = **99.39** as WAIS-IV IQ.

(2) The conversions that surround (+/−10 points) the WAIS-III raw score total of 115.6 are 106SS = 97IQ and 126SS = 109IQ. Therefore, a range of 20SS = 12 IQ points. 9.6/20 = 0.48 × 12 = 5.76 IQ points; and 97 + 5.76 = **102.76** as WAIS-III IQ.

(3) Difference 102.76 – 99.39 = 3.37 as the gain over 11 years.

Notes to Table AII2 (cont.)

(4) The actual WAIS-III mean (Wechsler, 2008a) is 102.9, so we have come gratifyingly close! Since that is an actual mean and our WAIS-IV estimate is eccentric in carrying over WISC-III subtests (and scoring vs. the WAIS-III tables), we will subtract the difference from the WAIS-III mean to get our simulated later performance: 102.90 – 3.37 = 99.53 as "WAIS-IV" mean.

Table AII3 WISC subtest and Full Scale IQ gains: 1947.5 to 2001.75

| | WISC to WISC-R (1947.5–72) | WISC-R to WISC-III (1972–89) | WISC-III to WISC-IV (1989–2001.75) | WISC to WISC-IV (1947.5–2001.75) | WISC to WISC-IV (1947.5–2001.75) |
|---|---|---|---|---|---|
| | Gain 24.5 yrs. (SD = 3) | Gain 17 yrs. (SD = 3) | Gain 12.75 yrs. (SD = 3) | Gain 54.25 yrs. (SD = 3) | IQ Gain 54.25 yrs. (SD = 15) |
| Information | 0.43 | −0.3 | 0.3 | 0.43 | 2.15 |
| Arithmetic | 0.36 | 0.3 | −0.2 | 0.46 | 2.30 |
| Vocabulary | 0.38 | 0.4 | 0.1 | 0.88 | 4.40 |
| Comprehension | 1.20 | 0.6 | 0.4 | 2.20 | 11.00 |
| Picture completion | 0.74 | 0.9 | 0.7 | 2.34 | 11.70 |
| Block design | 1.28 | 0.9 | 1.0 | 3.18 | 15.90 |
| Object assembly | 1.34 | 1.2 | [0.93] | [3.47] | [17.35] |
| Coding | 2.20 | 0.7 | 0.7 | 3.60 | 18.00 |
| Picture arrangement | 0.93 | 1.9 | [1.47] | [4.30] | [21.50] |
| Similarities | 2.77 | 1.3 | 0.7 | 4.77 | 23.85 |
| SUM[a] | 11.63 | 7.9 | 6.1 | 25.63 | |
| SUM[b] | 11.63 | 7.9 | 5.3 | 24.83 | |

Table AII3 (*cont.*)

| | Subtest Sums | Full Scale IQ | Gain | Rate/year |
|---|---|---|---|---|
| WISC | 100.00 | 100.00 | – | – |
| WISC-R | 111.63 | 107.63 | 7.63 | 0.311 |
| WISC-III | 119.53 | 113.00 | 5.47 | 0.322 |
| WISC-IV[a] | 125.63 | 117.63 | 4.63 | 0.363 |
| WISC-IV[b] | 124.83 | 116.83 | 3.83 | 0.300 |

*Notes:*

(1) It is customary to score subtests on a scale in which the SD is 3, as opposed to IQ scores, which are scaled with SD set at 15. To convert to IQ, just multiply subtest gains by 5, as was done to get the IQ gains in the last column.

(2) As to how the Full Scale IQs at the bottom of the table were derived:

1. The average member of the WISC sample (1947–48) was set at 100.
2. The subtest gains by the WISC-R sample (1972) were summed and added to 100: 100 + 11.63 + 111.63.
3. The appropriate conversion table was used to convert this sum into a Full Scale IQ score. The WISC-III table was chosen so that all samples would be scored against a common measure. That table equates 111.63 with an IQ of 107.63.
4. Thus the IQ gain from WISC to WISC-R was 7.63 IQ points.
5. Since the period between those two samples was 24.5 years, the rate of gain was 0.311 points per year (7.63 divided by 24.5 = 0.311).
6. The subsequent gains are also calculated against the WISC sample, which is to say they are cumulative. By the time of the WISC-IV, closer to 2002 than 2001, you get a total IQ gain of somewhere between 16.83 and 17.63 IQ points over the whole period of 54.25 years. Taking the mid-point (17.23 points) gives an average rate of 0.318 points per year, with some minor variation (as the table shows) from one era to another.

*Sources:* Flynn, 2000, Table 1; Wechsler, 2003, Table 5.8; Wechsler, 1992, Table 6.8.

Adapted from Flynn (2006a) – used with permission: ArtMed Publishers.

[a] With values for OA and PA at those bracketed (see text).

[b] With values for OA and PA put at 0.80 for both (see text).

Table AII4 Adjusting National IQs on WISC-III to allow for US gains over time

Full Scale IQ

| Nation | Date | Lag (years) | Points to be deducted | IQ unadjusted | IQ adjusted |
|---|---|---|---|---|---|
| France | 2000 = 1998 | 3 | 3 × 0.3 = 0.9 | 105.3* | 104.2 |
| UK | 1999 = 1997 | 2 | 2 × 0.3 = 0.6 | 103.7 | 103.1 |
| Germany | 2006 = 2004 | 9 | 9 × 0.3 = 2.7 | 102.9* | 100.2 |
| America | 1997 = 1995 | nil | nil | 100.0 | 100.0 |

Performance IQ

| Nation | Date | Lag (years) | Points to be deducted | IQ unadjusted | IQ adjusted |
|---|---|---|---|---|---|
| France | 2000 = 1998 | 3 | 3 × 0.34 = 1.0 | 107.2 | 106.2 |
| UK | 1999 = 1997 | 2 | 2 × 0.34 = 0.7 | 104.3 | 103.6 |
| Germany | 2006 = 2004 | 9 | 9 × 0.34 = 3.1 | 103.6 | 100.5 |
| America | 1997 = 1995 | nil | nil | 100.0 | 100.0 |
| Spain | 1999 = 1997 | 2 | 2 × 0.34 = 0.7 | 97.8 | 97.1 |
| Finland | 2005 = 2003 | 8 | 8 × 0.34 = 2.7 | 95.8 | 93.1 |

* Roivainen gives results for only seven subtests and, using these, I pro-rated to estimate Full Scale IQs.

*Notes:*

(1) US Full Scale IQ gains have been put at a rate of 0.3 points per year as described in the text.

(2) US Performance IQ gains have been put at a rate of 0.34 points per year as described in the text.

a score below 100 showing the reverse. Since all these nations had standardized the WAIS-III some years after America did so, I had to deduct from their advantage (or add to their disadvantage) the IQ gains America would have made over the intervening periods. Table AII4 (see page 243) details how her values were translated into those that appear in Box 16.

# Appendix III: Tables and comments relevant to adult/child IQ trends and bright taxes/bonuses (see Chapter 5)

Box 18 in Chapter 5 compares IQ gains between 1950–51 and 2005 on three subtests of the WAIS and WISC. It is derived from Table AIII1. That in turn is based on Tables AII2 and AII3 in Appendix II.

From Tabe AIII1, we can derive Table AIII2, which covers the full 54.25 years and puts the subtests in a hierarchy running from the subtest on which adult gains most exceeded child gains (vocabulary) to the subtest on which child gains most exceeded adult gains (block design). Box 18 in Chapter 5 includes only three of these subtests: vocabulary, information, and arithmetic. These tables are on pages 246 and 247.

Figure 2 in Chapter 5 showed how tertiary education and the parent/child vocabulary gap increased between 1947 and 2002. I will reproduce that figure here and add some comments (see Figure 4) on page 247.

The "index of some tertiary education" shows the rising percentage of Americans aged 25 years and over who had one year of tertiary education or more. The actual percentages are as follows: 12.1% in 1947; 22.9% in 1972; 38.4% in 1989; and 52.0% in 2002 (Current Population Surveys, 1940–2007). The slope was contrived simply to show a rise in the percentage with some tertiary education about double the vocabulary gain for adults over the same period. It has no more justification than the fact that

Table AIII1 WISC vs. WAIS subtest IQ gains over 54.25 years

| | 1950.5–75 | | 1975–92 | | 1992–2004.75 | | 1950.5– 2004.75 | | IQ gain difference (SD = 15) |
|---|---|---|---|---|---|---|---|---|---|
| | WI | WA | WI | WA | WI | WA(1) | WI | WA | WA – WI = Dif. |
| Information | 0.43 | **1.1** | –0.3 | **0.0** | 0.3 | **0.58** | 0.43 | **1.68** | 8.40 – 2.15 = 6.25 |
| Arithmetic | 0.36 | **1.0** | 0.3 | **–0.3** | – 0.2 | **0.00** | 0.46 | **0.70** | 3.50 – 2.30 = 1.20 |
| Vocabulary | 0.38 | **1.8** | 0.4 | **0.6** | 0.1 | **1.16** | 0.88 | **3.56** | 17.80 – 4.40 = **13.40** |
| Comprehension | 1.20 | **1.8** | 0.6 | **0.5** | 0.4 | **0.46** | 2.20 | **2.76** | 13.80 – 11.00 = 2.80 |
| Picture completion | 0.74 | **1.8** | 0.9 | **0.4** | 0.7 | **1.04** | 2.34 | **2.24** | 11.20 – 11.70 = –0.50 |
| Block design | 1.28 | **1.0** | 0.9 | **0.7** | 1.0 | **0.35** | 3.18 | **2.05** | 10.25 – 15.90 = –5.65 |
| Object assembly | 1.34 | **1.3** | 1.2 | **0.9** | – | | – | | Small |
| Coding | 2.20 | **1.8** | 0.7 | **1.2** | 0.7 | **0.23** | 3.60 | **3.23** | 16.15 – 18.00 = –1.85 |
| Picture arrangement | 0.93 | **0.8** | 1.9 | **0.6** | – | | – | | Perhaps minus |
| Similarities | 2.77 | **2.2** | 1.3 | **0.9** | 0.7 | **0.81** | 4.77 | **3.91** | 19.55 – 23.85 = –4.30 |
| Totals | 11.63 | **14.6** | 7.9 | **5.5** | (3.7) | **(4.63)** | (17.86) | **(20.13)** | 100.65 – 89.30 = 11.35(2) |
| Full Scale IQ gains | 7.63 | **7.5** | 5.37 | **4.2** | 4.63 | **3.91** | 17.63 | **15.61** | 15.61 – 17.63 = –2.02 |

*Notes:*

(1) WA(1) gains are WAIS gains over a period of 11 years projected to cover the last 12.75-year period of the WISC (as described in the text). This of course slightly increases the total WAIS gains estimated for the whole period of 1950.5 to 2004.75.

(2) The total difference of IQ points gained on all comparable subtests is 11.35 points greater for the WAIS than the WISC. Divided by eight subtests, this gives an average difference of 1.42 IQ points in favor of WAIS gains. Compare this to the result of using the norms tables in Appendix II, namely, 2.02 points in favor of WISC gains. It may be that WAIS gains matched WISC gains.

Table AIII2 WISC vs. WAIS subtests: Ranked by magnitude of difference between adult and schoolchild gains

| | Difference in points (SD = 15) | Difference in percentages |
|---|---|---|
| | WA – WI = Dif. | WA/WISC × 100 = Dif. |
| Vocabulary | 17.80 – 4.40 = 13.40 | 17.80/4.40 = 405 |
| Information | 8.40 – 2.15 = 6.25 | 8.40/2.15 = 391 |
| Comprehension | 13.80 – 11.00 = 2.80 | 13.80/11.00 = 125 |
| Arithmetic | 3.50 – 2.30 = 1.20 | 3.50/2.30 = 152 |
| Picture completion | 11.20 – 11.70 = –0.50 | 11.20/11.70 = 96 |
| Coding | 16.15 – 18.00 = –1.85 | 16.15/18.00 = 92 |
| Similarities | 19.55 – 23.85 = –4.30 | 19.55/23.85 = 82 |
| Block design | 10.25 – 15.90 = –5.65 | 10.25/15.90 = 64 |

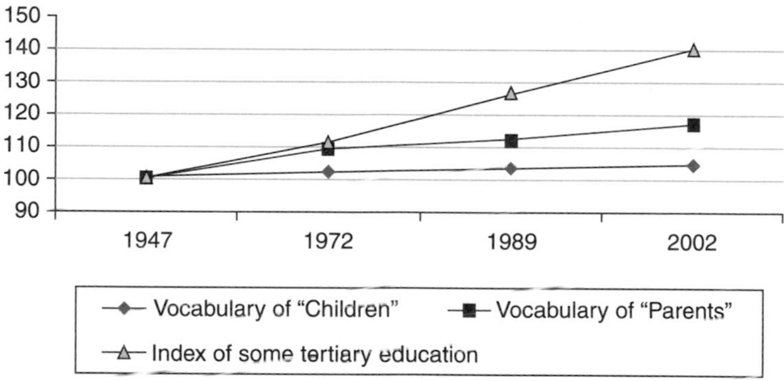


*Figure 4 As the percentage with some tertiary education rises, the gap between "parent" and "child" vocabulary expands.*

the correlation between the two cannot be perfect. The rationale of referring to WAIS vocabulary gains as the gains of "parents" and the WISC vocabulary gains as the gains of "their children" is described in the text.

The years refer to when WISC standardization samples were tested. However, the number of years between testings was the same for the WISC and WAIS except during the last period. In it, there were 12.75 years between when the WISC-III and WISC-IV samples were tested; but there were only 11 years between when the WAIS-III and WAIS-IV samples were tested. If the WAIS gain in that last period were multiplied by 12.75/11, it would be increased by 0.80 points (5 × 12.75/11 = 5.80). That would increase the widening gap between adult and schoolchild vocabulary gains from 12.6 IQ points (17.0–4.4) to 13.4 points (17.8–4.4). This adjustment was done in Table AIII1 above but has not been done here.

Box 19 in Chapter 5 estimates the effect of the expansion of tertiary education between 1953–1954 and 2000–2001 on adult vocabulary (WAIS) gains over that period. It is derived from Table AIII3.

The text spells out the logic of the table and this in turn clarifies the arithmetic:

(1) Those at IQ 79 repesent people between the ages of 16–17 and 20–24 who were not affected by the expansion of tertiary education between 1953 asnd 2000.
(2) Those at IQs 121 and 146 represent people between the ages of 16–17 and 20–24 who were most likely to be affected by the expansion of tertiary education betwecn 1953 and 2000.
(3) Therefore, D1 or the difference between the vocabulary gains (from ages 16–17 to 20–24) of IQ 79 and IQs 121 & 146 **in 2000** minus D2 or the difference between the vocabulary gains (from ages 16–17 to 20–24) of IQ 79 and IQ 121 & 146 **in 1953** equals the effects of more tertiary education over that period. The best approximation of 2000 is to average values from the WAIS-III (1995) and the WAIS-IV (2006).
(4) The arithmetic from the above table: D1 is 1.300 – 0.680 = 0.620 SS points or 3.100 IQ points. D2 is 1.815 – 1.750 = 0.065 SS points or 0.325 IQ points. And D1 minus D2 is

Table AIII3 Effect of tertiary education on vocabulary: Comparing effects as measured by the WAIS (1953–54) and as measured by the average of the WAIS-III (1995) and the WAIS-IV (2006) – (1995 & 2006 = 2000–01)

| | | Vocabulary gain between ages 16–17 and 20–24 (Scaled Scores points: SD = 3) | | | |
|---|---|---|---|---|---|
| | IQ | WAIS (1953–54) | WAIS-III (1995) | WAIS-IV (2006) | Average WIII & WIV (2000–01) |
| – 2 SD | MR | 0.00 | 1.00 | 0.75 | 0.875 |
| **– 1 SD (non-T)** | **79** | **1.75** | 0.50 | 0.86 | **0.680** |
| Median | 100 | 1.69 | 0.63 | 0.86 | 0.745 |
| + 1SD (T) | 121 | 1.80 | 1.33 | 1.20 | 1.265 |
| + 2SD (T) | 146 | 1.83 | 1.17 | 1.50 | 1.335 |
| **Ave. (T)** | **121 & 146** | **1.815** | 1.25 | 1.35 | **1.300** |
| Difference T–non-T (SD = 3) | | 0.065 | 0.75 | 0.49 | 0.620 |
| Converted to IQ pts. (SD = 15) | | **0.325** | 3.750 | 2.450 | **3.100** |
| Subtracting WAIS difference | | – | 3.425 | 2.125 | **2.775** |

*Notes:*

**(non-T)** refers to IQ levels unlikely to have entered university in either 1953 or 2000.

**(T)** refers to IQ levels likely to have entered university in greater numbers between 1953 and 2000.

Impact of expansion of tertiary education: 2.775 points.

As percentage of adult vocabulary gain 1953–54 to 2000–01: 2.775/14.935 = **18.6%**.

*Sources:* Wechsler, 1955, pp. 101–103; 1981, pp. 142–144; 1997a, pp. 181–184; 2008a, pp. 206–208.

3.100 IQ points – 0.325 IQ points = 2.775 IQ points. This last is our estimate of the effect of the expansion of tertiary education on adult vocabulary gains between 1953 and 2000.

Table AIII4 GSS (General Social Survey): Vocabulary gains from 1978 to 2006

| Items correct | 1978 (%) | SDs above or below mean | 2006 (%) | SDs above or below mean | SD difference favoring 2006 | IQ points |
|---|---|---|---|---|---|---|
| 0 to 4 | 24.4 | 0.694 below | 18.3 | 0.904 below | 0.210 | 3.15 |
| 0 to 5 | 40.3 | 0.246 below | 35.5 | 0.372 below | 0.126 | 1.89 |
| 0 to 6 | 60.9 | 0.277 above | 56.5 | 0.164 above | 0.113 | 1.70 |
| 0 to 7 | 76.6 | 0.726 above | 75.0 | 0.674 above | 0.052 | 0.78 |

*Notes:*
Average of comparisons: 1.88 IQ points
Average after compensation for obsolete item (omitting group "0 to 7"): 2.25 points
*Source:* General Social Surveys (2009), Cumulative File for wordsum 1972–2006.

Under the heading "Active versus passive vocabulary" in Chapter 5, I claim that the General Social Survey shows that between 1978 and 2006, adult Americans gained only the equivalent of 1.88 IQ points for passive vocabulary; or 2.25 points if allowance is made for an item that may have become less familiar and therefore more difficult. These estimates are derived from Table AIII4.

This table gives the percentages at four performance levels on the GSS vocabulary test in 1978 and 2006. It then uses these percentages to compare the four cutting lines in terms of their distance above or below the mean (measured in SDs). Averaging the four comparisons shows that the 2006 sample was superior by 0.125 SDs or 1.88 IQ points. One outdated item may have prevented the 2006 sample from getting really high scores. If you compensate by ignoring the top-scoring group in favor of the bottom three, the average of their gains is 0.150 SDs or 2.25 IQ points. Even the latter falls short of the gain that WAIS samples registered over those 28 years. See Table AII2 in Appendix II. It gives a W-R (1978) to W-III (1995) gain of 0.6 SS points; and a W-III (1995) to W-IV (2006) gain of 1.0 SS point. These total to a 1.6 SS gain or an 8 IQ point gain between 1978 and 2006.

Since the GSS measures passive vocabulary and the WAIS active vocabulary, the adult passive gains are at best only 28 percent of the active (2.25 divided by 8.00 = 0.28).

Box 23 in Chapter 5: Box 22 in the text summarizes the steps of how Box 23 is derived. I will illustrate these by deriving the values in the Verbal Ability section of Box 23.

First step: Using the relevant WAIS-IV tables, record the raw scores by age for each subtest. I have used similarities as an example.

Similarities

| | 16–17 | 18–19 | 20–24 | 25–29 | 30–34 | 35–44 | 45–54 | 55–64 | 65–69 | 70–74 | 75–79 | 80–84 | 85–89 |
|---|---|---|---|---|---|---|---|---|---|---|---|---|---|
| −1 SD | 17 | 18 | 18.5 | 19.5 | 19.5 | 19.5 | 19.5 | 18.5 | 17.5 | 16.5 | 15.5 | 14.5 | 13.5 |
| MED | 23 | 23.5 | 24.5 | 25 | 25.5 | 26 | 26 | 25.5 | 24.5 | 23.5 | 22.5 | 21.5 | 20.5 |
| +1 SD | 27.5 | 28.5 | 29.5 | 30 | 30.5 | 31 | 31 | 30.5 | 30 | 29 | 28 | 27 | 26 |
| +2 SDs | 31 | 32 | 33 | 34 | 34 | 34 | 34 | 34 | 34 | 33 | 32 | 31 | 30 |

Second step: Convert the raw scores into Scaled Scores (SD = 3). All ages are converted as if they were aged 16–17 (using the WAIS-IV table for those ages). This gives age trends from ages 16–17 to ages 85–90 for each IQ level, namely, −1 SD, median, +1 SD, and +2 SDs. I have used the three Verbal subtests as an example.

Scaled Score trends with age at four IQ levels for the WAIS-IV Verbal subtests

| | 16–17 | 18–19 | 20–24 | 25–29 | 30–34 | 35–44 | 45–54 | 55–64 | 65–69 | 70–74 | 75–79 | 80–84 | 85–89 |
|---|---|---|---|---|---|---|---|---|---|---|---|---|---|
| **–1 SD** | | | | | | | | | | | | | |
| SIM | 7 | 7+ | 7.5 | 8 | 8 | 8 | 8 | 7.5 | 7+ | 7 | 6 | 6 | 5.5 |
| VOC | 7 | 7+ | 8 | 8 | 8.5 | 9– | 9– | 9– | 8.5 | 8+ | 8 | 7.5 | 7+ |
| INF | 7 | 7 | 7 | 7 | 7 | 7.5 | 9 | 8– | 8– | 8– | 6+ | 6+ | 6– |
| **MED** | | | | | | | | | | | | | |
| SIM | 10 | 10.3 | 11 | 11.3 | 11.7 | 12 | 12 | 11.7 | 11 | 10.3 | 9.7 | 9 | 8.5 |
| VOC | 10 | 10.3 | 10.9 | 11.3 | 11.7 | 12.2 | 12.5 | 12.5 | 12.2 | 11.9 | 11.6 | 11.3 | 10.9 |
| INF | 10 | 10 | 10 | 10 | 10 | 10.3 | 11 | 11 | 11 | 11 | 10.3 | 9.7 | 9 |
| **+1 SD** | | | | | | | | | | | | | |
| SIM | 13 | 13.5 | 14.5 | 15 | 15.5 | 16 | 16 | 15.5 | 15 | 14 | 13+ | 13– | 12 |
| VOC | 13 | 13+ | 14+ | 15 | 16– | 16.5 | 17– | 17– | 16+ | 16+ | 16– | 15+ | 15 |
| INF | 13 | 13 | 13+ | 13+ | 13+ | 14– | 14 | 14.5 | 14.5 | 14.5 | 14 | 13.5 | 13 |
| **+2 SDs** | | | | | | | | | | | | | |
| SIM | 16 | 17 | 18 | 19– | 19– | 19– | 19– | 19– | 19– | 18 | 17 | 16 | 15 |
| VOC | 16 | 17 | 17.5 | 18+ | 19– | 19 | 19 | 19 | 19 | 19 | 19 | 19– | 18.5 |
| INF | 16 | 16 | 16 | 16 | 17 | 17 | 18 | 18 | 18 | 18 | 18 | 17 | 17 |

Third step: Average the Scaled Scores of the Verbal subtests to get the age trend for the Verbal index.

Scaled Score trends with age at four IQ levels for the WAIS-IV Verbal index

| | 16–17 | 18–19 | 20–24 | 25–29 | 30–34 | 35–44 | 45–54 | 55–64 | 65–69 | 70–74 | 75–79 | 80–84 | 85–89 |
|---|---|---|---|---|---|---|---|---|---|---|---|---|---|
| **−1 SD** | 7.00 | 7.00 | 7.50 | 7.67 | 7.83 | 8.17 | 8.67 | 8.17 | 7.83 | 7.67 | 6.67 | 6.50 | 6.17 |
| **MED** | 10.00 | 10.20 | 10.63 | 10.87 | 11.13 | 11.50 | 11.83 | 11.73 | 11.40 | 11.07 | 10.53 | 10.00 | 9.47 |
| **+1 SD** | 13.00 | 13.17 | 13.83 | 14.33 | 14.83 | 15.50 | 15.67 | 15.17 | 14.83 | 14.33 | 14.44 | 13.83 | 13.67 |
| **+2 SDs** | 16.00 | 16.67 | 17.17 | 17.67 | 18.33 | 18.33 | 18.67 | 18.67 | 18.67 | 18.33 | 18.00 | 17.33 | 16.83 |

Fourth step: Convert Scaled Scores into IQ scores. SS set the mean at 10 and SD at 3. IQ scores set the mean at 100 and SD at 15. Look at −1 SD. The value for ages 16–17 becomes 85 (100 − 1 SD). The value for ages 35–44 becomes 90.9. Calculations: (1) 8.17− 7.00 = 1.17 or the SS gain by those ages; (2) 1.17/3 = 0.39 or the gain in SDs; (3) 0.39 × 15 = 5.85 or the gain in IQ points; (4) 85 + 5.9 = 90.9 as the IQ value for ages 35–44. The Verbal section of Box 23 from Chapter 5 selects certain ages for emphasis, but all its values can now be derived.

The WAIS-IV: Trends with age for Wechsler cognitive abilities (SD = 15)

| | 16–17 | 35–44 | 55–64 | 65–69 | 70–74 | Gain or loss | 85–90 | Gain or loss |
|---|---|---|---|---|---|---|---|---|
| **Verbal** | | | | | | | | |
| −1 SD | 85.0 | 90.9 | 90.9 | 89.2 | 88.3 | **+3.3** | 80.8 | **−4.2** |
| Median | 100.0 | 107.5 | 108.7 | 107.0 | 105.4 | **+5.4** | 97.3 | −2.7 |
| +1 SD | 115.0 | 127.5 | 128.4 | 125.9 | 124.2 | **+9.2** | 118.3 | +3.3 |
| +2 SDs | 130.0 | 141.7 | 143.3 | 143.3 | 141.7 | **+11.7** | 134.2 | **+4.2** |
| | | | | | Bonus | 8.4 | Bonus | 8.4 |

Table AIII5 WAIS to WAIS-IV. Bright bonuses and bright taxes averaged

| Age 72 | WAIS (1953–54) | W-R (1978) | W-III (1995) | W-IV (2006) | Average | Difference between intelligence levels |
|---|---|---|---|---|---|---|
| **Verbal** | | | | | | |
| −1 SD | **−3.3** | **+1.7** | **+2.7** | **+3.3** | **+1.05** | – |
| Median | −5.0 | +0.9 | +3.3 | +5.4 | +1.15 | +0.10 |
| +1 SD | −3.3 | +1.7 | +6.6 | +9.2 | +3.55 | +2.40 |
| +2 SDs | **+0.9** | **+7.5** | **+8.4** | **+11.7** | **+7.13** | +3.58 |
| Bonus | 4.2 | 5.8 | 5.9 | 8.4 | 6.08 | – |
| **Memory** | | | | | | |
| −1 SD | **−6.3** | **−5.0** | **−5.0** | **−3.7** | **−5.00** | - |
| Median | −8.7 | −2.5 | −3.8 | −4.7 | −4.92 | +0.08 |
| +1 SD | −7.5 | + 1.2 | −5.0 | −5.0 | −4.08 | +0.84 |
| +2 SDs | **−2.5** | **+ 2.5** | **−5.0** | **−2.5** | **−1.87** | +2.21 |
| Bonus | 3.8 | 7.5 | Neutral | 1.2 | 3.13 | – |
| **Analytic** | | | | | | |
| −1 SD | **−10.0** | **−12.5** | **−12.4** | **−13.3** | **−12.05** | – |
| Median | −15.0 | −20.0 | −18.3 | −17.5 | −17.70 | −5.65 |
| +1 SD | −17.5 | −20.0 | −20.8 | −20.0 | −19.58 | −1.88 |
| +2 SDs | **−22.5** | **−20.0** | **−19.2** | **−22.5** | **−21.05** | −1.47 |
| Tax | 12.5 | 7.5 | 6.8 | 9.2 | 9.00 | – |
| **P. Speed** | | | | | | |
| −1 SD | **−20.0** | **−20.0** | **−20.0** | **−15.0** | **−18.75** | – |
| Median | −35.0 | −25.0 | −22.5 | −19.5 | −25.50 | −6.75 |
| +1 SD | −40.0 | −30.0 | −23.7 | −20.0 | −28.43 | −2.93 |
| +2 SDs | **−40.0** | **−35.0** | **−32.6** | **−21.2** | **−32.20** | −3.77 |
| Tax | 20.0 | 15.0 | 12.6 | 6.2 | 13.45 | – |

| Age 87/88 | WAIS (1953–54) | W-R (1978) | W-III (1995) | W-IV (2006) | Average | Difference between intelligence levels |
|---|---|---|---|---|---|---|
| **Verbal** | No data | No data | | | | |
| −1 SD | – | – | **−4.2** | **−4.2** | **−4.20** | – |
| Median | – | – | −4.2 | −2.7 | −3.45 | +0.75 |
| + 1 SD | – | – | −5.0 | +3.3 | −0.85 | +2.60 |
| + 2 SDs | – | – | **0.0** | **+4.2** | **+2.10** | +2.95 |
| Bonus | – | – | 4.2 | 8.4 | 6.30 | – |

Table AIII5 (*cont.*)

| Age 87/88 | WAIS (1953–54) | W-R (1978) | W-III (1995) | W-IV (2006) | Average | Difference between intelligence levels |
|---|---|---|---|---|---|---|
| **Memory** | No data | No data | | | | |
| −1 SD | – | – | **−6.3** | **−11.2** | **−8.75** | – |
| Median | – | – | −10.0 | −12.4 | −11.20 | −2.45 |
| +1 SD | – | – | −12.5 | −16.2 | −14.35 | −3.15 |
| +2 SDs | – | – | **−15.0** | **−11.2** | **−13.10** | +1.25 |
| Tax | – | – | 8.7 | Neutral | 4.35 | – |
| **Analytic** | No data | No data | | | | |
| −1 SD | – | – | **−13.3** | **−21.6** | **−17.45** | – |
| Median | – | – | −21.6 | −25.9 | −23.75 | −6.30 |
| +1 SD | – | – | −28.3 | −31.6 | −29.95 | −6.20 |
| +2 SDs | – | – | **−30.9** | **−35.8** | **−33.35** | −3.40 |
| Tax | – | – | 17.6 | 14.2 | 15.90 | – |
| **P. Speed** | No data | No data | | | | |
| −1 SD | – | – | **−27.5** | **−28.8** | **−28.15** | – |
| Median | – | – | −33.2 | −32.2 | −32.70 | −4.55 |
| +1 SD | – | – | −38.7 | −35.0 | −36.85 | −4.15 |
| +2 SDs | – | – | **−40.0** | **−40.0** | **−40.0** | −3.15 |
| Tax | – | – | 12.5 | 11.2 | 11.85 | – |

Box 25 in Chapter 5 averages results from all four versions of the WAIS. It presents an overall comparison between the bright tax for Analytic Ability and the bright bonus for Verbal Ability, both at ages 72 (70–74) and 87–88 (85–90). It selects from a master table that averaged the bright taxes/bonuses for all four of the WAIS indexes respectively. To derive it, the reader must duplicate the four steps used to analyze the WAIS-IV Verbal data when analyzing the whole of the WAIS, WAIS-R, and WAIS-III data. The master table is Table AIII5.

# Appendix IV: Tables and comments relevant to gender and Raven's (see Chapter 6)

Box 30 in Chapter 6 selects values (those in bold) from Table AIV1.

The predictions at the bottom of the table are discussed in the text. Table AIV1 uses the male SD to calculate the difference between the male and female means. That is because it is common to both the gender parity hypothesis and the male superiority hypothesis. As an example of the calculations, take the first row. It shows a male advantage of 0.48 male SDs (1.80 divided by 3.73 = 0.4826). That is inflated by the fact that the within-sample male SD is only 0.6 of the population SD (the bottom 50 percent of the male population falls below the IQ threshold). So 0.4826 × 0.6 = 0.2895 SDs. That times 15 = 4.34 IQ points, or the value in the table.

Under the heading "What does the data say?" Chapter 6 asserts that certain population values are a **perfect fit** for the university results. The values:

Population of males: mean IQ = 100; SD = 15; university threshold = 100

Population of females: mean = 100; SD = 14.62; university threshold = 96.

The calculations:

(1) Showing that 60.8 percent of females are eligible for university: a threshold 4 points below the mean, with an SD of 14.62, puts the threshold at 0.274 SDs below the mean (4 divided by 14.62 = 0.274). That equals 60.8 percent of the population.

Table AIV1 Recent university samples

| | | | Means | | Difference (M – F) | | | SDs | | |
|---|---|---|---|---|---|---|---|---|---|---|
| Place | Date | No. | Male | Female | Raw | Male SDs | IQ pts. (× 0.6 & × 15) | M | F | F/M % |
| **Standard Progressive Matrices (* = short form)** | | | | | | | | | | |
| 1. Canada | 2000 | 111 | 16.57* | 14.77* | 1.80 | 0.48 | **4.34** | 3.73 | 3.87 | **104** |
| 2. S. Africa (W) | 2000 | 136 | 54.44 | 53.33 | 1.11 | 0.24 | **2.19** | 4.57 | 3.76 | **82** |
| 3. USA | 1998 | 124 | 55.26 | 53.77 | 1.49 | 0.49 | **4.44** | 3.02 | 3.60 | **119** |
| 4. USA | 1998 | 218 | 22.5* | 21.6* | 0.90 | 0.24 | **2.13** | 3.80 | 3.69 | **97** |
| **Advanced Progressive Matrices** | | | | | | | | | | |
| 5. Canada | 1998 | 506 | 23.00 | 21.68 | 1.32 | 0.27 | **2.45** | 4.85 | 5.11 | **105** |
| 6. Spain | 2002 | 604 | 23.90 | 22.40 | 1.50 | 0.31 | **2.81** | 4.80 | 5.30 | **110** |
| 7. USA | 2004 | 2,222 | 25.78 | 24.22 | 1.56 | 0.33 | **2.93** | 4.80 | 5.30 | **110** |
| 8. Spain | 2004 | 1,970 | 24.19 | 22.73 | 1.46 | 0.27 | **2.47** | 5.37 | 5.47 | **102** |
| 9. Spain | 2004 | 339 | 24.57 | 23.32 | 1.25 | 0.30 | **2.72** | 4.13 | 4.52 | **109** |
| **Summary Comparisons** | | | | | | | | | | |
| | | Standard Progressive Matrices – Averages | | | | | 3.27 | | | 101 |
| | | Standard Progressive Matrices – Weighted averages | | | | | 3.05 | | | 100 |
| | | Advanced Progressive Matrices – Averages | | | | | 2.68 | | | 107 |

| | | | |
|---|---|---|---|
| | Advanced Progressive Matrices – Weighted averages | 2.70 | 107 |
| | All – Averages | **2.94** | **104** |
| | All – Weighted averages | **2.73** | **106** |
| **Predictions** | | | |
| | Gender parity with lower female threshold | 2.98 | 110 |
| | Male advantage with common threshold | 1.67 | 90 |

*Sources:* 1. Silverman *et al.*, 2000; 2. Rushton & Skuy, 2000; 3. Lovaglia *et al.*, 1998; 4. Crucian & Berenbaum, 1998; 5. Bors & Stokes, 1998; 6. Colom & Garcia-Lopez, 2002; 7. Lynn & Irwing, 2004; 8. Abad *et al.*, 2004; 9. Colom, Escorial, & Rebello, 2004.

(2) So 39.2 percent is gone and that lifts the mean by 0.6322 SDs. That times 14.62 = 9.24 points, which added to 100 makes the university sample mean 109.24.
(3) By definition, 50 percent of males are eligible for university.
(4) So the bottom 50 percent is gone and that lifts the mean by 0.7980 SDs. That times 15 = 11.97 IQ points, which added to 100 makes the university sample mean 111.97.
(5) Subtracting the female mean (109.24) from the male mean (111.97) gives a male advantage of **2.73 points.** This is a perfect fit for the male advantage in Table AIV1.
(6) With 39.2 percent gone, the female university SD is reduced to 0.6537 of the population SD. That times 14.62 = 9.557 points.
(7) With 50 percent gone, the male university SD is reduced to 0.6028 of the population SD. That times 15 = 9.042 points.
(8) Dividing the female SD (9.557) by the male SD (9.042) = 1.057, which means that the female SD is **106 percent** of the male SD. This is a perfect fit for the female percentage in Table AIV1.

Under the heading "What does the data say?" Chapter 6 asserts that it is impossible to reconcile the university data with the hypothesis of a common IQ threshold for the genders. There is a trade-off here. Every attempt to reconcile the male mean IQ advantage renders the female SD advantage even less reconcilable, and vice versa.

First, we will give population values that would reconcile the university mean IQ advantage of males: Female mean = 91; female SD = 15; female threshold = 100.

(1) Showing that only 27.43 percent are eligible for university: a threshold that is 9 points above the mean (100 – 91) puts the threshold at 0.600 SDs above the mean (9 divided by 15 = 0.600). That equates with 27.43 percent of the population.

(2) So 72.57 percent are gone and that lifts the mean by 1.2144 SDs. That times 15 = 18.22 points. That added to 91 makes the female university mean = 109.22.
(3) That subtracted from the male university mean of 111.97 = **2.75 points**, close to the 2.73 in Table AIV1.
(3) With 72.57 percent gone, the female university SD is reduced to 0.50275 of the population SD. That times 15 = 7.541 points. The female SD divided by the male university SD of 9.042 = 0.834.
(4) So the university female SD would be only **83 percent** of the male SD. As Table AIV1 shows, it is in fact 106 percent. So we have lost ground in reconciling the female SD advantage! A discrepancy of 90 compared to 106 has become a discrepancy of 83 compared to 106.

Second, we will attempt to give population values that reconcile the university SD advantage of females. Female mean = 95; female SD = 17.34; female threshold = 100.

(1) Showing that only 38.67 percent are eligible for university: a threshold that is 5 points above the mean (100 – 95), with an SD of 17.34, puts the threshold at 0.288 SDs above the mean (5 divided by 17.34 = 0.288). That equates with 38.67 percent of the population.
(2) So 61.33 percent are gone and that reduces the female university SD to 0.5526 percent of the population SD. That times 17.34 = 9.582 points. That divided by the male university SD of 9.042 = **1.06**, equal to the percentage in Table AIV1.
(3) With 61.33 percent gone, that lifts the mean by 0.9895 SDs. That times 17.34 = 17.16 points. That added to 95 = 112.16.
(4) The female mean (112.16) subtracted from the male mean (111.97) = –0.19 points. So we have lost ground in reconciling the male mean advantage! We wanted a male

advantage of 2.73 points and have got a female advantage of **0.19 points.** The discrepancy is now fully 2.92 points.

All of this assumes we can trust the university data we have got. Let us assume that its values are inaccurate and make assumptions about better values that would help the common threshold hypothesis. We will posit that male university students really have a mean advantage of only 1.67 points, which is exactly what is predicted by a female population mean of 95 combined with a common university threshold of 100. And we will cut the female university students SD advantage in half, that is, from 106 percent to 103 percent. And we will assume a female population SD that will give the desired 103. So: female mean = 95; female SD = 16.88; female threshold = 100.

(1) Showing that only 38.36 percent are eligible for university: a threshold 5 points above the mean (100 – 95), with an SD of 16.88, puts the threshold at 0.296 SDs above the mean (5 divided by 16.88 = 0.296). That equates with 38.36 percent of the population.

(2) So 61.64 percent are gone and that reduces the female university SD to 0.55124 percent of the population SD. That times 16.88 = 9.305. That divided by the male university SD of 9.042 = **1.03**, which we set as our target.

(3) With 61.64 percent gone, that lifts the mean by 0.9951 SDs. That times 16.88 = 16.80 points, which added to 95 = 111.80.

(4) The female mean (111.80) subtracted from the male mean (111.97) = 0.17 points. We posited that the male advantage could not be less than 1.67 points, so we have fallen far short of that with virtual IQ parity among university students. As usual rectifying one value (the female SD advantage) has made it impossible to rectify the other value (the male mean advantage).

In sum, the data as it stands gives a 2.73-point male IQ advantage among university students. To defend the common threshold hypothesis, we are forced to assume that the data are so defective that there is in fact gender parity among university students. However, the most economical population values to fit such parity would be to assume gender parity in the general population, with both males and females at a mean of 100, an SD of 15, and a common threshold of 100. It would only be if we found higher female variance in both the general population and among university students, that we might suspect a female IQ deficit in the general population.

Lynn has been looking for the wrong values to evidence his hypothesis. If females face a common cutting line that is above their population mean, while males do not, an unknown higher female population variance would tend to deceive us by generating mean parity among the selected university groups. But we could unmask the deception by finding female SD superiority both in the general population and among the selected university groups (at say the 103 percent level). There is a lesson here that may save a lot of time. University samples are useless for making inferences about the general population – until we have information about the general population, and that makes university samples irrelevant. University samples are worth studying primarily because they tell us interesting things about university students.

To return to the world as it is, unless the data for current university students in advanced nations is grossly inaccurate, the existence of a lower female threshold is beyond debate. Let us hope that more data will establish its size. My estimate is from 3 to 5 IQ points with 4 as my best guess.

Box 31 in Chapter 6 selects values from Table AIV2. The values in bold appear in the box.

Table AIV2 OECD data on reading used to predict IQ thresholds and means for female university students

| 1 | 2 | 3 | 4 | 5 | 6 | 7 |
|---|---|---|---|---|---|---|
| Nation/s | F – M raw score (reading) | SD | Female SD advantage | Female pts. advantage (SD = 15) | Female IQ deficit threshold | Female IQ deficit mean |
| OECD | 38 | 98.7 | .3850 | 5.78 | 2.89 | 1.97 |
| Austria | 45 | 98.7 | .4559 | 6.84 | 3.42 | 2.33 |
| Belgium | 40 | 98.7 | .4053 | 6.08 | 3.04 | 2.07 |
| Canada | 32 | 98.7 | .3242 | 4.86 | 2.43 | 1.65 |
| Denmark | 30 | 98.7 | .3040 | 4.56 | 2.28 | 1.55 |
| Finland | 51 | 98.7 | .5167 | 7.75 | 3.88 | 2.64 |
| France | 35 | 98.7 | .3546 | 5.32 | 2.66 | 1.81 |
| Germany | 42 | 98.7 | .4255 | 6.38 | 3.19 | 2.17 |
| Iceland | 48 | 98.7 | .4863 | 7.29 | 3.65 | 2.48 |
| Ireland | 34 | 98.7 | .3445 | 5.17 | 2.58 | 1.75 |
| Italy | 41 | 98.7 | .4154 | 6.23 | 3.12 | 2.12 |
| Netherlands | 24 | 98.7 | .2433 | 3.65 | 1.82 | 1.24 |
| Norway | 46 | 98.7 | .4661 | 6.99 | 3.50 | 2.38 |

| | | | | | | |
|---|---|---|---|---|---|---|
| Spain | 35 | 98.7 | .3546 | 5.32 | 2.66 | 1.81 |
| Sweden | 40 | 98.7 | .4053 | 6.08 | 3.04 | 2.07 |
| Switzerland | 31 | 98.7 | .3141 | 4.71 | 2.36 | 1.60 |
| UK | 29 | 98.7 | .2938 | 4.41 | 2.20 | 1.50 |
| **USA** | – | – | .4400 | **6.60** | **3.30** | **2.24** |
| **Argentina** | 54 | 128.4 | .4266 | **6.31** | **3.15** | **2.14** |
| **Australia** | 37 | 93.5 | .3957 | **5.94** | **2.97** | **2.02** |
| **Estonia** | 46 | 83.1 | .5534 | **8.30** | **4.15** | **2.82** |
| **Israel** | 42 | 126.2 | .3329 | **4.99** | **2.50** | **1.70** |
| **New Zealand** | 37 | 105.4 | .3511 | **5.27** | **2.63** | **1.79** |

*Sources:* 1. USA: USDE (2003) 2. All others: PISA (2006), Table 6.1c

The values in Box 31 labeled "W/C Europc" are the average of all the nations from Austria to the Untied Kingdom (with Canada included). As the table shows, I calculated the female reading advantage in these nations by using the SD of the OECD as a whole. This gives a common metric for anyone who wants to compare these nations to one another. Data for the USA were not available from the OECD, but the Nation's Report Card shows that the median for girls' reading proficiency was at the 67th percentile of the boys' curve, which means that the US gender gap is a bit high but comparable to several nations in the table. For the nations from Argentina to New Zealand, I used SDs specific to each nation as these are of special interest. Once you have the female reading advantage in SDs, (column 4), multiplying that by 15 gives the equivalent in IQ points (column 5).

Multiplying that in turn by 0.50 estimates how many IQ points females could spot males and secure university entry (column 6). This assumes a correlation between reading proficiency and IQ at 0.50. Jensen (1980, p. 325) gives 0.58 but warns that the value is lower for lower SES subjects. The difference in the IQ threshold of two groups is greater than the resulting mean IQ difference. Therefore, in the final column in Table AIV2, I multiply the threshold difference by 0.68. This is the value if one-third of males attend university, and would differ nation by nation. Even if male and female IQs were identical in the general population, nations herein would show a female threshold for university 3 points below the male, and a 2-point IQ deficit for female university students.

Even though females on average have slightly lower IQs than males, the same noncognitive factors that boost female high-school grades above male should continue to operate at university. Therefore, I would predict that, despite their IQ deficit, university women would get higher grades than males. This is borne out by US graduation rates: these stand at 66 percent for women and 59 percent for men. Coates and

Draves (2006) present only one study of university GPAs. At Truman State University, from 1999 to 2002, women enjoyed a GPA advantage of about 0.23 points all the way from their Freshman year to their Senior year. Over this period, Senior-year women averaged at 3.34 and males at 3.11. Such an advantage would mean a large disparity in terms of students who got 3.5 or better (half As and half Bs).

Box 32 in Chapter 6 selects values from Table AIV3. Values in bold appear in the box.

The age categories match the census categories, so that adjustments can be made for those missing from the in-school population. See the text for an illustration of the calculations (using ages 15–19 as an example). The complete raw data are given in Table AIV4.

Under the heading "Argentina," Chapter 6 promises more detail about the La Plata sample. Ten schools were chosen at random, subject to substitutions that made them representative as to location (radiating out from the city's center) and type (usual secondary school, or technical, or fine arts). There are five levels of schooling, ranging from the first level (ages 13–14) to the fifth level (ages 17–18), and from each school, one class was randomly chosen at each level, giving a total of 50 classes. La Plata has both a state university and a private university that offer degree courses of five to six years; and 32 tertiary institutes that offer four-year diploma courses. All were sampled in proportion to their share of total tertiary student numbers.

Box 33 in Chapter 6 selects values from Table AIV5. The values in bold appear in the box.

"SA" appended to a group means the sample is from South Africa. (T) and (UT) distinguish the timed and untimed Australian administrations of the SPM. The administration of

Table AIV3 La Plata, male/female means by age

| | Male | | Female | | |
|---|---|---|---|---|---|
| Ages | Raw score | IQ | Raw score | IQ | IQ adj. |
| **13–14** | 46.82 | 100.00 | 46.87 | **100.12** | **100.12** |
| **15–19** | 49.29 | 100.00 | 49.36 | **100.17** | **100.79** |
| **20–24** | 51.18 | 100.00 | 51.16 | **99.95** | **100.39** |
| **25–29** | 51.03 | 100.00 | 51.08 | **100.13** | – |
| **30** | 49.80 | 100.00 | 49.93 | **100.31** | – |
| 13–30 | 49.86 | 100.00 | 49.92 | 100.14 | 100.39 |
| 15–24 | 50.26 | 100.00 | 50.28 | 100.06 | 100.59 |
| 15–19 | 49.29 | 100.00 | 49.36 | 100.17 | 100.79 |

Table AIV4 Argentine raw data

| | Male | | | Female | | |
|---|---|---|---|---|---|---|
| Ages | Mean | SD | No. | Mean | SD | No. |
| 13–14 | 46.82 | 6.26 | 116 | 46.87 | 6.03 | 117 |
| 15–16 | 48.48 | 6.11 | 119 | 48.40 | 5.99 | 120 |
| 17–18 | 49.39 | 5.25 | 114 | 49.60 | 5.48 | 116 |
| 19–20 | 51.27 | 4.40 | 113 | 51.20 | 4.35 | 116 |
| 21–22 | 50.85 | 4.87 | 120 | 50.80 | 4.93 | 122 |
| 23–24 | 51.30 | 5.31 | 106 | 51.41 | 5.46 | 111 |
| 25–30 | 50.83 | 5.19 | 148 | 50.90 | 5.23 | 157 |
| Totals | | | 836 | | | 859 |

*Note:* As Chapter 6 says, using the raw data (without adjustment for male bias), the largest male advantage is 0.08 raw score points (ages 15–16). Divided by 6.26 (unattenuated SD) = 0.0128 SDs, and times 15 = 0.19 IQ points.

Table AIV5 Male/female means by age for New Zealand, Australia, and South Africa (four ethnic groups)

| Nation & age | Gender | Raw score | IQ | IQ (adj.) | Number | F/M ratio |
|---|---|---|---|---|---|---|
| New Zealand 15–16 | Male | 49.33 | 100.00 | | 223 | – |
| | Female | 49.93 | **101.37** | (101.37) | 277 | |
| Australia 14.5–16.5 | Male | 45.40 (T) | 100.00 | | 548 | 1.04 |
| | Female | 45.30 (T) | **99.78** | **100.11** | 718 | |
| | Male | 47.80 (UT) | 100.00 | | 636 | 1.04 |
| | Female | 47.53 (UT) | **99.41** | **99.74** | 663 | |
| White SA 15 | Male | 45.18 | 100.00 | | 490 | 1.10 |
| | Female | 45.34 | **100.38** | **100.80** | 566 | |
| Indian SA 15 | Male | 43.01 | 100.00 | | 530 | – |
| | Female | 40.97 | **96.38** | (96.38) | 533 | |
| Colored SA 15–16 | Male | 37.50 | 100.00 | | 386 | – |
| | Female | 35.86 | **97.36** | (97.36) | 381 | |
| Black SA 16–17 | Male | 29.29 | 100.00 | | 554 | – |
| | Female | 25.96 | **95.29** | (95.29) | 539 | |

the SPM elsewhere was untimed. The bracketed values under "IQ adj." were actually left unadjusted.

All nations took Raven's at roughly the same time, so raw scores are comparable across nations. For South Africa, I have converted raw score differences (between male and female) into IQs using the SD of whichever sex had the larger SD at the earliest secondary school age available. This produced tiny differences from Lynn's values.

The ratio of F/M is: the females in school as a percentage of the total number of females in the age cohort; divided by the male percentage. For white South Africa, sample ratios have been assumed to be identical to population ratios and the adjusted female IQ should be taken as a rough estimate. Census data for nonwhite groups were not sufficiently accurate, particularly for blacks, to derive adjusted IQs.

Box 34 in Chapter 6 selects values from Table AIV6. The values in bold appear in the box. The lower percentiles in the table have to be reduced by 1 to get the box values for percentiles missing.

The sample percentages do not quite add up to 100% because only the principal percentiles selected by the samples are given. For example, the male sample for age 16 was: 8.22% from grade 8 (percentiles 27–36); 91.32% from grade 10 (percentiles 64–87); and 0.46% from grade 12.

The correction for male bias in the Estonian data would have been impossible without Olev Must, the distinguished Estonian scholar, who supplied valuable information and comment. As I know from our long correspondence, it is not easy to explain what is going on in the table below. But the fruitful understanding he and I eventually reached emboldens me to try.

In order to quantify the biases, I constructed 14 normal curves: one for each sex at each age from 12 to 18. The curves are based on age-cohort size data, age-cohort in-school data, and age data for the samples tested (Statistikaamet, 2001, pp. 54–55;

Table AIV6 Adjustment of the Estonian female mean IQs

| | Percentiles of age cohort in academic cohort | | Percentiles of age cohort in sample (with sample percentages) | | Male bias IQ pts. | | |
|---|---|---|---|---|---|---|---|
| Age | F | M | F | M | | F IQ | F IQ (adj.) |
| **12** | **2–100** | **2–100** | 43–90 (100%) | 37–93 (100%) | **−0.48** | **107.40** | **106.92** |
| **13** | **2–100** | **2–100** | 7–42 (90%) | 10–40 (97%) | nil | **104.38** | **103.11** |
| | | | 89–100 (10%) | 92–100 (3%) | **−1.27** | | |
| **14** | **3–100** | **4–100** | 4–7 (3%) | 7–14 (7%) | +0.27 | **100.18** | **100.76** |
| | | | 41–85 (97%) | 45–89 (92%) | +0.31 | | |
| | | | | | **+0.58** | | |
| **15** | **6–100** | **9–100** | 12–40 (71%) | 23–50 (83%) | +0.38 | **102.79** | **103.06** |
| | | | 82–100 (29%) | 90–100 (14%) | −0.11 | | |
| | | | | | **+0.27** | | |
| **16** | **13–100** | **21–100** | 15–19 (2%) | 27–36 (8%) | +0.48 | **98.14** | **100.40** |
| | | | 45–78 (98%) | 64–87 (91%) | +1.78 | | |
| | | | | | **+2.26** | | |
| **17** | **22–100** | **39–100** | 29–46 (38%) | 53–65 (47%) | +0.92 | **99.15** | **100.12** |
| | | | 78–100 (61%) | 86–100 (49%) | +0.05 | | |
| | | | | | **+0.97** | | |
| **18** | **36–100** | **56–100** | 55–80 (99%) | 72–87 (98%) | **+1.22** | **99.55** | **100.77** |

2003; Allik, private communication, December 31, 2002). All data were coordinated to eliminate differences in terms of the time of collection.

The curves are an attempt to rank the components of each age cohort ranging from best (those in the academic stream who were a year or more ahead for their age) all the way down to the worst (those who had dropped out of school entirely), so as to create an academic quality hierarchy. Assuming a correlation between academic performance and IQ, I could then calculate how much difference it made that the Estonian age samples often omitted either the very best students, or the worst students, or some of both.

Take the curves populated by all females aged 16 and by all males aged 16 respectively. In each case, I assumed that the top percentiles were those who were a grade or more ahead for their age (16-year-olds in grade 11 and above). I assumed that the next highest percentiles were those who were typical (16-year-olds who were in grade 10). Next I put those who were a grade or more behind for their age (16-year-olds in grade 9 and below). I assumed that the bottom percentiles were the nonacademic group. The fact that the nonacademic group is a mix of vocational students and those who have dropped out of school entirely creates a problem. Perhaps some of the vocational students are better academically than those in the academic stream who are a grade behind their age group.

Still, the ranking is roughly correct and greatly simplifies the calculations. By keeping the academic stream and the nonacademic group separate, we can calculate: first, a correlation between speed of progress through the academic steam and IQ – a tool needed to allow for the fact that the sample often omits the speediest; second, a correlation between being in the academic stream and IQ – a tool needed to allow for the fact that the sample omits the nonacademic group entirely.

To exemplify how an age-cohort curve illuminates sampling omissions, I will extract from Table AIV6 the cohort that was aged 16.

| | Percentiles of age cohort in academic cohort | | Percentiles of age cohort in sample (with sample percentages) | | Male bias IQ pts. | | |
|---|---|---|---|---|---|---|---|
| Age | F | M | F | M | | F IQ | F IQ (adj.) |
| 16 | 13–100 | 21–100 | 15–19 (2%)<br>45–78 (98%) | 27–36 (8%)<br>64–87 (91%) | +0.48<br>+1.78<br>Total<br>+2.26 | 98.14 | 100.40 |

From census data, it can be shown that only 88.12% of 16-year-old females were attending academic secondary schools, so the bottom 12 percentiles of the female curve are omitted; similarly, it can be shown that fully the bottom 20 percentiles of males are omitted – and this advantages males. Within the academic stream, grade 10 was tested but grade 11 was not. Therefore, over 90% of the 16-year-olds the sample captured are in the 10th grade and it includes only one 16-year-old who had reached the 11th grade or above. Which is to say that the sample misses virtually all of the precocious students who were one or more grades ahead of their age group; and they, of course, constitute the top percentiles of the age-16 curve. As for the differential impact on the genders: the sample omits all females above the 78th percentile; but it omits only those males above the 87th percentile – this again advantages males.

To summarize the male advantage at age 16: fewer of their top percentiles are missing and more of their bottom percentiles are missing. (Constructing the curve for age 18 posed a special problem: it had to include those who had already graduated from gymnasia or keskkools by that age; it would hardly make sense to count graduates as having opted out of the academic stream!)

Correcting the male biases required two correlations: one between IQ and persisting in the academic stream; and one between IQ and speed of progress through academic schools. For the former, I assumed correlations of 0.59 at age 14, 0.45 at age 15, and 0.26 for ages 16–18. For the latter, I will assume a correlation of 0.50. These values will be defended in a moment.

For now we will present an example of how the mathematics of a normal curve plus our correlations allow us to estimate the magnitude of the male bias. Estimates are given separately for the effects of "dropouts" (the omission of the nonacademic group) on male bias and the effects of sampling (sampling only every other grade). "Dropouts" refers to the nonacademic group: those who are not in gymnasia or keskkools.

Calculations for the 16-year-old age cohort

Females

I. Dropouts = bottom 11.88%
   (1) Bottom 11.88% of normal curve gone raises mean by (+)0.2257 SDs
   (2) Effect of dropouts: +0.2257 × 0.26 (cor. with IQ) = +0.0587; that × 15 =

**+0.88 IQ points**

II. Portion of in-school sample from 8th grade (1.90%)
   (1) Omits percentiles 11.89–13.88: raises mean by (+)0.0315 SDs
   (2) Omits percentiles 18.74–100.00: lowers mean by (−)1.4370 SDs
   (3) Net loss = −1.4055 SDs; times 0.0190 (portion of sample) = – 0.0267 SDs

III. Portion of in-school sample from 10th grade (98.10%)
   (1) Omits percentiles 11.89–43.86: raises mean by (+)0.4771 SDs
   (2) Omits percentiles 78.02–100.00: lowers mean by (–)0.3796 SDs
   (3) Net gain = 0.0975 SDs; times 0.9810 (portion of sample) = +0.0956 SDs

IV. Effect of in-school sample: – 0.0267 (8th grade) & +0.0956 (10th grade) = +0.0689 SDs; that × 0.5 (cor. with IQ) = +0.03445; that × 15 = **+0.52 IQ points**

Males

I. Dropouts = bottom 19.85%
   (1) Bottom 19.85% of normal curve gone raises mean by (+)0.3485 SDs
   (2) Effect of dropouts: +0.3485 × 0.26 (cor with IQ) = +0.0906; that × 15 =

**+1.36 IQ points**

II. Portion of in-school sample from 8th grade (8.22%)
   (1) Omits percentiles 19.86–25.64: raises mean by (+)0.0840 SDs
   (2) Omits percentiles 35.69–100.00: lowers mean by (–)1.0449 SDs
   (3) Net loss = – 0.9609 SDs; times 0.0822 (portion of sample) = –0.0790 SDs

III. Portion of in-school sample from 10th grade (91.32%)
   (1) Omits percentiles 19.86–62.89: raise mean by (+)0.6701 SDs
   (2) Omits percentiles 86.70–100.00: lowers mean by (–)0.2479 SDs
   (3) Net gain = 0.4222 SDs; times 0.9132 (portion of sample) = +0.3856 SDs

IV. Effect of in-school sample: – 0.0790 (8th grade) & +0.3856 (10th grade) = +0.3066 SDs; that × 0.5 (cor. with IQ) = +0.1533 SDs; that × 15 = **+2.30 IQ points**

Male bias

I. Advantage from dropouts: 1.36 (male gain) – 0.88 (female gain) = **0.48 IQ points**. This is the value shown in the "table extract" above.

II. Advantage from sampling: 2.30 (male gain) – 0.52 (female gain) = **1.78 IQ points.** This is the value shown in the "table extract" above.

III These values are also entered (for age 16) in Table AIV6 under "Male bias IQ points" from dropouts and sample respectively.

It remains to justify the correlations between IQ and academic status used.

*First, justifying the correlations between IQ and not being in the academic stream:* As we have seen, *The Bell Curve* gives 0.59 as the correlation between IQ and staying in school. When transferring that value to other societies, I lowered it to 0.50 to be conservative. But Estonia is a special case meriting lower values still because of the presence of full-time vocational school students among the "dropouts" from the academic stream. I decided to discount the correlation to a maximum degree so as to avoid dispute. I will assume that the vocational stream has just as high a mean IQ as the academic stream. Unless this is true, the size of the correlation is too low and adjustment of female IQ upward too modest. And unless the high quality of its vocational stream makes Estonia unique, it is unlikely to be true.

In any event, I adjusted the correlation as follows. At age 14, all dropouts are genuine so a correlation of **0.59** stands. After that age, as the quality of the "dropouts" improves (by way of including vocational students), I reduce the correlation.

At age 15, vocational students are 24% of the "dropouts," so I multiply by 0.76: 0.59 × 0.76 = **0.45**. At ages 16–18, vocational students average about 56.5% of the "dropouts," so I multiply by 0.435: 0.59 × 0.435 = **0.26** (all data from Statistikaamet, 2001, pp. 139–140). Since these adjustments are crude to say the least, I used a proper statistical method to check the value of 0.26. It was reassuring that it showed that 0.26 was probably too low.

As the percentage of those in the academic stream falls, the variance or SD of the group also falls. I used the attenuation of the SD to calculate a correlation.

(1) Divide the SD at ages 16 to 18 by the SD at ages 14 to 15 and get a percentage. The result is 74% (5.01 divided by 6.78). But the percentage has been affected by the fact that at both ages 14 to 15 and 16 to 18, rising ceiling effects lower the SD. When both are adjusted, the true result is 87% (7.81 divided by 8.96).

(2) In other words, at ages 16 to 18, when the 29.25% at the bottom of the academic curve are missing, this reduces the SD of the IQ curve by 13%. Therefore, there has to be some correlation between the two curves. If the correlation were nil, cutting the tail off the first curve would have no effect on the SD of the second.

(3) Calculate what the effect would be if the correlation were perfect. Were that so, cutting the bottom 29.25% off the academic curve would have lowered the SD of the IQ curve by just over 29%.

(4) The relationship between the actual loss of SD and the ideal loss of SD is almost linear. If it were simply linear, dividing the ideal by the actual would give the correlation; and 13% divided by 29.4% gives 0.44 as the correlation. The true value is 0.40. In sum, there is absolutely no doubt that there is a strong correlation between persisting

in the academic stream and IQ. The value of 0.26 used for ages 16–18 is, if anything, an underestimate.

There is also indirect evidence that 0.26 as the value for ages 16 to 18 is too low. First, the Estonian academic-stream sample has a mean score on Raven's that looks well above a plausible national average. For example, its mean is fully 0.639 SDs (or 4.29 Raven's points) above that of nearby Lithuania (Lynn *et al.*, 2002b; Lynn & Kazlauskaite, 2002). Second, the Raven's SD of the Estonian sample is foreshortened at age 16 as if cut by a knife, and this is the age at which young people begin opting out of the academic stream in large numbers. Such a radical truncation of variance can only mean that a large tail has suddenly been lopped off.

*Second, justifying the correlations between IQ and speed of progress through school:* Table AIV7 shows that whether the sample overrepresented precocious students (a grade or more ahead for their age) or backward students (behind) was a potent factor at all ages. Raven's performance and speed of progress through school were highly correlated: the Pearson gives 0.733 and the Spearman gives 0.643. The former is probably to be preferred because the distribution of the two factors is close to bivariant normal. The correlation is unlikely to be below 0.70.

However, the fact that we are correlating only 12 pairs suggests caution, as the wide confidence intervals show. Conservative as usual, in all calculations of bias, I used 0.50. This is the mid-point within the confidence interval of the lower correlation (the Spearman). The correlations for female and male are virtually the same. I was quite unprepared for correlations of this magnitude. Let us hope for more Estonian data on this point.

To understand Table AIV7, look at the first row, which compares females aged 12 and 13. This is the notorious

Table AIV7 Correlation between IQ and speed of progress through school. Comparing Raven's score differences with sample quality differences based on speed of progress by age (students differentiated by one year of age).

| Comparing ages x and x + 1 | Gender | Score difference in SDs (& rank order) | Sample quality difference in SDs (& rank order) |
|---|---|---|---|
| 12 & 13 | Female | −0.0969 (1) | −1.0419 (2) |
| 17 & 18 | Male | −0.0045 (2) | −0.2572 (6) |
| 17 & 18 | Female | +0.0223 (3) | −0.3371 (5) |
| 16 & 17 | Male | +0.0283 (4) | −0.0070 (7) |
| 14 & 15 | Male | +0.0596 (5) | −0.5537 (3) |
| 16 & 17 | Female | +0.0954 (6) | +0.2094 (8) |
| 12 & 13 | Male | +0.1043 (7) | −1.1479 (1) |
| 15 & 16 | Female | +0.1699 (8) | +0.3115 (9) |
| 14 & 15 | Female | +0.2340 (9) | −0.4978 (4) |
| 13 & 14 | Female | +0.2504 (10) | +0.8326 (11) |
| 15 & 16 | Male | +0.4799 (11) | +0.5644 (10) |
| 13 & 14 | Male | +0.5306 (12) | +1.0426 (12) |

*Correlations:*
Pearson: 0.733 Confidence interval (95%) is 0.275–0.920 (mid-pt. 0.60)
Spearman: 0.643 Confidence interval (95%) is 0.110–0.889 (mid-pt. 0.50)

comparison where age 13 had a lower raw score on Raven's than age 12, by fully 0.0969 SDs. Therefore, the difference is entered as a minus in the column "Score difference in SDs." It is the worst scoring discrepancy between ages to be found, so it gets a rank order of 1. Hence the entry: – 0.0969 (1).

We now look at the quality of the female 12-year-old and 13-year-old in-school samples. From Table AIV6 (the previous table), we find that the age 12 sample included percentiles 43 to 90 of the age cohort, a highly elite sample. The age 13 sample included percentiles 7 to 42 and 89 to 100, a very substandard sample. Thanks to its percentiles, the 12-year-olds got a bonus of +0.4645 SDs. Due to its percentiles, the 13-year-olds were penalized by −0.5774 SDs. So the total difference in sample quality between the two years was −1.0419 SDs, and this is entered in our table in the column "Sample quality difference in SDs." Since this is the second largest discrepancy in sample quality we have, it is followed by a 2. Hence the full entry is −1.0419 (2).

To allow the values to be checked, here are the calculations:

I. Score difference between ages 12 and 13
  (1) Raven's mean for females age 12 = 48.13
  (2) Raven's mean for females age 13 = 47.48
  (3) 47.48 minus 48.13 = (−)0.65 as score loss between ages 12 and 13
  (4) −0.65 divided by 6.71 (Raven's SD – see text) = **−0.0969** as score difference between ages 12 and 13 expressed in SDs

II. Sample quality difference between ages 12 and 13
  (1) Due to the percentiles sampled, the age 12 in-school female sample had its mean raised by (+)0.4645 SDs.
  (2) Due to the percentiles sampled, the age 13 in-school female sample had its mean lowered by (−)0.5774 SDs.
  (3) +0.4645 (age 12) & – 0.5774 (age 13) give **−1.0419** as sample quality difference between ages 12 and 13 expressed in SDs.

Once we have all the values entered in Table AIV7, the calculation of the Pearson and Spearman correlations is straightforward. A final reminder of why sample quality from age to age varied so much in the Estonian samples: partly, it was a result of omitting those not in the academic stream, although this was not important for ages 12 and 13. It took effect beginning at age 16 when increasing numbers opted for vocational training. At age

12 and 13, we see only the effects of testing every other grade. As the reader knows, testing grade 6 but not grade 7 had profound effects. It gave a sample of female 12-year-olds that excluded the lower percentiles (dropouts and those lagging behind) and a sample of female 13-year-olds that excluded the higher percentiles (those in their normal grade). It is hardly accidental that the more sample quality was loaded against 13-year-olds, the more their performance suffered.

# Appendix V: Wonderful paper on causes of Raven's gains

As this book was going to press, I was sent a paper that advances our knowledge of what goes on in the minds of people today so that they score much better on Raven's than previous generations. Hitherto my explanation of why similarities scores had increased was more adequate than my explanation of why Raven's scores had increased. As to the latter, I could say only that the utilitarian habits of mind of our ancestors tied their use of logic to the concrete world of physical objects, while the scientific ethos we live in made using logic on symbols and abstractions (often far removed from the concrete) more congenial.

Fox and Mitchum have written a paper that adds substance to the explanation of Raven's gains: mainly that Raven's (they used the Advanced Progressive Matrices Test) scores between generations rise on items that are further and further away from taking images at face value and more toward ascribing them symbolic significance. In my system, the sociological key is that utilitarian manipulation of the real world means that the representational image of objects is primary. If you are hunting, you do not want to shoot a cow rather than a deer. If a bird is camouflaged by being in a bush, you flush it out so its shape can be clearly seen. On the other hand, what Raven's often asks you to do is to divine relations that emerge only if you "take liberties" with the images presented.

I offer a series of analogies (the first three are my own) to illustrate the point.

(1) Dogs are to domestic cats as wolves are to (wild cats). Presented with representational images of various animals, I doubt that people in 1900 would have any more difficulty than we have in selecting the picture of a wild cat as the right answer.

(2) ■ is to ◆ as 🡅 is to (🡥) where the alternatives were 🡅 - 🡆 - 🡇 - 🡥. Here you must ignore everything about an image except its shape and position. Just as the square has been rotated a half turn, so has the arrow.

(3) □ is to / as O is to ( | ) where the alternatives are ∅ - Θ - | - ⊗. Here you must ignore everything but the number of dimensions: the analogy compares two-dimensional shapes to one-dimensional shapes and all else is irrelevant. All representational images are of course three-dimensional, so such a contrast requires being well removed from them.

(4) &#B is to B&# as T&T is to ## _. This is an item from Fox and Mitchum that illustrates the kind of analogical thinking you must do on the Advanced Raven's.

Note that the right answer in the fourth item has been left blank. Since no alternatives were presented to choose from, you had to deduce that "&" is the correct answer. I got it right, which was reassuring given that I have turned 78, by reasoning as follows. In the first half of the analogy, all that has altered is the sequence of symbols: labeling them 1, 2, 3, they have become 3, 1, 2. Applying that to the second half of the analogy, T&T changes to TT&. Clearly you are supposed to ignore the fact that the doubled letter (TT) has changed to a doubled symbol (##), so the right answer is ##&. This would really discriminate between the generations. We have moved far away from the "habit of mind" of taking pictorial images at face value, indeed, we are interested only in their sequence and treat images as interchangeable if the logic of the sequence demands it.

The key is this: anyone fixated on the literal appearance of the image "T", as a utilitarian mind would tend to be, would simply see no logical pattern. If we turn to a Wechsler subtest such as vocabulary, the etiology of any enhanced scores over time would be entirely different: people would have to accumulate a larger core vocabulary and get no bonus from the shift from utilitarian toward "scientific" thinking. The fact that both Raven's and vocabulary are heavily *g*-loaded would have no relevance. How salutary that everything is beginning to fall into place.

Fox and Mitchum classify Raven's items in ascending order of "relational abstraction," more specifically: "for analogical mapping when relations between objects are unrelated to objects themselves." In example #(4) the answer can be derived only if one ignores that a "T" is a "T." Their core assumption was that "analogical mapping of *dissimilar* objects is more difficult than mapping *similar* objects" (italics mine). I certainly found this to be true. The fact "TT&" had to be translated into "##&" rendered the item harder to solve. And if I were my father (born in 1885), and wedded to taking images at face value for reasons of utility, I suspect I would have found it insuperable.

They analyzed the performance of two samples of young adults, tested in 1961 and circa 2006 respectively. They found that as the degree of deviation toward the abstract increased, items were less predictive of performance within the two generations than between the two generations.

My bald summary of their research design and my interpretation of their results (in my own terms) do not capture the sophistication they brought to bear. For example, a corollary of their analysis is that Raven's gains over time will not be factor invariant. Thus, we again see that lack of factor invariance is compatible with enhanced problem-solving skills over time. They also caution against treating the latent variables of factor analysis as causes, and I would add that it is more dubious still to treat them as if they monopolized the role of significant cause. New social priorities act as causes (remember the decathlon) even if the gains on the various events do not tally with factor loadings.

Read the paper. But we are finally making progress in pinpointing just what changes in our minds (the authors prefer: changes in the cognitive phenomena that comprise knowledge-based skills) were the proximate causes of the huge rise in Raven's scores over the last century.

# References

Abad, F. J., Colom, R., Rebello, I., & Escorial, S. (2004). Sex differential item functioning in the Raven's Advanced Progressive Matrices: Evidence for bias. *Personality and Individual Differences*, 36: 1459–1470.

Adam, S., Bonsang, E., Germain, S., & Perelman, S. (2007). Retirement and cognitive reserve: A stochastic frontier approach to survey data. CREPP Working Paper 2007/04.

American Federation for Aging Research (AFAR): Neurobiology of Aging Information Center (2009). *What Cognitive Changes Take Place with Age?* (Google: AFAR: Neurobiology Cognitive Changes).

Batterjee, A. A. (2011). Intelligence and education: The Saudi case. *Mankind Quarterly*, 52: 133–190.

Batterjee, A. A., Khaleefa, O., Yousef, K., & Lynn, R. (in press). An increase of intelligence in Saudi Arabia, 1977–2010. *Intelligence*.

Baxendale, S. (2010). The Flynn effect and memory function. *Journal of Clinical and Experimental Neuropsychology*, 32: 699–703.

Benson, C., & Clay, E. with Michael, F. V., & Robertson, A. W. (2001). *Dominica: Natural Disasters and Economic Development in a Small Island State*. Washington, DC: Overseas Development Institute, The World Bank.

*Berry* v. *Epps*, 2006 WL 2865064 (N.D.Miss.) October 5, 2006.

Blair, C., Gamson, D., Thorne, S., & Baker, D. (2005). Rising mean IQ: Cognitive demand of mathematics education for young children, population exposure to formal schooling, and the neurology of the prefrontal cortex. *Intelligence*, 33: 93–106.

Bors, D. A., & Stokes, T. L. (1998). Raven's Advanced Progressive Matrices: Norms for first year university students and the development of a short form. *Educational and Psychological Measurement*, 58: 382–398.

Bouvier, U. (1969). *Evolution des cotes à quelques tests* [Evolution of scores from several tests]. Brussels: Belgian Armed Forces, Center for Research Into Human Traits.

*Bowling* v. *Commonwealth of Kentucky*, 163 S.W.3d 361 (Ky.) April 22, 2005.

Brand, D. (1987). The new whiz kids: Why Asian Americans are doing so well, and what it costs them. *Time*, August 31.

*Butler* v. *Quarterman*, 576 F.Supp.2d 805 (S.D.Tex.) September 4, 2008.

Cavalli-Sforza, L. L. (1997). Genes, peoples and languages. *Proceedings of the National Academy of Science*, 94: 7719–7724.

Ceci, S. J., & Williams, W. M. (2010). Sex differences in math-intensive fields. *Current Directions in Psychological Science*, 19: 275–279.

Chen, J., Zheng, H., Bei, J.-X., Sun, L., Jia, W., Li, T., Zhang, F., Seielstad, M., Zeng, Y.-X., Zhang, X., & Liu, J. (2009). Genetic structure of the Han Chinese population revealed by genome-wide SNP variation. *The American Journal of Human Genetics*, 85: 775–785.

Clarke, S. C. T., Nyberg, V., & Worth, W. H. (1978). *Technical Report on Edmonton Grade III Achievement: 1956–1977 Comparisons.* Edmonton, Canada: University of Alberta.

Coates, J., & Draves, W. A. (2006). *Smart Boys, Bad Grades*. River Falls, WI: Learning Resources Network (LERN).

*Coleman* v. *State*, 2010, WL 118696 (Tenn.Crim.App.) January 13, 2010.

*Coleman* v. *State*, 2011, 341, S.W.3rd (Tenn.Sup.Ct.) April 2011.

Colom, R., Escorial, S., & Rebello, I. (2004). Sex differences on the Progressive Matrices are influenced by sex differences on spatial ability. *Personality and Individual Differences*, 37: 1289–1293.

Colom, R., Flores-Mendoza, C. E., & Abad, F. J. (2007). Generational changes on the Draw-a-Man test: A comparison of Brazilian urban and rural children tested in 1930, 2002, and 2004. *Journal of Biosocial Science*, 39: 79–89.

Colom, R., & Garcia-Lopez, O. (2002). Sex differences in fluid intelligence among high school graduates. *Personality and Individual Differences*, 32: 445–452.

Colom, R., Lluis Font, J. M., & Andres-Pueyo, A. (2005). The generational intelligence gains are caused by decreasing variance in the lower half of the distribution: Supporting evidence for the nutrition hypothesis. *Intelligence*, 33: 83–92.

Crucian, G. P., & Berenbaum, S. A. (1998). Sex differences in right hemisphere tasks. *Brain and Cognition*, 36: 377–389.

Current Population Surveys (1940–2007). Table A-1. Years of school completed by people 25 years and over, by age and sex (selected years).

Daley, T. C., Whaley, S. E., Sigman, M. D., Espinosa, M. P., & Neumann, C. (2003). IQ on the rise: The Flynn effect in rural Kenyan children. *Psychological Science*, 14: 215–219.

Deary, I. J., Penke, L., & Johnson, W. (2010). The neuroscience of human intelligence differences. *Nature Reviews Neuroscience*, 11: 2001–2011.

Deary, I. J., Weiss, A., & Batty, G. A. (2011). Intelligence and personality as predictors of illness and death: How researchers in differential psychology and chronic disease epidemiology are collaborating to understand and address health inequalities. *Psychological Science in the Public Interest*, 11: 53–79.

de Lemos, M. M. (1988). The Australian standardization of the Standard Progressive Matrices. Paper presented at the ACER Seminar on Intelligence, Melbourne, August 24–26, 1988.

Diamond, J. (1998). Japanese roots. *Discover Magazine*, June 1, 1998.

Dickens, W. T., & Flynn, J. R. (2006a). Black Americans reduce the racial IQ gap: Evidence from standardization samples. *Psychological Science*, 17: 913–920.

(2006b). Common ground and differences. *Psychological Science*, 17: 923–924.

Duckworth, A. L., & Seligman, M. E. P. (2006). Self-discipline gives girls the edge: Gender differences in self-discipline, grades, and achievement test scores. *Journal of Educational Psychology*, 98: 198–208.

Ee, J. (1961). Chinese migration to Singapore, 1896–1941. *Journal of Southeast Asian History*, 2: 33–51.

Emanuelsson, I., Reuterberg, S.-E., & Svensson, A. (1993). Changing differences in intelligence? Comparisons between groups of thirteen-year-olds tested from 1960 to 1990. *Scandinavian Journal of Educational Research*, 37: 259–277.

Eppig, C., Fincher, C. L., & Thornhill, R. (2010). Parasite prevalence and the worldwide distribution of cognitive ability. *Proceedings of the Royal Society*. Published online: http://dx.doi.org/10.1098/rspb.2010.0973.

Erickson, K. I., Kim, J. S., Suever, B. L., Voss, M. W., Francis, B. M., & Kramer, A. F. (2008). Genetic contributions to age-related decline in executive function: A 10-year longitudinal study of COMT and BDNF polymorphisms. *Frontiers of Human Neuroscience*, 2: 1–9.

*Ex Parte Blue*, 230 S.W.3d 151 (Tex.Crim.App.) March 7, 2007.

Floyd, R. G., Clark, M. H., & Shadish, W. R. (2008). The exchangeability of IQs: Implications for professional psychology. *Professional Psychology: Research and Practice*, 39: 4514–4523.

Flynn, J. R. (1980). *Race, IQ, and Jensen*. London: Routledge.

(1984). The mean IQ of Americans: Massive gains 1932 to 1978. *Psychological Bulletin*, 95: 29–51.

(1985). Wechsler intelligence tests: Do we really have a criterion of mental retardation? *American Journal of Mental Deficiency*, 90: 236–244.

(1987). Massive IQ gains in 14 nations: What IQ tests really measure. *Psychological Bulletin*, 101: 171–191.

(1991a). *Asian Americans: Achievement beyond IQ*. Hillsdale, NJ: Erlbaum.

(1991b). Reaction times show that both Chinese and British children are more intelligent than one another. *Perceptual and Motor Skills*, 72: 544–546.

(1998a). IQ gains over time: Towards finding the causes. In U. Neisser (ed.), *The Rising Curve: Long-Term Gains in IQ and Related Measures*. Washington, DC: American Psychological Association, pp. 25–66.

(1998b). Israeli military IQ tests: Gender differences small; IQ gains large. *Journal of Biosocial Science*, 30: 541–553.
(1998c). WAIS-III and WISC-III: IQ gains in the United States from 1972 to 1995; how to compensate for obsolete norms. *Perceptual and Motor Skills*, 86: 1231–1239.
(1999a). Evidence against Rushton: Genetic loading of WISC-R subtests and causes of between-group IQ differences. *Personality and Individual Differences*, 26: 373–379.
(1999b). Reply to Rushton: A gang of *g*s overpowers factor analysis. *Personality and Individual Differences*, 26: 391–393.
(2000). IQ gains, WISC subtests, and fluid *g*: *g* theory and the relevance of Spearman's hypothesis to race (followed by Discussion). In G.R. Bock, J.A. Goode, & K. Webb (eds.), *The Nature of Intelligence (Novartis Foundation Symposium 233)*. New York: Wiley, pp. 202–227.
(2006a). O efeito Flynn: repensando a inteligência e aquilo que a afeta [The Flynn effect: Rethinking intelligence and what affects it]. In C. Flores-Mendoza & R. Colom (eds.), *Introdução à psicologia das diferenças individuais* [Introduction to the psychology of individual differences]. Porto Alegre: ArtMed, pp. 387–411. English translation available from author: jim.flynn@stonebow.otago.ac.nz.
(2006b). Tethering the elephant: Capital cases, IQ, and the Flynn effect. *Psychology, Public Policy, and Law*, 12: 170–178.
(2007). *What Is Intelligence? Beyond the Flynn Effect*. New York: Cambridge University Press.
(2008). *Where Have All the Liberals Gone? Race, Class, and Ideals in America*. New York: Cambridge University Press
(2009a). Requiem for nutrition as the cause of IQ gains: Raven's gains in Britain 1938 to 2008. *Economics and Human Biology*, 7: 18–27.
(2009b). The WAIS-III and WAIS-IV: Daubert motions favor the certainly false over the approximately true. *Applied Neuropsychology*, 16: 1–7.
(2009c). *What Is Intelligence? Beyond the Flynn Effect* (Expanded paperback edn.). New York: Cambridge University Press.

(2010). Problems with IQ gains: The huge vocabulary gap. *Journal of Psychoeducational Assessment*, 28: 412–433.

(in press). *How to Improve Your Mind: Twenty Keys to Unlock the Modern World.* Oxford: Wiley-Blackwell.

Flynn, J. R., & Rossi-Casé, L. (2011). IQ gains in Argentina between 1964 and 1998. *Intelligence*, 40: 145–150.

Flynn, J. R., & Weiss, L. G. (2007). American IQ gains from 1932 to 2002: The significance of the WISC subtests. *Journal of International Testing*, 7: 209–224.

Fox, M. C., & Mitchum, A. L. (under review). *A Knowledge-Based Theory of Rising Scores on "Culture-Free" Tests.*

*Furman* v. *Georgia*, 408 U.S. 238 (1972).

Gardner, H. (1983). *Frames of Mind.* New York: Basic Books.

General Social Surveys (2009). Cumulative File for wordsum 1972–2006.

Genovese, J. E. (2002). Cognitive skills valued by educators: Historic content analysis of testing in Ohio. *Journal of Educational Research*, 96: 101–114.

Goldstein, R. (1983). *The Mind–Body Problem.* New York: Penguin.

Gorton, W. A., & Diels, J. (2010). Is political talk getting smarter: An analysis of presidential debates and the Flynn effect. *Public Understanding of Science*, 20: 578–594.

*Green* v. *Johnson*, 2006 WL 3746138 (E.D.Va.) December 15, 2006.

*Green* v. *Johnson*, 2007 WL 951686 (E.D.Va) March 26, 2007.

Greenfield, P. (1998). The cultural evolution of IQ. In U. Neisser (ed.), *The Rising Curve: Long-Term Gains in IQ and Related Measures*, Washington, DC: American Psychological Association, pp. 81–123.

Gresham, F. M., & Reschly, D. J. (2011). Standard of practice and Flynn effect testimony in death penalty cases. *Intellectual and Developmental Disabilities*, 49: 131–140.

Gurian, M. (2001). *Boys and Girls Learn Differently!* San Francisco: Jossey-Bass.

*Hall* v. *Quarterman*, 2009 WL 612559 (N.D.Tex.) March 9, 2009.

Harris, S. R., Fox, H., Wright, A. F., Hayward, C., Starr, J. M., Whalley, L. J., & Deary, I. J. (2006). The brain-derived neurotrophic factor Val66Met polymorphism is associated with age-related change in reasoning skills. *Molecular Psychiatry*, 11: 505–513.

Haworth, C. M. A., Wright, M. J., Luciano, M., Martin, N. G., de Geus, E. J. C., van Beijsterveldt, C. E. M., Bartels, M., Posthuma, D., Boomsma, D. I., Davis, O. S. P., Kovas, Y., Corley, R. P., DeFries, J. C., Hewitt, J. K., Olson, R. K., Rhea, S.-A., Wadsworth, S. J., Iacono, W. G., McGue, M., Thompson, L. A., Hart, S. A., Petrill, S. A., Lubinski, D., & Plomin, R. (2010). The heritability of general cognitive ability increases linearly from childhood to young adulthood. *Molecular Psychiatry*, 15: 1112–1120.

Heckman, J. J., & Rubenstein, Y. (2001). The importance of non-cognitive skills: Lessons from the GED testing program. *American Economic Review*, 91: 145–149.

Heckman, J. J., Stixrud, J., & Urzua, S. (2006). The effects of cognitive and noncognitive abilities on labor market outcomes and social behavior. *Journal of Labor Economics*, 24: 411–482.

Herrnstein, R. J., & Murray, C. (1994). *The Bell Curve: Intelligence and Class in American Life*. New York: Free Press.

*Holladay* v. *Allen*, 555 F.3d 1346 (11th Cir.) January 30, 2009.

Howard, R. W. (1999). Preliminary real-world evidence that average intelligence really is rising. *Intelligence*, 27: 235–250.

*Howell* v. *State*, 151 S.W.3d 450, 458 (Tenn.) November 16, 2004.

INDEC (Instituto Nacional de Estaditica y Censos) (2002). School attendance from the Argentine census. Unpublished.

*In re Mathis*, 483 F.3d 395 (5th Cir.) April 2, 2007.

*In re Salazar*, 443 F.3d 430, 433 (5th Cir.) March 17, 2006.

Irwing, P., & Lynn, R. (2005). Sex differences in means and variability on the Progressive Matrices in university students: A meta-analysis. *British Journal of Psychology*, 96: 505–524.

Japan Reference (2011). The origins of the Japanese people. Accessed August 26, 2011.

Jensen, A. R. (1973). *Educability and Group Differences*. London: Methuen.

(1980). *Bias in Mental Testing*. London: Methuen.

(1998). *The g Factor: The Science of Mental Ability*. Westport, CT: Praeger.

(2011). The theory of intelligence and its measurement. *Intelligence*, 39: 171–177.

Johnson, S. (2005). *Everything Bad Is Good for You: How Today's Popular Culture Is Actually Making Us Smarter.* New York: Rimerhead Books.

Jung, J., Kang, H., Cho, Y. S., Oh, J. H., Ryu, M. H., Chung, H. W., Seo, J.-S., Lee, J.-E., Oh, B., Bhak, J., & Kim, H.-L. (2010). Gene flow between the Korean Peninsula and its neighboring countries. *PLoS ONE*, 5: e11855.

Kagitcibasi, C., & Biricik, D. (2011). Generational gains on the Draw-a-Person IQ scores: A three-decade comparison from Turkey. *Intelligence*, 39: 351–355.

Karmona, A. J. (2003). Censo Nacional de Pob: Departamento La Plata (National Census of Population: Department La Plata). Unpublished.

Khaleefa, O., Abdelwahid, S. B., Abdulradi, F., & Lynn, R. (2008). The increase of intelligence in Sudan 1964–2006. *Personality and Individual Differences*, 45: 412–413.

Khaleefa, O., Sulman, A., & Lynn, R. (2009). An increase of intelligence in Sudan, 1987–2007. *Journal of Biosocial Science*, 41: 279–283.

Kolmos, J., & Breitfelder, A. (2008). Height of US-born non-Hispanic children and adolescents ages 2–19, born 1942–2002 in the NHANES samples. *American Journal of Human Biology*, 20: 60–71.

Laird, C., & Whitaker, S. (2011). The use of IQ and descriptions of people with intellectual disabilities in the scientific literature. *British Journal of Developmental Disabilities*, 57: 175–183.

Lamb, S. (2003). Figures derived from the Y95 Cohort of the Longitudinal Surveys of Australian Youth (The Y95 cohort comprises a nationally representative sample of students who were in Year 9 in 1995). Unpublished.

*Ledford* v. *Head*, 2008 WL 754486 (N.D.Ga.) March 19, 2008.

Liu, J., Yang, H., Li, L., Chen, T., & Lynn, R. (2012). An increase of intelligence measured by the WPPSI in China, 1984–2006. *Intelligence*, 40: 139–144.

Lovaglia, M. J., Lucas, J. W., Houser, J. A., Thye, S. R., & Markovsy, B. (1998). Status process and mental ability test scores. *American Journal of Sociology*, 104: 195–228.

Luria, A. R. (1976). *Cognitive Development: Its Cultural and Social Foundations.* Cambridge, MA: Harvard University Press.

Lynn, R. (1982). IQ in Japan and the United States shows a growing disparity. *Nature*, 297: 222–223.

(1987). The intelligence of Mongoloids: A psychometric, evolutionary, and neurological theory. *Personality and Individual Differences*, 8: 813–844.

(1989). Positive correlation between height, heads size, and IQ: A nutrition theory of the secular increases in intelligence. *British Journal of Educational Psychology*, 59: 372–377.

(1990). The role of nutrition in secular increases in intelligence. *Personality and Individual Differences*, 11: 273–275.

(1993). Nutrition and intelligence. In P. A. Vernon (ed.), *Biological Approaches to the Study of Intelligence.* Norwood, NJ: Ablex.

(1994). Sex differences in intelligence and brain size: A paradox resolved. *Personality and Individual Differences*, 17: 257–271.

(1998a). In support of nutrition theory. In U. Neisser (ed.), *The Rising Curve: Long-Term Gains in IQ and Related Measures.* Washington, DC: American Psychological Association, pp. 25–66.

(1998b). Sex differences in intelligence: A rejoinder to Mackintosh. *Journal of Biosocial Science*, 30: 529–532.

(1998c). Sex differences in intelligence: Some comments on Mackintosh and Flynn. *Journal of Biosocial Science*, 30: 555–559.

(1999). Sex differences in intelligence and brain size: A developmental theory. *Intelligence*, 27: 1–12.

(2002a). Racial and ethnic differences in psychopathic personality. *Personality and Individual Differences*, 32: 273–316.

(2002b). Sex differences on the Progressive Matrices among 15–16 year olds: Some data from South Africa. *Personality and Individual Differences*, 33: 669–677.

(2009). Fluid intelligence but not vocabulary has increased in Britain, 1979–2008. *Intelligence*, 37: 249–255.

Lynn, R., Allik, J., Pullman, H., & Laidra (2002a). A study of intelligence in Estonia. *Psychological Reports*, 91: 1022–1026.

(2002b). Sex differences on the Progressive Matrices among adolescents: Some data for Estonia. *Personality and Individual Differences*, 34: 669–679.

Lynn, R., & Irwing, P. (2004). Sex differences on the Progressive Matrices: A meta-analysis. *Intelligence*, 32: 481–498.

Lynn, R., & Kazlauskaite, V. (2002). A study of IQ in Lithuania. *Psychological Reports*, 95: 611–612.

Lynn, R., & Vanhanen, T. (2002). *IQ and the Wealth of Nations*. Westport, CT: Praeger.

(2006). *IQ and Global Inequality*. Augusta, GA: Washington Summit.

Mackintosh, N. J. (1998). Reply to Lynn. *Journal of Biosocial Science*, 30: 533–539.

Maguire, E. A., Gadian, D. G., Johnsrude, I. S., Good, C. D., Ashburner, J., Frackowiak, R. S. J., & Frith, C. D. (2000). Navigation-related structural change in the hippocampi of taxi drivers. *Proceedings of the National Academy of Sciences*, 97: 4398–4403.

Mahdi, W. (2010). Oil is no gold mine for jobs in Saudi. *The National*, March 2, 2010.

Martonell, R. (1998). Nutrition and the worldwide rise in IQ scores. In U. Neisser (ed.), *The Rising Curve: Long-Term Gains in IQ and Related Measures*. Washington, DC: American Psychological Association, pp. 183–206.

Meisenberg, G., Lawless, E., Lambert, E., & Newton, A. (2005). The Flynn effect in the Caribbean: Generational change of cognitive test performance in Dominica. *Mankind Quarterly*, 46: 29–69.

(2006). Determinants of mental ability on a Caribbean island, and the mystery of the Flynn effect. *Mankind Quarterly*, 46: 273–312.

Mills, C. Wright (1959). *The Sociological Imagination*. London: Oxford University Press.

Mintz, S. (2004). *Freaks, Geeks, and Cool Kids: American Teenagers, Schools, and the Culture of Consumption*. New York: Routledge.

*Moore* v. *Quarterman*, 454 F.3d 484 (5th Cir.) June 29, 2006.

Mosler, D., & Catley, B. (1998). *America and Americans in Australia*. Westport, CT: Praeger.

Murphy, R., te Nijenhuis, J., & van Eeden, R. (2008, December). The Flynn effect in South Africa. Paper presented at the Ninth

Annual Conference of the International Society for Intelligence Research (ISIR), Georgia, United States of America.

Must, O., Must, A., & Raudik, V. (2003). The secular rise in IQs: In Estonia, the Flynn effect is not a Jensen effect. *Intelligence*, 31: 461–471.

*Neal* v. *State*, 256 S.W.3d 264 (Tex.Crim.App. June 18, 2008).

Neisser, U., ed. (1998). *The Rising Curve: Long-Term Gains in IQ and Related Measures*, Washington, DC: American Psychological Association.

Nijman, E., Scheirs, J., Prinsen, M., Abbink, C., & Blok, J. (2010). Exploring the Flynn effect in mentally retarded adults by using a nonverbal intelligence test for children. *Research in Developmental Disabilities*, 31: 1404–1411.

Nisbett, R., Aronson, J., Blair, C., Dickens, W. T., Flynn, J. R., Halpern, D. F., & Turkheimer, E. (2012). Intelligence: New findings and theoretical developments. *American Psychologist*, 67: 130–159.

Nunn, J. (1999). *John Nunn's Chess Puzzle Book*. London: Gambit.

Owen, K. (1992). The suitability of Raven's Standard Progressive Matrices for various groups in South Africa. *Personality and Individual Differences*, 13: 149–160.

*People* v. *Superior Court of Tulare County*, 21 Cal.Rptr.3d 542 (Cal. Ct.App.) December 6, 2004.

*People* v. *Superior Court of Tulare County*, 155 P.3d 259 (Cal.) April 12, 2007.

Pietschnig, J., Voracek, M., & Formann, A. K. (2010). Pervasiveness of the IQ rise: A cross-temporal meta-analysis. *PLoS ONE*, 5: e14406.

PISA (2006). *Science Competencies for the Modern World*. Paris: OECD – Programme for International Science Assessment.

Raven, J. (1986). *Manual for Raven's Progressive Matrices and Vocabulary Scales* (research supplement No. 3). London: H. K. Lewis.

Raven, J., & Court, J. H. (1989). *Manual for Raven's Progressive Matrices and Vocabulary Scales* (research supplement No. 4). London: H. K. Lewis.

Raven, J. C., Court, J. H., & Raven, J. (1986). *Manual for Raven's Progressive Matrices and Vocabulary Scales: Section 2 – Coloured Progressive Matrices.* London: H. K. Lewis.

Raven, J., Rust, J., & Squire, A. (2008). *Manual: Coloured Progressive Matrices and Crichton Vocabulary Scale.* London: NCS Pearson.

Reid, N., & Gilmore, A. (1988). The Raven's Standard Progressive Matrices in New Zealand. Paper presented at the ACER Seminar on Intelligence, Melbourne, August 24–26, 1988.

Resnick, S. M., Lamar, M., & Driscoll, I. (2007). Vulnerability of the orbitofrontal cortex to age-associated structural and functional brain changes. *Annals of the New York Academy of Sciences,* 1121: 562–575.

*Rivera* v. *Dretke*, 2006 WL 870927 (S.D.Tex.) March 31, 2006.

Roid, G. H. (2003). *Stanford–Binet Intelligence Scales*, 5th edn. *Technical Manual.* Itasca, IL: Riverside.

Roivainen, E., (2009). European and American WAIS-III norms: Cross-national differences in performance subtest scores. *Intelligence*, 38: 187–192.

Rönnlunda, M., & Nilsson, L-G. (2009). Flynn effects on sub-factors of episodic and semantic memory: Parallel gains over time and the same set of determining factors. *Neuropsychologia*, 47: 2174–2180.

Rosenau, J. N., & Fagan, W. M. (1997). A new dynamism in world politics: Increasingly skilled individuals? *International Studies Quarterly*, 41: 655–686.

Rossi-Casé, L. (2000). The recent standardization of Raven's Standard Progressive Matrices in La Plata; and information concerning the 1964 standardization of Raven's Standard Progressive Matrices in La Plata. Unpublished.

Rushton, J. P. (1995). *Race, Evolution, and Human Behavior: A Life History Perspective.* New Brunswick, NJ: Transaction.

Rushton, J. P., & Jensen, A. R. (2010). Editorial: The rise and fall of the Flynn effect as a reason to expect a narrowing of the black/white IQ gap. *Intelligence*, 38: 213–219.

Rushton, J. P., & Skuy, M. (2000). Performance on Raven's matrices by African and white university students in South Africa. *Intelligence*, 28: 251–266.

Rutter, J. M. (2000). Comments in discussion on James R. Flynn. In Bock, Goode, & Webb (eds.), *The Nature of Intelligence*, pp. 222–223.

Saudi Press Association (2011). Census shows Kingdom's population at more than 27 million. *The Saudi Gazette*, August 15, 2011.

Schneider, D. (2006). Smart as we can get? *American Scientist*, 94: 311–312.

Schooler, C. (1998). Environmental complexity and the Flynn effect. In U. Neisser (ed.), *The Rising Curve: Long-Term Gains in IQ and Related Measures*. Washington, DC: American Psychological Association, pp. 67–79.

Shayer, M., Coe, R., & Ginsburg, D. (2007). 30 years on – a large anti-'Flynn effect'? The Piagetian test *Volume and Heaviness* norms 1975–2003. *British Journal of Educational Psychology*, 77: 25–41.

Shayer, M., & Ginsburg, D. (2009). 30 years on – a large anti-'Flynn effect'? (II): 13 and 14 year olds. Piagetian tests of formal operations norms 1976–2006/7. *British Journal of Educational Psychology*, 79: 409–418.

Shi, H., & Su, B. (2009). Origin of modern humans in East Asia: Clues from the chromosome. *Frontiers of Biology in China*, 4: 241–247.

Silverman, I., Choi, J., Mackewn, A., Fisher, M., Moro, J., & Olshansky, E. (2000). Evolved mechanisms underlying wayfinding: Further studies on the hunter-gatherer theory of spatial sex difference. *Evolution and Human Behavior*, 21: 201–213.

Silverman, W., Miezejeski, C., Ryan, R., Zigman, W., Krinsky-McHale, S., & Urv, T. (2010). Stanford–Binet and WAIS IQ differences and their implications for adults with intellectual disability. *Intelligence*, 38: 242–248.

Sowell, Elizabeth R., Thompson, Paul M., & Toga, Arthur W. (2004). Mapping changes in the human cortex throughout the span of life. *Neuroscientist*, 10: 372–392.

*State* v. *Burke*, 2005 WL 3557641 (Ohio App. 10 Dist.) December 30, 2005.

Statistikaamet [Statistical Office of Estonia] (2001). *Haridus* (Education) *2000/2001*. Tallinn, Estonia.

(2003). Data from Census, March 31, 2000: Gender cohorts ages 12–18 by ethnic group.

Steen, R. G. (2009). *Human Intelligence and Medical Illness: Assessing the Flynn Effect*. New York: Springer.

Sternberg, R. J. (1988). *The Triarchic Mind: A New Theory of Human Intelligence*. New York: Penguin.

(2006). The Rainbow Project: Enhancing the SAT through assessments of analytic, practical, and creative skills. *Intelligence*, 34: 321–350.

Sternberg, R. J., Forsythe, G. B., Hedlund, J., Horvath, J. A., Wagner, R. K., Williams, W. M., Snook, S. A., & Grigorenko, E. L. (2000). *Practical Intelligence in Everyday Life*. New York: Cambridge University Press.

Storfer, M. D. (1990). *Intelligence and Giftedness: The Contributions of Heredity and Early Environment*. San Francisco, CA: Jossey-Bass.

Sundet, J. M., Barlaug, D. G., & Torjussen, T. M. (2004). The end of the Flynn effect? A study of secular trends in mean intelligence test scores of Norwegian conscripts during half a century. *Intelligence*, 32: 349–362.

Sundet, J. M., Eriksen, W., Borren, I., & Tambs, K. (2010). The Flynn effect in sibships: Investigating the role of age differences between siblings. *Intelligence*, 38: 38–44.

Sundet, J. M., Tambs, K., Harris, J. R., Magnus, P., & Torjussen, T. M. (2005). Resolving the genetic and environmental sources of the correlation between height and intelligence: A study of nearly 2,600 Norwegian male twin pairs. *Twin Research Human Genetics*, 8: 307–311.

Teasdale, T. W., & Owen, D. R. (1989). Continued secular increases in intelligence and a stable prevalence of high intelligence levels. *Intelligence*, 13: 255–262.

(2000). Forty-year secular trends in cognitive abilities. *Intelligence*, 28: 115–120.

te Nijenhuis, J., Cho, S. H., Murphy, R., & Lee, K. H. (2008). The Flynn effect in South Korea. Paper presented at the Ninth Annual Conference of the International Society for Intelligence Research (ISIR), Georgia, United States of America.

te Nijenhuis, J., Murphy, R., & van Eeden, R. (2011). The Flynn effect in South Africa. *Intelligence*, 39: 456–467.

*Thomas* v. *Allen*, 2009 WL 0912869 (N.D.Ala.) April 21, 2009.

*Thomas* v. *Allen* (11th Cir.) May 27, 2010.

Thorndike, R. L., Hagen, E. P., & Sattler, J. M. (1986). *The Stanford–Binet Intelligence Scale*, 4th edn. *Technical Manual*. Chicago: The Riverside Publishing Company.

Tsai, S. J., Hong, C. J., Yu, Y. W., & Chen, T. J. (2004). Association study of a brain-derived neurotrophic factor (BDNF) Val66Met polymorphism and personality trait and intelligence in healthy young females. *Neuropsychobiology*, 49: 13–16.

Tuddenham, R. D. (1948). Soldier intelligence in World Wars I and II. *American Psychologist*, 3: 54–56.

USDE (2003). Department of Education, Institute of Education Sciences, National Center for Educational Statistics. *The Nation's Report Card: Reading 2002*, NCES 2003–521, by W. S. Grigg, M. C. Daane, Y. Jin, & J. R. Campbell. Washington, DC.

US Department of Education (2000). Office of Educational Research and Improvement, National Center for Educational Statistics. *NAEP 1996 Trends in Academic Progress*, NCES 97–985r, by J. R. Campbell, K. E. Voelkl, & P. L. Donahue. Washington, DC.

(2001). *The Nation's Report Card: Mathematics 2000*, NCES 2001–517, by J. S. Braswell, A. D. Lutkus, W. S. Grigg, S. L. Santapau, B. Tay-Lim, & M. Johnson. Washington, DC.

*United States* v. *Davis*, 611 F.Supp.2d 472 (E.D.Md) April 24, 2009.

*United States* v. *Paul Hardy*, Fed. Dis. Ct. (E. D. of Louisiana) November 24, 2010.

*United States* v. *Parker*, 65 M.J. 626 (N.M.Ct.Crim.App.) February 28, 2007.

Verguts, T., & De Boeck, P. (in press). A knowledge-based theory of rising scores on "culture-free" tests. *Psychological Review*.

Vineland (2006). Pre-publication data from the Vineland-II manual courtesy of S. Sparrow, Ph.D., Professor Emerita and Senior Research Scientist, Yale Child Study Center.

Vroon, P. A. (1984). Raven's score distribution of Dutch draftees. Personal communication, November 5, 1984.

Wai, J., & Putallaz. M. (2010). Sex Differences: A 30-year examination from the right tail of the ability distribution. *Intelligence*, 38: 412–423.

*Walker* v. *Kelly*, 593, F.3d 319 (4th Cir.) January 27, 2010.

*Walker* v. *True*, 399, F.3d 315 (4th Cir.) February 17, 2005.

*Walton* v. *Johnson*, 407, F.3d 285 (4th Cir.) April 28, 2005.

Wechsler, D. (1955). *Wechsler Adult Intelligence Scale: Manual*. New York: The Psychological Corporation.

(1981). *Wechsler Adult Intelligence Scale*, rev. edn. *Manual*. New York: The Psychological Corporation.

(1992). *Wechsler Intelligence Scale for Children*, 3rd edn. *Manual* (Australian adaptation). San Antonio, TX: The Psychological Corporation.

(1997a). *Wechsler Adult Intelligence Scale*, 3rd edn. *Manual*. San Antonio, TX: The Psychological Corporation.

(1997b). *Wechsler Adult Intelligence Scale*, 3rd edn. *Technical and Interpretive Manual*. San Antonio, TX: The Psychological Corporation.

(2003). *The WISC-IV Technical Manual*. San Antonio, TX: The Psychological Corporation.

(2008a). *Wechsler Adult Intelligence Scale*, 4th edn. *Manual*. San Antonio, TX: Pearson.

(2008b). *Wechsler Adult Intelligence Scale*, 4th edn. *Technical and Interpretive Manual*. San Antonio, TX: Pearson.

Weyl, N. (1966). *The Creative Elite in America*. Washington, DC: Public Affairs Press.

Wicherts, J. M., Dolan, C. V., Hessen, D. J., Oosterveld, P., van Baal, G. C. M., Boomsma, D. I., & Span, M. M. (2004). Are intelligence test measurements invariant over time? Investigating the Flynn effect. *Intelligence*, 32: 509–538.

*Wiley* v. *Epps*, 668 F.Supp.2d 848 (N.D.Miss.) November 5, 2009.

*Williams* v. *Campbell*, 2007 WL 1098516 (S.D.Ala.) April 11, 2007.

*Winston* v. *Kelly*, 624 F.Supp.2d 478, May 30, 2008.

*Winston* v. *Kelly*, 592 F.3d 535 (4th Cir.) January 27, 2010.

Wright, Quincy (1955). *The Study of International Relations.* New York: Appleton-Century-Crofts.

Young, G. W. (2012). Understanding Flynn and honoring Atkins: The Flynn effect should apply in capital determinations of mental retardation or intellectual disability. *Vanderbilt Law Review*, March 2012.

Zhong, H., Shi, H., Qi, X.-B., Duan, Z.-Y., Tan, P.-P., Jin, L., Su, B., & Runlin, Z. M. (2010). Extended Y-chromosome investigation suggests postglacial migrations of modern humans into East Asia via the northern route. *Molecular Biology and Evolution*, 28: 717–727.

# Subject index

# Name index